Corporate Social Responsibility and International Development

Corporate Social Responsibility and International Development

Is Business the Solution?

Michael Hopkins

London • Sterling, VA

First published by Earthscan in the UK and USA in 2007

Reprinted 2007, 2008

Copyright © Michael Hopkins, 2007

ISBN: 978-1-84407-356-6   hardback
        1-84407-356-4   hardback

Typesetting by Composition & Design Services
Printed and bound in the UK by Antony Rowe Ltd, Chippenham, Wiltshire
Cover design by Susanne Harris
Cover photos by the author – Canary Wharf, London and a Vocational School
Residence near Hanoi, Vietnam

For a full list of publications please contact:

Earthscan
8–12 Camden High Street
London, NW1 0JH, UK
Tel: +44 (0)20 7387 8558
Fax: +44 (0)20 7387 8998
Email: earthinfo@earthscan.co.uk
Web: **www.earthscan.co.uk**

22883 Quicksilver Drive, Sterling, VA 20166-2012, USA

Earthscan publishes in association with the International Institute for Environment
and Development

A catalogue record for this book is available from the British Library

Library of Congress Cataloging-in-Publication Data

Hopkins, Michael, 1945 Nov. 16-
    Corporate social responsibility and international development : are
corporations the solution? / Michael Hopkins.
        p. cm.
    ISBN-13: 978-1-84407-356-6 (hardback)
    ISBN-10: 1-84407-356-4 (hardback)
    1. Social responsibility of business–Developing countries. 2. International
business enterprises–Moral and ethical aspects–Developing countries.
3. Economic assistance–Developing countries. I. Title. HD60.5.D44H67 2006
658.4'08–dc22

                                                              2006011978

The paper used for the text pages of this book
is FSC certified. FSC (the Forest Stewardship
Council) is an international network to promote
responsible management of the world's forests.

Printed on totally chlorine-free paper

Contents

List of Figures, Tables and Boxes

Figures

Tables

Boxes

Acknowledgements

Jawahir has again been with me during the evolution of another book which could not have been written without her moral and intellectual support. Thanks to Adrian Payne, Emilio Klein and Armand Pereira for providing detailed comments as well as to Gerry Rodgers and Hernando de Soto for their kind remarks on an earlier version. The book could not have been written without my partner, and brother, Ivor holding up our company, MHC International Ltd, while this brother indulged his love of writing.

Preface
Corporate Social Responsibility (CSR) and International
Development: Is Business the Solution?

Governments and their international arms, the agencies grouped under the
umbrella of the United Nations (UN), have failed in their attempts to rid
the planet of under-development and poverty. Whether they like it or not,
corporations are involved in development. Large corporations, with their
power and economic strength, have taken a dominant position in society.
They will, as this book argues, need to take much more responsibility for
development than ever before.

After more than 60 years since the foundation of the UN in 1945 and
US$1 trillion (1000 billion US dollars) in development aid, 2.65 billion
people – or nearly half the people on the planet – still live on less than $2 a
day and the figures have grown over the past decade. Indeed, some of the
poorest economies are going backwards. In Africa – from the War on Poverty to Live Aid – much publicity and private sector support has been gathered through harnessing the photogenic power of actors and pop singers.
This is because it was in sub-Saharan Africa, over the period 1981–2001,
when gross domestic product (GDP) per capita shrank 14 per cent, poverty
rose from 41 per cent to 46 per cent by 2001, and an additional 150 million
people fell into extreme poverty!

So has the UN failed?

As Kofi Annan remarked in his speech on the restructuring of the UN in
March 2006: 'I am expected to be the world's chief diplomat, and to run a
large and complex organisation in my spare time.' The UN, in fact, punches
above its weight. The UN is actually a small organization. The total operating expenses for the entire UN system – including the World Bank, International Monetary Fund (IMF) and all the UN funds, programmes and
specialized agencies – came to around $18 billion a year at the turn of the
21st century. This is less than the size of many multinational enterprises
(MNEs) – General Electric, for instance, had a market capitalization of

$350 billion in 2004, and Exxon Mobil had profits of around $32 billion in 2005 – and is dwarfed by military expenditure: $80 billion a year just on Iraq by the US in 2005.

Since the UN's founding, there has been a fourfold increase in peace-keeping, with 80,000 peacekeepers and a $5 billion budget – a depressing example of the failure of development efforts. The budget for the UN's core functions – the Secretariat operations in New York, Geneva, Nairobi, Vienna and five Regional Commissions – is around $1.25 billion a year. This is about 4 per cent of New York City's annual budget – and nearly $1 billion less than the yearly cost of Tokyo's Fire Department. It is $3.7 billion less than the annual budget of New York's State University system!

Thus, its lack of resources which, in turn, is intimately tied up with the politicization of its actions by powerful member states who don't seem to know better, has left it in poor shape to tackle the pressing issues of under-development today. As the seemingly incessant need for 'transparency' and 'accountability' of the UN's actions bites through misdirected assistance, it will see its power to influence development continue to reduce.

At the micro level, large corporations are doing more and more to assist in development. It is at the macro, policy level, where corporations are reluctant to act but where their critics urge them to perform – for instance oil company receipts that are retained in developing countries continue to be managed poorly in encouraging development. The macro level is an area where the UN family can be a partner to corporations and is likely to grow in importance.

This book is not an attack on the UN – my overall impression is that it does a good job on development, even at times outstanding. But, with the very small resources at its disposal its direct impact on development is, unfortunately, a mere drop in the ocean.

So what is likely to happen next? Hard economics is losing way to softer versions. Culture and ethnicity have dominated recent world events and this trend is likely to continue. Focusing on purely economic growth for countries or profits for companies will, of course, be uppermost in our leaders' minds. But the softer undercurrents of change, such as Corporate Social Responsibility (CSR), will require new, inspired leadership.

And the UN? The UN will remain under-funded as long as it is used as a political football by the major powers to serve their own short-term interests, and will not be able to deliver its many excellent development initiatives.

Can the power, money and reach of large corporations do a better job on development?

Obviously, the main concern of business is not the development of the under-developed parts of the world. Yet, there are many aspects of its work that could be placed at the service of the planet. Prahalad and Hart (2002) have attracted attention through their work *The Fortune at the Bottom of the Pyramid*.[1] Their argument is that the key to unlocking this potential is for MNEs to use technology to produce affordable products for the poor. But this only covers the supply of products to the poor, not how the poor are going to pay for them, that is, the demand side. The argument in this book is that looking at development through a CSR lens could, by examining both the supply and demand aspects of corporations and development, untap many more concerns than solely the consumption of the poor, that is to say *CSR can untap the fortune from development!*

So what can be gained from CSR?

CSR, at its simplest, is treating its stakeholders in a socially responsible way. Since shareholders and the environment are also stakeholders, then CSR must address economic and environmental concerns as well as social ones – more on this in Chapter 2.

The CSR route is a way in which major global problems can be resolved. The expanding CSR movement has shown companies that their responsibilities do not lie simply in making profits, what is important is *how* profits are made. It is relatively easy to argue the obverse that corporations should stick to making profits and leave development for governments. This, though, is a dance to the death, since the market left purely to profit maximization will not, as things are, fulfil major social roles such as reducing unemployment, creating primary and secondary education for all and tackling the major diseases of the developing world.

Only time will tell how vigorously corporations will take on this new challenge. To a certain extent MNEs will engage in development simply to ward off problems such as rising energy prices, resentment at off-shoring, consumer boycotts and the like. They should be cajoled and persuaded to take on the wider challenge of development. How they do this, if they decide to go forward, is still the subject of intense discussion. My suggestions as to what they should do are given in the last chapter of this book.

MNEs are already involved in development

In fact, MNEs are already involved, in one way or another, in development. Their involvement can be characterized by three broad types of activity:

■ *Type I:* Charitable donation to a 'good' cause in a developing country, that is, development philanthropy.

---

[1] S. K. Prahalad and S. L. Hart (2002) *The Fortune at the Bottom of the Pyramid*, Strategy+Business, McLean, VA, First Quarter, Booz Allen Hamilton Inc.

■ *Type II:* Development inside the company that initiates new products for developing countries, or invests in a developing country to take advantage of cheap labour or special skills or natural resources such as oil and, in turn, directly impacts upon the profits of the whole organization.
■ *Type III:* Activities that promote sustainable development and anti-poverty initiatives that might also be in addition to Type II activities. These activities serve to promote development but do not immediately impact on a company's bottom line. They are carried out to enhance a company's reputation and contribute to wider development objectives.

Thus, many if not all, of the largest corporations are involved in development in some way. Many of these efforts, to date, stem from their philanthropic interests with few direct benefits to the company itself except, of course, for public relations (PR) purposes. Chapter 3 will give many examples of what corporations are doing in development as well as covering some of the development activities of large companies such as Microsoft, Wal-Mart, Unilever, British American Tobacco (BAT), Shell and BP. The examples given in the chapter, and these are only a subset of the enormous efforts going on worldwide, show that large private corporations are heavily involved in development. Not perfectly, but it can be concluded that although profits need to be made, companies have realized that economies must be encouraged to develop and it is this need that is prompting companies to be realistic about how pro-poor their policies are.

The book covers what is happening on CSR and development within developing countries themselves. It is still early days, but there are many activities that can be reviewed in the burgeoning number of regionally focused websites and newsletters devoted to CSR across the world from China, the Philippines, India to Brazil. These are covered, partially, in Chapter 9. There is also a growing academic literature on CSR in developing countries as interest in the whole field has exploded despite, it must be admitted, a lack of consensus on what CSR means across different countries.

Another area starting to promote development, which is covered in Chapter 11, is socially responsible investment (SRI), one of the fastest growing forms of investment. In the US alone, from 1995 to 2003, assets involved in social investing, through screening of retail and institutional funds, shareholder advocacy and community investing, have grown 40 per cent faster than all professionally managed US investment assets. Investment portfolios involved in SRI grew by more than 240 per cent from 1995 to 2003, compared with the 174 per cent growth of the overall universe of assets under professional management.

Is CSR really the answer?

It is, of course, easier to dispose than to propose, which leads to Chapter 6 concerning addressing some of the common criticisms of the CSR concept.

It is most likely that CSR will transform into different concepts but not disappear entirely. Since the realm of business in society is so crucial, CSR and its associated tools will eventually become embedded in all organizations rather like environment concerns are right now. Consequently, in the future, there will be less talk about CSR simply because it will become part of routine daily operations.

So what next for MNEs?

Corporate philanthropy can lead to sustainable development, but often it does not, as explained in Chapter 5. CSR can help in assessing the merits of philanthropy and therefore:

- Companies should abandon all philanthropy which is outside a CSR framework.
- Companies should work hand-in-hand with governments to promote economic and social development.
- Companies should develop a CSR vision that includes an overall strategy for the company's place in development.
- Companies should work (a) with the government in their host country to see how the government's anti-poverty policy can be enhanced, and (b) with local UN and non-governmental organizations (NGOs) to increase the efficiency of development initiatives, including ensuring their tax contributions are used wisely.

Final remark on CSR

CSR is one of, if not *the* most important issue of our time. The power and strength of corporations can be harnessed for positive developments. This is not always so, as can be seen in the case of the major tragedy of the modern era – Iraq.

Could CSR have prevented the Iraq war? Yes! The relations between Halliburton, Bechtel, Carlyle and many other corporations in a CSR world would have been intensively examined. Stakeholders would have been held publicly accountable, and socially irresponsible actions such as supporting war efforts for personal gain would have been stamped out. Naïve? Perhaps. But right now, large corporations are more powerful than the UN, and more powerful than many nation states. Therefore, CSR is a more urgent issue than it has ever been before.

List of Acronyms and Abbreviations

ADCE	Associação de Dirigentes Cristãos de Empresas do Brasil (Brazil)
AICC	African Institute of Corporate Citizenship
AR	Accountability Rating
ARMM	Autonomous Region of Muslim Mindanao (the Philippines)
AU	African Union
AWDCs	Afghan Women's Development Centers
BAA	Business Action for Africa
BDA	business development activities
CBO	community-based organization
CER	corporate environmental responsibility
CERES	Coalition for Environmentally Responsible Economies
CFR	corporate financial responsibility
CII	Confederation of Indian Industry
CITEVE	Technological Centre for the Textile and Clothing Industries (Portugal)
CPI	Corruption Perceptions Index
CR	corporate responsibility
CSD	corporate social development
CSI	corporate social investment
CSM	Centre for Social Markets
CSR	corporate social responsibility
CSu	Corporate Sustainability
DAWN	Diabetes, Attitudes, Wishes and Needs
DJSI	Dow Jones Sustainability Index
ECGD	Export Credits Guarantee Department (UK)
ECLT	Eliminating Child Labour in Tobacco Growing Foundation
EITI	Extractive Industries Transparency Initiative
EP	Equator Principles
EPZ	export processing zone
ETEF	Empowerment through Energy Fund
ETI	Ethical Trading Initiative
EU	European Union
FAO	Food and Agriculture Organization (UN)

FEMA	Federal Emergency Management Agency
FDI	Foreign Direct Investment
FIs	financial institutions
FICCI	Federation of Indian Chambers of Commerce and Industry
FLA	Fair Labour Association
FMCG	fast-moving consumer-goods
FTE	full-time equivalent
GDP	gross domestic product
GLPNet	Global Learning Portal Network
GRI	Global Reporting Initiative
GSBI	Global Social Benefit Incubator
GSL	Global Student Leadership
HNP	Health, Nutrition and Population
ICLS	ILO core labour standards
IDB	Inter-American Development Bank
IDS	Institute of Development Studies (University of Sussex, UK)
IFC	International Finance Corporation
ILO	International Labour Organization
IMF	International Monetary Fund
IOE	International Organisation of Employers
ISO	International Standards Organisation
IUCN	International Union for the Conservation of Nature
JPO	Junior Professional Officer
LDC	less-developed country
MDG	Millennium Development Goals
MMV	Medicines for Malaria Venture
MNC	multinational company
MNE	multinational enterprise
MOU	Memorandum of Understanding
NGO	non-governmental organization
NLC	National Labor Committee (US)
ODA	Official Development Assistance
OECD	Organization for Economic Co-operation and Development
OPSP	Oficina Presidencial de Seguimiento a Proyectos
PAT	Profits After Tax
PFI	Private Finance Initiative
PIC	Personal Internet Communicator
PPP	Private–Public Partnerships
PR	public relations
PSP	private sector participation
RI	Relief International
SDC	Swiss Agency for Development and Cooperation
SECO	State Secretariat for Economic Affairs
SF	Shell Foundation
SHS	solar home systems
SIM	societal issues in management

SME	small to medium-sized enterprise
SOEs	State Operated Enterprises
SRI	socially responsible investment
SSACI	Swiss–South African Co-operation Initiative
SUVs	sports utility vehicles
T&A	transparency and accountability
TEAM	Television Education for the Advancement of Muslim Mindanao
TI	Transparency International
TII	Technology, Innovation and Initiative
TNC	transnational corporations
UDHR	Universal Declaration of Human Rights
UEF	Uganda Energy Fund
UI	Unilever Indonesia
UN	United Nations
UNAIDS	the joint United Nations Programme on HIV/AIDS
UNCTAD	United Nations Conference on Trade and Development
UNDP	United Nations Development Programme
UNEP	United Nations Environment Programme
UNHCR	United Nations High Commission for Refugees
UNIAPAC	International Christian Union of Business Executives
WBCSD	World Business Council for Sustainable Development
WBI	World Bank Institute
WHO	World Health Organization
WTN	World Technology Network
UNOPS	United Nations Office for Project Services
UNESCO	United Nations Educational, Scientific and Cultural Organization
UN/DESA	United Nations Department of Economic and Social Affairs
UNGC	United Nations Global Compact
UKSIF	UK Social Investment Forum

Can CSR Pave the Way for Development?

2.65 billion, or nearly half the people on the planet, live on less than $2 a day and the figures have grown over the past decade. (World Bank Data)

In the seventies I believed that if a company ran an efficient operation with sound staff development, employment, safety and environmental policies, did not bribe anyone, paid our taxes honestly and in the country where income was earned and engaged in a reasonable amount of community development, our responsibilities stopped there. It was the responsibility of government to use the revenue generated. The Economist newspaper still holds to this line. But we now know that where revenue is mis-spent or stolen over long periods by governments, people turn to the company and say 'You made money, but there is little in the country to show for it.' To protest that we paid our taxes is of no avail. It may not be our responsibility, but it becomes our problem. If we want the sort of functioning society in which we can do business, we need to work with others to create the capacities and conditions which sound governance requires. (Sir Mark Moody Stuart, Chairman, Anglo American PLC)[1]

Introduction

If the business of business is business, why should corporations be involved in development? The two quotes above show why. The main proposition of this chapter is that governments and their international arms, the agencies grouped under the umbrella of the United Nations (UN), have failed in their attempts to rid the planet of under-development and poverty. Large corpo-

---

[1] Personal communication, 18 February 2006.

rations with their power and economic strength have taken a dominant position in society. They will, as this book argues, need to take much more responsibility for development than ever before. This chapter will also spell out why development, as seen through the lens of Corporate Social Responsibility (CSR) is a useful tool to promote economic development.

CSR provides a platform for corporations to be involved in economic development in ways that can be much more powerful than has been hitherto thought of. Economic development means improving the well-being of disadvantaged people wherever they may be. Most, of course, can be found in developing countries but many can also be found in the developed and oil-rich countries – the deep south of the US, the north-west of England, the south of France around Marseilles, the poor of Turkmenistan or Uzbekistan; refugees in Saudi Arabia – the list tragically goes on. There is no need, though, for this scandalous situation to be either countenanced or allowed to continue.

The meaning of development

'Development' itself is a much maligned term. Until the late 1960s, development was considered by most economists to be the maximization of economic growth. It was really only in 1969 that Dudley Seers finally broke the growth fetishism of development theory.[2] Development, he argued, was a social phenomenon that involved more than increasing per capita output. Development meant, in Seers' opinion, eliminating poverty, unemployment and inequality as well. Seers' work at the University of Sussex was quickly followed by a focus on structural issues such as dualism, population growth, inequality, urbanization, agricultural transformation, education, health, unemployment, basic needs, governance, corruption and the like, all of which began to be reviewed on their own merits, and not merely as appendages to an underlying growth thesis.[3]

The main proposition of this chapter is that governments and their international arms, the international agencies grouped under the umbrella of the UN (which also includes the Bretton Woods institutions: the World Bank, International Monetary Fund (IMF) and their newest recruit – the World Trade Organization) have failed in their attempts to rid the planet of under-development, widespread inequalities and poverty. After half a cen-

---

[2] I was fortunate enough to have the late Professor Seers, founder and first Director of the Institute of Development Studies (IDS) at the University of Sussex, as my mentor and friend at IDS, Sussex in the early 1970s. See some of his ideas on development at http://cepa.newschool.edu/het/schools/develop.htm.

[3] See, for instance, the discussion in Hopkins, M. and Van Der Hoeven, R. (1983) *Basic needs in Development Planning*, Aldershot, Gower.

tury and US$1 trillion (1000 billion US dollars) in development aid, more than 2 billion people still live on less than $2 a day and, indeed, some of the poorest economies are going backwards.[4]

Can corporations fill the gap?

Before addressing the issue of corporations and development, it is worth putting the power of corporations into context. Bestriding the world, these large companies command immense power and reach – the biggest, in terms of revenues as of January 2005, was Wal-Mart which is worth around $300 billion in terms of sales and made $10.3 billion in pre-tax profits in 2004. Most major multinational enterprises (MNEs) are domiciled in the developed world and are owned and controlled largely by citizens of these countries, with 10 of the world's top 15 companies having their base in the US (Figure 1.1). There are developing world MNEs too, although numbers

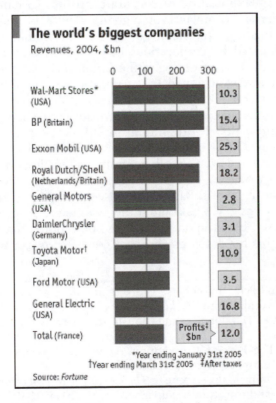

Figure 1.1 *Size of top MNEs by country*

---

[4] Simon Caulkin, 13 March 2005, The Observer.

are small with only around 30 figuring in the Fortune 500 list of largest companies.[5] More than in 2001, when an UNCTAD (United Nations Conference on Trade and Development) list of the largest MNEs included only four companies from developing countries – Hutchinson Whampoa, Singtel, Cemex and LG Electronics.[6] This trend is expected to continue as companies from developing countries (especially in Asia) increasingly internationalize their operations, not just within the region but also worldwide.

These figures mean nothing on their own, of course, but note that the World Bank lends around US$15–20 billion a year while the annual budget of oft-cited UN agencies such as the ILO (International Labour Office) is only US$0.25 billion, 100 times smaller than the annual profits of Exxon Mobil for the year 2004 (see Figure 1.1). Both the World Bank and ILO figures are tiny compared with the power and wealth of the largest corporations.

A large portion of world trade – figures vary but some estimates put this at 40–50 per cent – is conducted either within the walls of MNEs or at their behest.[7] Their role in development has only recently been acknowledged because it was accepted that corporations were thought to have as their main focus the maximization of corporate profits. To date, corporations have been generous in philanthropic giving – witness the large amounts dedicated and raised for the victims of the Asian tsunami. Around US$400 million was donated by corporations in the US in only a few weeks in early 2005.[8] In the UK, according to the *London Evening Standard*, about US$15 million was contributed by corporations – such as US$3 million from the giant Swiss bank UBS, which set up a UBS Tsunami Relief Fund to bring together individual contributions from staff and clients worldwide. In fact the 500 largest global corporations in 2004 took a record $7.5 trillion in revenue and earned $445.6 billion in profit.[9] If MNEs followed governments and contributed even a modest amount on the lines of 0.3 per cent of net income, this would have allocated $13.37 billion for development – just a little less than the World Bank's annual contribution. Therefore, on the basis of ability to pay, MNEs could if they wanted to.

So size shows, based upon figures for 2004 alone, that MNEs can be a powerful engine for development if, of course, this can be proven to be

---

[5] Leslie Sklair and Peter T Robbins, 'Global Capitalism and Major Corporations from the Third World', *Third World Quarterly*, vol 23, no 1, pp81–100, 2002.

[6] UNCTAD (2004) 'Development and Globalization – Facts and Figures', (Geneva), p40.

[7] Anup Shah, 'The Rise of Corporations', www.globalissues.org/TradeRelated/Corporations/Rise.asp, accessed 17 July 2006.

[8] According to a tally on the website of *The Chronicle of Philanthropy* trade newspaper, http://philanthropy.com/free/update/2005/01/2005010502.htm, accessed 5 February 2005.

[9] Riva Krut (2005) *Understanding Corporate Social Responsibility after the 2004 Pacific Tsunami: An argument for a financial target for MNE contributions*, New York, Cameron Cole.

in their interest *and* they have the wherewithal to get involved in development. Both these topics will be discussed below, the former under the business case for MNEs in development and the latter under CSR.

It is also worth noting that, according to the KPMG International Survey of Corporate Responsibility Reporting 2005,[10] there has been a dramatic change in the type of corporate responsibility (CR) reporting, which has changed from purely environmental reporting up until 1999, to sustainability reporting (social, environmental and economic), and which has now become mainstream among the largest companies. The KPMG report states that:

- Although the majority (80 per cent) in most countries still issue separate CR reports, there has been an increase in the number of companies publishing CR information as part of their annual reports.
- At a national level, the two top countries in terms of separate CR reporting are Japan (80 per cent) and the United Kingdom (71 per cent). The highest increases in the 16 countries in the survey are seen in Italy, Spain, Canada, France and South Africa. There have been significant decreases in Norway and Sweden.
- The typical industrial sectors with relatively high environmental impact continue to lead in reporting. At the global level, more than 80 per cent of the 250 companies examined are reporting in the electronics and computers, utilities and automotive and gas sectors. While, at the national level, over 50 per cent of the 100 companies studied are reporting in the utilities, mining, chemicals and synthetics, oil and gas, forestry and paper and pulp sectors. But the most remarkable is the financial sector, which shows more than a twofold increase in reporting since 2002.
- The survey, which includes a detailed analysis of the reports of the 250 Global companies, focused on the reasons behind their commitment to corporate responsibility and what influenced the content of the reports. The conclusion that may be drawn is that business drivers are diverse, both economic (75 per cent) and ethical (50 per cent). The top three reported economic drivers are innovation and learning, employee motivation and risk management and reduction, with about 50 per cent of companies reporting these as motivating factors.
- Independent assurance remains a valuable part of reporting. In 2005, the number of reports with an assurance statement increased to 30 per cent (G250) and 33 per cent (N100) from 29 per cent and 27 per cent respectively in 2002. Major accountancy firms continue to dominate the Corporate Responsibility assurance market with close to 60 per cent of the statements.

---

[10] www.foundation-development-africa.org/africa_corporate_social_investment/increase_in_csr_reporting.htm accessed 1 March 2006.

Has the UN really failed?

Governments and their main instruments, such as the UN, have failed in tackling under-development. As I will show in Chapter 4, poverty has increased according to certain measures over the past decade. The UN and its agencies are not entirely to blame for the situation, since they must do what their member governments tell them. These, in general, have been incredibly inconsistent over the years with some, such as the US, downright hostile – more on this in Chapter 10. In fact some parts of the UN, the UNDP (United Nations Development Programme) for instance, despite over-programming and bureaucracy, does have a sound knowledge of development, as can be attested in its annual *Human Development Reports* and associated national publications. But governments have only managed to find about US$1 billion for the UNDP, a drop in the ocean when it is considered that the UNDP works in more than 180 countries.

For instance, the UK's approach to the UN is one of 'accountability and transparency', a mantra that no one can dispute.[11] But when one looks in detail at what this means, one finds that the UN and its agencies have increasing difficultly in acting simply because their every action is now double and triple checked. Paralysis cannot be far away.

The assumption, especially after the Iraq 'oil for food' scandal, is that the UN and its agencies cannot be trusted and, when they can, that they are inefficient. This does not mean that everything they have done is worthless. Far from it. It is just that the effort has been minuscule in comparison with the resources and technology required.

There was a glimmer of hope that governments may start to take development more seriously than ever before. The UK government placed the problem of under-development as one of the two key issues in the G8 meeting held in Gleneagles, Scotland in July 2005. It addressed at least one part of the problem, that of impoverished nations having huge debts to pay.

The sum proposed by Gordon Brown, then UK finance minister, to settle the debts of some impoverished African countries was significant at US$55 billion. Under the deal, the World Bank, the International Monetary Fund and the African Development Fund would immediately write off 100 per cent of the money owed to them by 18 nations – a total of $40 billion.

---

[11] When the Minister of State for Work and Pensions was pressed by the author at the ILO conference in the summer of 2005 to explain why the UK, along with the US, had vetoed the ILO budget, he explained that it was because there was a need for more 'transparency and accountability' because there was too much waste. In principle this sounds fine but in practice these simple ideas drive the organizations into the ground by giving more power to the bureaucrats and less to the innovative thinkers. The ILO told me that their managers spend three times as much time on 'accountability' issues as they did three years ago and that productive programmes have suffered significantly.

Brown also said that up to 20 other countries could be eligible if they met strict targets for good governance and tackling corruption.

US$55 billion is only 20 per cent of the market capitalization of General Electric, just one of hundreds of MNEs. Further, many banks and investment brokers have been earning large fees in lending this money to the developing world and receiving interest when corrupt developing world politicians and their cronies transfer their own profits to banks and financial institutions abroad. There is certainly a smile on the face of Swiss bankers – shares of the largest Swiss bank UBS rose 5 per cent during May and June 2005 – partly due at least to the fact that many of their African clients now have deposits but no debts!

And the fact remains that the proportion of GDP going to development from the rich nations has been stuck at around 0.3 per cent ever since the target of 1 per cent was set. The US, for instance, only spends 0.16 per cent of its GDP on development and much of that goes to Israel and Eygpt. Curiously, many of the 'American people' are convinced that its government spends 25 per cent of its budget on development aid! (Somberg, 2005)[12]

When Mayor Giuliani was elected for the first time in New York, he wanted to turn the UN building into an hotel. His aides pointed out very rapidly that if he did, then the east side of New York would have to close many of the existing hotels and restaurants because the business from the UN was so important. Rough calculations show that for each dollar spent by the US on the UN, it receives US$3 back via spending from all the conferences and international travel initiated by the UN. Further, it was pointed out to Mayor Giuliani that the budget of the New York health department was bigger both in terms of people and expenditure than the United Nations' overall budget serving over 200 countries around the world!

New way could be CSR

Given the rise in prominence of CSR, is there now mileage for corporations to be more involved in development than hitherto? There is more interest from corporations than even a decade or so ago in being involved in development, although much of this interest to date has been in philanthropy (charitable giving) rather than development per se. Development is a wider concept than purely philanthropy, as I argue in Chapter 5. Development projects are much more complicated than charitable donations, where cash is given directly for a school or hospital, however welcome these seem to be. Development means working with local partners as well as the public institutions to create sustainable projects. Much of development, and prob-

---

12 B. Somberg (2005) 'the world's most generous misers', *Third World Traveler*, October, www.thirdworldtraveler.com/Foreign_Policy/Most_Generous_Misers.html, accessed 11 August 2006.

ably the most effective – albeit unsung, is purely creating capacity, since the best development projects are those which help people to help themselves – teaching people how to fish instead of simply giving them a fish.

Clearly, corporations are not experts in 'development' and tend to make many of the mistakes that were made in the post-Second World War crusade against under-development by aid agencies. There are plenty of stories of companies providing direct grants to projects that are unsustainable or that simply offer corrupt members of host governments an opportunity for personal gain. For instance, Coca Cola funded a hospital in Mozambique that was beautifully built and filled with the latest, modern equipment. When Coca Coal executives returned to the site a few months later, the hospital was being used as housing for the many homeless people in the area and much of the equipment had been 'sold'.

Clearly, to move the case forward, large corporations must also see that there is a business case to be involved in development. The business case for MNEs to be involved in CSR has been made and this should be extended to incorporate development.[13]

To suggest this case let us look at CSR in more detail. The attraction of CSR is that it is a systems approach, which states that the problem is defined and the system's boundary delineated so that all the important influences on resolving the problem are taken into consideration.[14] Many of the criticisms of CSR, as will be seen in Chapter 2, stem from problems with concepts and definitions. Now business, in general, is more concerned to stay in business and be profitable than to be involved in such seemingly academic discussions. This is unusual, since business is usually an area where detail is vitally important – a company cannot prepare accounts, sell pharmaceuticals, computer software, copper tubing, and so on without knowing the exact definition of the product being sold.

Yet, somehow, management concepts are manipulated with ease to fit in with one pre-conceived notion or other that will please the chairman or the companies' shareholders. This translates into a confusing set of definitions for the same concept. For instance, some define CSR as a systems approach taking into account both internal and external stakeholders, while others define it as purely voluntary. This confusion is compounded by a proliferation of terminology in the area of business in society– corporate sustainability, corporate citizenship, corporate responsibility, business responsibility, business social responsibility, business reputation, the ethical corporation, sustainable business and so on. However, without a common language we don't really know that our dialogue with companies is being heard and

---

[13] See for instance, Michael Hopkins and Roger Crowe, *Corporate Social Responsibility: Is there a business case?*, ACCA, 2003; see www.accaglobal.com/pdfs/members_pdfs/publications/csr03.pdf.
[14] John Clark et al (1975) *Global Modelling: A Systems Approach*, Guildford, UK, John Wiley.

interpreted in a consistent way. These flaws lead some companies to consider CSR as purely corporate philanthropy while others dismiss the notion entirely. But there are some, such as Shell, BP-Amoco, the Co-operative Bank and so on that see CSR as a new corporate strategic framework.

The definition that is appealing is the stakeholder definition:

> *CSR is concerned with treating the stakeholders of the firm ethically or in a socially responsible manner. Stakeholders exist both within a firm and outside. The aim of social responsibility is to create higher and higher standards of living, while preserving the profitability of the corporation, for its stakeholders both within and outside the corporation.*[15]

Most of us have a good idea what is meant by ethics but it is the identification of the stakeholders of a company that has sparked intense debate. As a minimum, they include those *within* the company: the board of directors, shareholders, investors, managers and employees; and those *outside* the company: suppliers, customers, the natural environment, government and local community.

The definition, of course, does not link directly into why corporations should be involved in development, although it does note that the key stakeholders outside a company – the government, the environment, the community, its customers and suppliers – must be involved as much as its own employees or shareholders. So why should corporations be involved in development?

Corporations and development

There are two inter-related issues: Why should corporations be interested in *development*? and Why choose the CSR route?

Corporations are already involved in development or, at least, in some aspects of development. These aspects can be characterized by three broad types of activity:

- *Type I:* Charitable donation to a 'good' cause in a developing country, i.e. development philanthropy.
- *Type II:* Development inside the company that initiates new products for developing countries, or invests in a developing country to take advantage of cheap labour or special skills or natural resources such as oil and, in turn, directly impacts upon the profits of the whole organization.

---

[15] Michael Hopkins (2003) *The Planetary Bargain: CSR Matters*, London, Earthscan.

■ *Type III:* Activities that promote sustainable development and anti-poverty initiatives that might be in addition to Type II activities. These activities serve to promote development but do not immediately impact on a company's bottom line. They are carried out to enhance a company's reputation and contribute to wider development objectives.

The case for corporations to be involved in Type I and II development does not need to be made on these pages. Our concern is with Type III development. Type III development can benefit a company in three main ways:

1   Type III activities have more impact than Type I, and go further than pure philanthropy to encourage sustainable development.
2   A company can enhance its reputation and reduce risk in the developing country where it has subsidiaries or suppliers.
3   The broader aim of development will eventually trickle down to a company's bottom line. Shareholders, of course, are generally interested in short-term profits and will be very wary of such ventures. But, more and more, companies will think longer term and see that poor development does not ensure the sustainability of their own operations.

The subject is controversial and even supporters of CSR draw the line at companies being too greatly involved in development. Indeed, a prominent development expert, Paul Streeten, argued that companies are best left to their own devices. Streeten says: *'only companies operating under near monopoly conditions could accept social responsibilities and continue to remain in business, unless they were able to put sufficient pressure to bear on their suppliers, competitors and contractors to follow suit.'*[16]

I cover the arguments against CSR in Chapter 6. But before that, and assuming that companies are interested in Type III development, would following the CSR route provide added value?

Why go the CSR route?

The CSR route can be attractive simply because the CSR movement has shown companies that their responsibilities do not lie purely in making profits, what is important is *how* profits are made. Once responsibility is accepted, the anticipation is that companies will move to *Corporate Social Development*. Such a concept is more action-orientated than CSR per se, and includes social actions for all stakeholders. Note that my CSR definition (see Chapter 2) has a wide definition of 'social' that also includes

---

[16] Novartis, 'Human right and the private sector', International Symposium Summary, p23, www.novartisfoundation.com/pdf/symposium_human_rights_report.pdf, accessed 11 August 2006.

environmental, financial, governance and economic concerns as well as those that are also normally considered 'social'.

The CSR route for corporate involvement in development is attractive due to the, at least nine, benefits of CSR that will both improve the financial bottom line *and* help to resolve the problem of under-development and poverty. These are:

1 A company's reputation is improved since it is built around key intangibles such as trust, reliability, quality, consistency, credibility, relationships and transparency, and tangibles such as investment in people, diversity and the environment.

2 Access to finance is greatly improved as socially responsible investment (SRI) becomes increasingly important. The creation of new financial indexes also supports these trends, for example FTSE4Good and the Dow Jones Sustainability Index (DJSI) publicly rank the major international companies according to their environmental and social performance (see Chapter 11).

3 CSR is an important factor for employee motivation and for attracting and retaining top quality employees.

4 Innovation, creativity, intellectual capital and learning are helped by a positive CSR strategy. Given that 80 per cent of the value of many new economy companies is now their intellectual capital, its preservation through the positive treatment of internal stakeholders is becoming more and more necessary.

5 Better risk management can be achieved by in-depth analysis of relations with external stakeholders. Factors such as new technologies and changing societal, regulatory and market expectations drive companies to take a broader perspective when analysing the range of risks they may encounter.

6 CSR positively helps in the building of relationships with host governments, communities and other stakeholders and can be of vital importance should the company encounter future difficulties with regard to its investment decisions. CSR gives a company a 'competitive' advantage over companies with poorer images.

7 Greater corporate social responsibility is linked to the heightened public debate on the benefits and shortcomings of globalization and the perceived role of business in this process. Those companies perceived to be socially responsible are, more and more, the companies of consumer choice.

8 The energy, technology and management skills learned and honed in large companies are increasingly being made available for the management of poverty alleviation through such instruments as the UN's Global Compact, Business in the Community and private and public partnerships.

9 There is a growing consensus for a *Planetary Bargain*, whereby beggar-thy-neighbour policies of companies through, among other means, using the cheapest labour and the most polluting industries are neither

in the interests of the companies concerned nor in the interests of their consumers.

Regarding this last point, as CSR gradually becomes embedded in large companies, the mixture of prediction and advocacy I made five years ago in my book *The Planetary Bargain* is gradually being achieved, much more quickly than I could have imagined even those few short years ago. In my book, my thesis was that CSR represents the decent treatment of stakeholders by the company. Nothing revolutionary in that, but the main point was that beggar-thy-neighbour policies by companies racing to the bottom to site their production in the location with the lowest common denominator in terms of wages, worker conditions, shoddy products, outrageous demands on the environment, corruption of local officials, disrespect for the human rights of its workers and local communities would simply be a poor strategy.

CSR is a complete opposite to beggar-thy-neighbour policies. This is because its positive impacts on stakeholders would mean that consumers would be able to earn adequate wages to purchase the products they produced; the environment would improve and create less drag on the company and its surroundings; improved governance would reduce transaction costs; human rights policies would provide dignity to workers and communities, and improve productivity in local outlets and facilities. Thus companies who refused to follow the socially responsible path would be 'outed' by a massive response from the invisible hand of consumers all over the world. This response would be fuelled by globalizing technologies and the spread of information whereby few secrets can be held for long, even in the remotest locations.

Of course, there are costs and limitations to the CSR approach and the idealisms behind the approach can also hinder its spread as hard-nosed businessmen try to squeeze every ounce out of cost-cutting and profit maximization. Yet, as the classic study *Built to Last* has shown, CSR companies perform better for shareholders in financial and market terms, carry less debt, and are long stayers.[17]

The CSR route to development

What are the main actions that corporations could take to enhance corporate social development (CSD)? I will consider those actions outside the company that are designed to improve the well-being of people in the host developing country and not actions within the company itself – a subject that I covered in my book *The Planetary Bargain*.

There are at least five main actions that MNEs can do to invoke CSD:

---

[17] James Collins and Jerry Porras (1994) *Built to Last*, HarperCollins, New York.

First, and of course many are doing this already, is to invest in developing countries and work toward allowing their exports to be freely imported into the rich countries – a huge and controversial issue that will play out for many decades to come. Will not these new imports hurt local markets in industrialized countries where the MNEs and many of their staff are located? Again, this is an issue that is being discussed vigorously in the development literature right now. This author's view is that the rich countries will innovate more quickly than the less-developed countries (LDCs) simply as a result of their higher level of skills and will continue to move into brain-intensive knowledge industries. As the LDCs start to move into these markets too, the economic growth that is being created will allow room for many and there is no particular reason for unemployment to rise drastically (that is another story).

Second, CSR is, for many, simply working with the local community. Clearly, improving local conditions is in the interest of MNEs to enhance reputation and preserve harmony. But these actions are not as easy as they seem on the surface. Three questions not easily answered are:

1   Where does the role of the MNE start and stop vis-à-vis the local community?
2   What are the key issues to be involved in?
3   Should MNEs be involved in human rights and if so, as many think, what are the limits?

Third, philanthropy has always been a big part of MNEs actions in LDCs (as will be discussed critically in Chapter 5). But so few of these actions are sustainable in the sense of whether, once the project has finished, its related activities will continue; this should not be confused with environmental sustainability.

Fourth, development assistance is key in many countries. This would best be done with existing development agencies, such as the UNDP, who have vast experience in development. Clearly, MNEs should not replace the UN nor government's own efforts. Simply, the power and wealth of MNEs need to be harnessed in positive development efforts. Should they be in addition to the taxes that MNEs pay anyway? Again, this is a more complicated subject than can be discussed here. Suffice to say that many tax contributions are handled poorly by governments, and MNEs can help governments to use their tax contributions more wisely while, at the same time, carrying out their own development projects in full consultation with the host government and UN agencies. Of course, another tax issue is 'where do corporates pay their taxes'?[18] Is rent-seeking behaviour on behalf of corporations to locate their tax contributions in favourable locations socially responsible? If corporations plough some of their money and ideas back

---

[18] As queried to me by Adrian Payne, personal communication, July 2006.

into global development, where they pay their taxes becomes less of an issue!

Fifth, improving people's skills in a myriad of ways is undoubtedly the best way to create sustainable development. Education, training, skill development, capacity development are all aspects of the same issue – improving human skills. There is no substitute and MNEs, with their wealth of experience in in-house training, have an enormous amount to contribute.

CSR can pave the way for development

Can CSR pave the way for development? The short answer is yes. CSR has paved the way for corporations to examine their wider role in society in ways that have never been done before. CSR is a systems concept that touches every part of a company and has both positive and negative effects. The wide role of CSR, coupled with the power and technological capacity of corporations, provides additional impetus for corporations and the private sector to be more involved in development than ever before. Clearly, governments will be the overall arbiter of development through the public purse, but their failure, along with their international partner the UN, in many developing countries has provided an empty space that must be filled by another entity – the private sector and its champions, the large corporations.

It is relatively easy to argue the obverse, that corporations should stick to making profits and leave development for governments. This, however, is a dance to the death, since the market left purely to profit maximization has been unable to fulfil social roles such as reducing unemployment, creating primary and secondary education for all, tackling the major diseases of the developing world and so on. Only time will tell whether corporations will take on this new challenge. To a certain extent MNEs will engage in development simply to ward off problems such as rising energy prices, resentment at off-shoring, consumer boycotts and so on. They should be cajoled and persuaded to take on the wider challenge of development; how they will do this if they decide to go forward are still subjects of intense discussion. My suggestions on what they should do are given in the last chapter of this book.

2

What is CSR all About and Where is it Going?

The lack of a widely agreed definition contributed to misunderstanding and cynicism towards the concept itself. If CSR means different things to different people then debate on its importance in strategy formulation and stakeholder management becomes confused, if not impossible.[1]

Introduction

The definition of CSR is clearly important as the quote above indicates.[2] For the purposes of this book, it is essential to know what I am talking about and why I believe CSR offers an opportunity to do much more on development than has been the case to date. In this chapter, therefore, I look at the various definitions and controversy surrounding CSR and conclude with what I think is the best definition of CSR.

My original CSR definition

A definition that I have used for some years is as follows:

> CSR is concerned with treating the stakeholders of the firm ethically or in a responsible manner. 'Ethically or responsible' means treating stakeholders in a manner deemed acceptable in

---

[1] Wan Saiful Wan Jan and Alan Gully: 'Defining Corporate Social Responsibility', presented at Conference on CSR, Middlesex University Business School, London, June 22 2005.

[2] Thanks to Sir Geoffrey Chandler and Prof. John Tepper Marlin for comments on an earlier draft. Both kindly gave me permission to use their comments as I saw fit but what remains is the responsibility of the author.

civilized societies. Social includes economic and environmental responsibility. Stakeholders exist both within a firm and outside. The wider aim of social responsibility is to create higher and higher standards of living, while preserving the profitability of the corporation, for peoples both within and outside the corporation.[3]

This definition is easier to criticize than to revise. Indeed, I am not sure that any definition of social phenomena ever reaches widespread agreement and I would be surprised if my lengthy definition would, anyway, be the definition of choice particularly given its length.[4]

Wordiness aside, the definition still does not cover all the key issues and there are at least ten concerns that are not elaborated in my definition. These are:

1   Who are the stakeholders?
2   Why include the word 'social' in the definition of a corporation's responsibility?
3   What is meant by 'ethical'?
4   Does 'treating stakeholders in a manner deemed acceptable in civilized societies' help to elaborate the word 'ethical'?
5   What is meant by a civilized society? Do any exist these days or did they ever?
6   What does responsible actually mean?
7   Is 'ethically' the same as 'responsible'?
8   Does social include economics and environment?
9   Why should a firm worry about 'outside' stakeholders?
10 Why should CSR care about creating higher standards of living for people outside the corporations?

---

[3] Michael Hopkins (2003) *The Planetary Bargain – CSR Matters*, London, Earthscan.

[4] I discussed in *The Planetary Bargain* the fact that corporate social responsibility is not a new issue. The social responsibility of business was not widely considered to be a significant problem from Adam Smith's time to the Great Depression. But since the 1930s, and increasingly since the 1960s, social responsibility has become 'an important issue not only for business but in the theory and practice of law, politics and economics'. See also A. B. Carroll (1979) 'A Three Dimensional Model of Corporate Social Performance', *Academy of Management Review*, vol 4, no 3, pp497–505; Dirk Matten and Jeremy Moon (2004) '"Implicit" and "Explicit" CSR A conceptual framework for understanding CSR in Europe', No. 29-2004 ICCSR Research Paper Series – ISSN1479-5124 Nottingham University; Marcel van Marrewijk (2003) 'Concepts and Definitions of CSR and Corporate Sustainability: Between Agency and Communion', *Journal of Business Ethics*, vol 44, pp95–105.

Market economy critique of CSR

As well as not elaborating on the above, the definition, in some eyes, also leaves out some key aspects. For instance, the word 'sustainability' is not mentioned. Neither, following a well-known definition (from the European Union (EU) and ILO), does it include the notion that CSR should be a 'voluntary' act of companies. Nor that CSR activities should be those of a company over and above its legal requirements.

But a clear definition is important, imperfect though it may be, otherwise there is complete confusion. This confusion is illustrated by a vigorous opponent of CSR, David Henderson. The editor of the *Journal of Financial Planning*, when interviewing Henderson, said: 'You've been described as the strongest critic of the CSR "movement". Are you totally against the concept of corporate social responsibility?' Henderson replied:

> *Not at all. But let's be clear about the differences between what I refer to as lowercase corporate social responsibility and upper case Corporate Social Responsibility. The former expects that businesses should act responsibly, which I have always supported. And the dialogue about how companies ought to behave is nothing new; it's been around for centuries. The latter is a dangerous new doctrine, which I oppose. Ardent advocates of CSR believe that what is involved is nothing less than a complete 'corporate transformation' and an entirely new concept of business's mission. If you look at economic history of the last 50 or 60 years, the role of business in a market economy is strongly positive and I see no reason to question or redefine it. Extraordinary advances have been made in countries that were previously seriously economically disadvantaged. My conclusion is that the material progress of people everywhere depends on the dynamism of the economies in which they live and work, and that rapid progress is now to be expected wherever the political and economic conditions exist for a market economy to operate efficiently. The adoption of CSR carries with it a high probability of cost increases and diminished performance.[5]*

Clearly, there is a lot of truth in this statement. But, when Henderson states: 'the role of business in a market economy is strongly positive and I see no reason to question or redefine it', one can only wonder at his absolute faith in the market economy. Countless examples of market failure exist, typified only recently by companies such as Union Carbide, Enron, WorldCom, and

---

[5] Anonymous (2005) *Journal of Financial Planning*, August, vol 18, no 8, p10.

the often overwhelming monopsonic power and strength of large corporations of which Microsoft and Wal-Mart are close examples.

My own position, as a proponent of CSR, is that the market economy works well when there is a level playing field. Companies compete poorly when there is a lack of information, when skills are distributed disproportionately, when transparency is cloudy or when laws favour the powerful over the weak. These latter items, and many more, are better controlled in richer nations than poor, in general. Although very friendly to the market economy, the George W. Bush administration has seen a substantial rise in poverty as laissez-faire[6] has been given its head.[7] Neatly encapsulating this latter view is the comment by Thomas Friedman (known for his generally supportive views of Bush) in the *New York Times* who wrote:

> *And then there are the president's standard lines: 'It's not the government's money; it's your money,' and, 'One of the last things that we need to do to this economy is to take money out of your pocket and fuel government.' An administration whose tax policy has been dominated by the toweringly selfish Grover Norquist – who has been quoted as saying: 'I don't want to abolish government. I simply want to reduce it to the size where I can drag it into the bathroom and drown it in the bathtub' – doesn't have the instincts for this moment.*[8]

Consequently, I believe CSR is a powerful tool, as I define it, for reducing the excesses of the private sector while, at the same time, ensuring its profitability.

The technique of setting up a 'straw man' and then knocking it down is a trick used by many bright, and sometimes scurrilous, people to make an argument. Henderson is no exception. Indeed, a Henderson definition is

---

[6] Perhaps if laissez-faire capitalism had been given its head then the situation may have been better – education levels the playing field, at which point markets can favour the many rather than the few. However, the Bush administration has created a huge fiscal imbalance through tax cuts that favour the rich, and defence spending increases, i.e. it is a very interventionist Government.

[7] Paul Harris (2006) '37 Million Poor Hidden in the Land of Plenty', *The Observer*, London, UK, 19 February. He noted that 'Americans have always believed that hard work will bring rewards, but vast numbers now cannot meet their bills even with two or three jobs. More than one in 10 citizens live below the poverty line, and the gap between the haves and have-nots is widening. That is 12.7 per cent of the population – the highest percentage in the developed world. They are found from the hills of Kentucky to Detroit's streets, from the Deep South of Louisiana to the heartland of Oklahoma. Each year since 2001 their number has grown. Under President George W. Bush an extra 5.4 million have slipped below the poverty line'.

[8] Thomas Friedman (2005) 'Osama and Katrina', Op-Ed column, *New York Times*, New York, US, 7 September.

awaited even of 'lowercase CSR'. As Henderson mentions himself when he writes in the same article quoted above:

> *So, just what is CSR and how are companies supposed to behave differently if they embrace it? There is no one good definition of CSR, and that's the problem. But I'll answer that by using some of the stock phrases that have come into use. CSR-oriented firms are supposed to embrace corporate citizenship and adopt as their goal 'sustainable development'. They must pursue sustainable development in conjunction with an array of different stakeholders – in fact, they should buy into multi-stakeholder engagement. This notion of sustainable development also doesn't have one good, accepted definition. CSR advocates call it working to meet the triple bottom line: financial, environmental, and social.*

Again, Henderson doesn't define CSR. If, for instance, he had taken my above definition he would see that embracing 'corporate citizenship' or 'sustainable development' are not there. This is not surprising, perhaps, since both concepts are fuzzy as I shall show next.

Corporate citizenship has been defined to be:

> **Corporate citizenship is about business taking greater account of its social and environmental – as well as its financial – footprints.**[9]

Thus this definition is more limited than my definition of CSR since it ignores the stakeholder issue and does not mention whether 'greater account' means acting responsibly (which I presume it does) nor does it say what is meant by 'greater'? Greater than before, greater than competitors or whatever?

More recently, Donna Wood and others have taken the concept of citizenship much further and introduced the notion of 'global business citizenship' where 'a global business citizen is a business enterprise (including its managers) that responsibly exercises its rights and implements its duties to individuals, stakeholders, and societies within and across national and cultural borders'.[10] This innovative view is similar to my definition of CSR and also takes the concept into the global sphere as I do in this book – 'The concept of global business citizenship takes the older, societally based notion of CSR into the global arena where national sovereignty no longer suffices for basic rule-setting and enforcement.'[11]

---

[9] Simon Zadek (2001) *The Civil Corporation*, London, Earthscan, p7.
[10] Donna J. Wood, Jeanne M. Logsdon, Patsy G. Lewellyn, Kim Davenport (2006) *Global Business Citizenship: A Transformative Framework for Ethics and Sustainable Capitalism*, Armonk, New York, M.E. Sharpe, p4.
[11] Donna J. Wood et al (2006) *ibid.*, p219.

Would corporate sustainability be a better concept than CSR?

Corporate sustainability arose out of the environmental movement and, in particular, the Brundtland Definition that emerged, in 1987, from the World Commission on Environment and Development (the Brundtland Commission). Its widely quoted definition of sustainable development is as follows:

> **Sustainable development is development that meets the needs of the present without compromising the ability of future generations to meet their own needs. (Brundtland Commission Report, p43)**

So, this definition was closely concerned with the longer-term issues of environment but has gradually come to be concerned with wider issues as well. In particular, many companies, not liking the implications of the word 'social' in CSR tend to use the notion of corporate sustainability which, in turn, is defined as:

> **corporate sustainability can be defined as meeting society's expectation that companies add social, environmental and economic value from their operations, products and services. (PriceWaterhouseCoopers)[12]**

Note, therefore, that corporate sustainability is similar to my CSR definition above and to that of corporate citizenship. However, it does not take into account stakeholders, ethics or responsible behaviour.

The notion of sustainability was originally thought of as development that seeks to be continuous amid worries that existing development will be resource constrained by the carrying capacity of earth's natural resources and eco-systems. The term sustainability first came to widespread acceptance, as noted above, in the Brundtland report in 1987. At that time the concept and study of sustainable development had hardly left the domain of environmentalists and ecologists. For instance, the Global Reporting Initiative (GRI) grew out of environmental work by the Coalition for Environmentally Responsible Economies (CERES) and, in June 2000, the United Nations Environment Programme (UNEP) produced the GRI Sustainability Reporting Guidelines that cover economic and social performance as well as the more 'traditional' environmental ones.

---

12 www.pwc.com/extweb/service.nsf/docid/C5CCD7A9C84C98E7852569040003 9DAF, accessed 14 August 2006.

But many companies have taken on board the notion of corporate sustainability and many are now producing 'sustainability reports'.[13] For instance, the Dow Jones Sustainability rankings put ABB as number one in the Dow Jones on its 'sustainability' index and notes that there is mounting evidence that the financial performance of sustainable companies that are performing well is superior to that of companies that are ranked lower.[14]

So, should Corporate Social Responsibility (CSR) now read Corporate Sustainability (CSu)? There is a strong semantic attraction for that since it is clear that the notion of sustainability has an attractive ring about it to hard-pressed CEOs trying to keep, and raise, shareholder value as well as keeping an eye on a plethora of social concerns, while responsibility appears, at face value, to be about the 'nice' things a company should do.

As the word 'sustainability' widens its acceptance outside the environmental movement to now include economic and social phenomena, it is probably true to say that CSR and CSu are two sides of the same coin, that is to say they are accepted as meaning the same thing even if they do not. Humpty Dumpty as Sir Geoffrey Chandler calls it, implying a cavalier use of words.[15] In fact there are probably few companies that are 'sustainable' – they may keep the same name but few are likely to go on and on. For instance, as oil runs out over the next hundred years or so, Shell may well be the world's biggest producer of hydrogen from seawater as well as of other renewables such as wind power. But Shell may not exist as the billions it gains from oil are harder to earn elsewhere.

However, excluding the word 'social' from CSR, leaving us with the phrase 'Corporate Responsibility' is, to use an ugly but apt expression, simply throwing the baby out with the bathwater. I define social to include economic and environmental (precedence is set by the fact that most universities have schools of social science that include sociology, economics, political science, environmental sciences, and so on). If the word 'social' is left out of CSR, then it is less clear what is implied. It could imply attention to corporate governance and agreeing to obey the law. But even that latter sentiment, although praiseworthy, falls down in many countries – for instance, Uzbekistan has rigorous laws about labour standards but, in practice, ignores most of them. Thus, corporate responsibility, without the

---

[13] See, e.g., Michael Hopkins (2000) 'Is Corporate Social Responsibility the Same as Corporate Sustainability?', MHCi Monthly Feature, December, www.mhcinternational.com.

[14] Unfortunately ABB's posture does not seem to be sustainable as evidenced by ABB moving its sustainability group into its PR function in mid 2005 while its former head, Christian Kornewall, moved to the World Business Council for Sustainable Development in Geneva (WBCSD).

[15] Personal communication cited with permission. Sir Geoffrey is founder-Chair of Amnesty International UK Business Group 1991–2001; former senior manager at Royal Dutch/Shell; former Director General of the UK National Economic Development Office.

qualifying word 'social' adds further confusion to what is now becoming a confusion of definitions.

Corporate social performance and responsiveness

Scholars in the US in the 'Business in Society' field (also known as Societal Issues in Management – SIM), as far back as 30 years ago, were concerned about how much social responsibility there should be in an enterprise, given that it is a social entity as well as a profit-making one. In 1975, Preston and Post suggested an approach that helped to establish the legitimacy of the field.[16] Business had been previously assumed to be an independent social force, which interacted with other social forces but was not influenced by them. Preston and Post pointed out that all social systems 'penetrate' and mutually affect one another. Employees, for example, do not exist wholly within a business, but also represent the external world and bring their own skills, understandings, prejudices and limitations to the workplace. Similarly, a manufacturing business buys certain raw materials, but freely 'uses' air and water in its processes. Practices, for instance, that take vast amounts of water from general usage or that emit residue into the atmosphere penetrate other aspects of society, and give society the legitimate right to examine the role of business in society.

Arguably, there is a case for replacing the word 'responsibility'. American academicians prefer the term 'performance' and use the term 'corporate social performance'. For instance, Preston and Post focused interest on a firm's ability to respond to social issues,[17] corporate social responsiveness, or 'CSR_2' as it was named by Frederick, the '$_2$' indicating responsiveness rather than responsibility.[18] Social responsiveness was defined by Frederick to be *the capacity of the corporation to respond to social issues*. As corporate social responsibility had already claimed, the acronym 'CSR', Frederick referred to corporate social responsiveness as 'CSR_2'.

Frederick observed that Preston and Post's models could not offer a means by which a business's fulfilment of its responsibilities to society could be measured. They proposed a conceptual shift to look at the responsiveness of business to social issues and sought to classify such responses as: 'reactive, defensive or responsive'. Thus a wholly different layer of analysis was added to simple responsibility within the general domain of ethical principles: a consideration of action was added.

---

[16] Lee E. Preston and J. E. Post (1975) *Private Management and Public Policy: The Principle of Public Responsibility*, Englewood Cliffs, NJ, Prentice-Hall, p3.
[17] Preston and Post, *ibid.*, p3.
[18] William C. Frederick (1978) 'From CSR_1 to CSR_2: The Maturing of Business-and-Society Thought', Working Paper, Katz Graduate School of Business, University of Pittsburgh.

Like Frederick, Donna Wood recognized that neither motivating principle nor 'responsiveness' lent itself to measurement, nor did either one take full cognisance of the roles of the stakeholders.[19] Clearly, both authors take on board the aphorism that 'what gets measured gets done'. I agree with that assertion but will not go into it in great detail here. Suffice to say that some phenomena are much easier to measure than others. Certainly, business (as well as governments) follow this age-old adage since we have a surfeit of financial information but much less on social issues, which are harder to measure in general.

Donna Wood sought a model that would include the outcomes of social responsiveness as actual indicators of corporate social performance. In her 1994 book (see footnote 19), Wood defined CSP as 'a business organization's configuration of: principles of social responsibility, processes of social responsiveness and observable outcomes as they relate to the firm's societal relationships'.

Clearly, replacing responsibility with the word development focuses on what corporations could do to achieve the development of social phenomena in and surrounding their company. Responsibility suffers from the notion of whose responsibility are we talking about? A responsible person can still break the law – witness the case of Judith Miller of *The New York Times* who spent 90 days in jail trying to preserve a journalist's guarantee of confidentiality to sources. Does that mean that if someone breaks the law and works for a particular company then that company is no longer considered socially responsible because one person in the company has broken the law and the company acquiesces? For instance, does the fact that *The New York Times* will re-hire Miller make it socially irresponsible? So, we can see that there is a problem with the word 'responsibility'. But the current meaning refers to a company endeavouring to be responsible toward its stakeholders that is, it works with them to achieve harmony while ensuring that such harmony does not bring the company to its knees. Clearly the case of low wages, as described in Chapter 8, means that paying low wages (but not starvation wages, nor slavery, nor through forced or coercive behaviour) to ensure the survival of a company should be acceptable as long as once the company is on the road to survival wages and conditions are adjusted accordingly. But legal issues are much more complicated – hence those who argue that a company's social responsibility is purely to obey the law cannot use that argument so simply.

---

[19] Donna J. Wood (1994) *Business and Society*, 2nd edn, New York, HarperCollins.

More CSR definitions

The UK definition

That confusion exists about definitions, even at the highest levels, is typified by a statement from the former UK Minister for CSR, Nigel Griffiths MP, when he wrote:

> *CSR, or corporate responsibility as I call it* [sic!], *is about the way businesses take account of their economic, social and environmental impacts in the way they operate – maximizing the benefits and minimizing the downsides.*[20]

In the same book, in a chapter by Tim Clement-Jones, we can find a more interesting and useful definition. Jones cites the UK government's Department of Trade and Industry-sponsored Corporate Responsibility Group who defined CSR as:

> **The management of an organization's total impact upon both its immediate stakeholders and upon the society within which it operates. CSR is not simply about whatever funds and expertise companies choose to invest in communities to help resolve social problems, it is about the integrity with which a company governs itself, fulfils its mission, lives by its values, engages with its stakeholders, measures its impacts and reports on its activities.**[21]

But is it not rather strange to have a definition stating what CSR is not rather than what it is? It is also strange to include new concepts such as 'mission', 'values', 'impacts' (on what one may ask?), and 'reports'. It includes the word 'stakeholder' without defining what is meant but, at least, does not appear to be too far away from my definition at the beginning of this book. However, it does lead me to question whether my own definition could not be improved by a clearer definition, at least, of stakeholder. I shall leave that discussion to the end of this piece, as I continue to look at other statements about CSR.

---

[20] Nigel Griffiths in John Hancock (ed.) (2004) *Investing in CSR – A Guide to Best Practice, Business Planning and the UK's Leading Companies*, London and Sterling, Kogan Page, pvi.

[21] Tim Clement-Jones in John Hancock (ed.) (2004) *ibid.*, p8.

WBCSD definition

Another prominent definition of CSR is the one by the World Business Council for Sustainable Development, which is as follows:

> **continuing commitment by business to behave ethically and contribute to economic development while improving the quality of life of the workforce and their families, as well as of the local community and society at large.**[22]

Here we see an attempt to include stakeholders (workforce, families, local community, society at large) and even to 'contribute to economic development'. More on the latter below, but it is clear that the WBSCD has a limited notion of who the stakeholders of a company should be. Again, more on this below.

EU definition

Even as companies struggle with voluntary principles and standards, which critics argue raise the cost of compliance, there is a gradual movement toward regulation. One part of this is coming from the EU but various drafts of its papers indicate the struggle within its walls between whether legislate or not.[23] Its green paper in July 2001 argued:

> *Corporate social responsibility should nevertheless not be seen as a substitute to regulation or legislation concerning social rights or environmental standards, including the development of new appropriate legislation. In countries where such regulations do not exist, efforts should focus on putting the proper regulatory or legislative framework in place in order to define a level playing field on the basis of which socially responsible practices can be developed.* (EU Green Paper, 18.7.2001)

However, after consultation, that paragraph was dropped from the EU's white paper published in July 2002. The EU even defined CSR as being voluntary when it said:

> **CSR is a concept whereby companies integrate social and environmental concerns in their business operations and in**

---

[22] www.wbcsd.org/DocRoot/RGk80O49q8ErwmWXIwtF/CSRmeeting.pdf, p6, accessed 14 August 2006.
[23] See Michael Hopkins 'CSR and Legislation', MHCi Monthly Feature, July 2002, www.mhcinternational.com.

their interaction with their stakeholders on a *voluntary* basis
[emphasis added][24]

In correspondence with one of the EU authors, I noted that the EU included
process in their CSR definition with the addition of 'on a voluntary basis'.
I suggested that the word 'voluntary' should be eliminated since you cannot then consider 'any' regulation however minor. The EU official kindly
replied that he thought that the definition is obviously a crucial point.

> *Our compromise was to use again the definition given in
> the Green paper, which puts stress on that CSR means going
> beyond obligations and thus is by nature voluntary. This focus
> reflects the approach adopted by the Commission, which is
> not to regulate CSR but to facilitate the dialogue between the
> stakeholders on CSR issues and to promote existing market
> developments. In 2004 we will have more evidence to judge
> what can be achieved through this approach.* (Note that the
> EU definition has not since changed.)

ILO definition

The ILO World Commission on the Social Dimension of Globalization
went as far as to distinguish between corporate governance and CSR
as two essentially different concepts. The former, the Commission states,
is:

> essentially concerned with issues of ownership and control of
> enterprises

but it then cites OECD principles of Corporate Governance that good corporate governance:

> helps to ensure that corporations take into account the inter-
> ests of a wide range of constituencies, as well as the communi-
> ties within which they operate.

The ILO Commission defined CSR to be:

> the voluntary initiatives enterprises undertake over and above
> their legal obligations.

---

[24] EU White Paper (July 2002).

The Commission report reflects the strong influence of a little known business organization, the International Organisation of Employers (IOE), whose view is that CSR is a set of:

> **initiatives by companies voluntarily integrating social and environmental concerns in their business operations and in their interaction with their stakeholders.[25]**

Moreover, in the IOE's own submission to the World Commission, the IOE sees CSR to be:

> **a core aspect of business activities throughout a company and recognizes CSR as a means of engagement with stakeholders in the various markets in which a company operates.**

It is interesting that the ILO World Commission document and IOE both see the legislative part of business in society as corporate governance, while the voluntary part as CSR. Not something I agree with, particularly since a major concern for multinationals is the issue of legislation. Many of the bigger companies, in fact, welcome some legislation since it helps to create a level playing field.

But the question is not whether CSR activities should be voluntary but where on the scale between no legislation and total legislation the pointer should be set. For instance, many companies are happy with rules about child labour and approach the ILO for guidance. But as Philip Jennings, the General Secretary of Union Network International noted:

> *Companies and governments overwhelmingly want the public both to believe in the ethical corporation and at the same time do not want to provide new legal backing for tighter ethical behaviour... But the ethics genie is out of the bottle and its operational principles are proving difficult to control. Another big change is that workers and citizens as stakeholders can now be involved directly with powerful corporations. Traditional global standards (ILO/OECD) are mainly administered through governments: their exercise is remote and complex.[26]*

Both the ILO and the IOE insist on voluntary initiatives for CSR. Yet, there will always be both voluntary and prescriptive rules for corporate behaviour including for social aspects since there is always some social legislation

---

[25] International Organisation of Employers (2003) 'Corporate Social Responsibility: An IOE Approach', 21 March, Geneva.

[26] Philip J. Jennings, UNI General Secretary, Union Network International, http://www.union-network.org/uniindep.nsf/0/0240DE313E8F1A64C1256E5A0043FA88? OpenDocument.

which limits what corporations can do or obliges them to do something such as respect minimum wages. Thus defining CSR as a set of voluntary initiatives misses the point that there is a dividing line between voluntary and obligatory. Both the ILO and the IOE could make a useful contribution by being clear on which issues require legislation and which do not. To a certain extent, the CSR and legislation issue is a red herring, since the most important point is that countries often have excellent social legislation but, in practice, the legislation is ignored.

And as Sir Geoffrey Chandler wrote in one of his comments on my regular 'Monthly Features':

> It is the word 'voluntary' which is my sticking point [when defining CSR]. Is honesty 'voluntary'? Are humane labour conditions when the law does not prescribe them 'voluntary'? There is a real difference between the normative and the voluntary. If indeed CSR is defined as something you can choose to do or not, then I shall start saving up for my funeral wreath for capitalism. Union Carbide voluntarily decided not to exercise due care over their Bhopal plant and thereby killed and maimed thousands of people.[27]

William Werther and David Chandler definition

William Werther and David Chandler have put a lot of thought into CSR and, in their book on strategic CSR, define CSR to be:

> **The broad concept that businesses are more than just for-profit seeking entities and, therefore, also have an obligation to benefit society.[28]**

This precise definition is encompassed by my definition above with two main exceptions. I specify further what is meant by society (through identifying stakeholders) and I state that corporation profits must be allowed. William Werther and David Chandler have a more cavalier approach to profits. Clearly, a company is going to be useless for all concerned if it is unprofitable. The key issues is not profits per se but how profits are made.

---

[27] Personal communication, June 2005, cited with permission.
[28] William B. Werther, Jr and David Chandler (2005) *Strategic Corporate Social Responsibility: Stakeholders in a Global Environment*, USA, Sage Publications.

Does my own definition hold water?

Sir Geoffrey Chandler has raised several important criticisms both of my definition of CSR and my link between CSR and development. He writes:

> *I still find your arguments confused by the absence of any clear definition of CSR. It still seems to be in your view something you add on. E.g. 'Adoption of CSR shows that large corporations have accepted that they cannot ignore their responsibility' and 'translating CSR into social development per se'. What is this magic additive? I would continue to argue that corporate responsibility is the conduct of operations in a manner that reflects international standards in the treatment of all stakeholders. I think the international values set out in the UDHR [Universal Declaration of Human Rights], the Convention on the Rights of the Child, and the core ILO conventions today set the ethical framework which we are entitled to expect companies to follow. And indeed it is those instruments which underlie the business principles of BP, Shell and a growing number (84 I think at the latest count) of major companies today.*
>
> *It's a point of departure. If indeed adopted by all companies (which is a long way from happening), it would really change the world. It is of course true that company operations can be conducted in a manner which assists the broader development of a country or community and that – as you say – requires discussion with the government of that country or that particular community This is not 'social development per se', which is the responsibility of governments: it is the sensitive aligning of company operations (which the company understands) with community needs which only the community can tell it and which will therefore require the involvement of that community. E.g. the building of roads for company use in a manner that helps, rather than hinders, the needs of a community. The suggestion that companies should deal with 'social development per se' plays into the hands of right-wing economists such as David Henderson who legitimately lampoon the wilder shores of CSR but in so doing throw out the baby of real corporate responsibility with the bathwater of misconceptions.*
>
> *This may be an objective for a society or an individual, but it is far too general and unspecific for a company. My own view is that corporate responsibility (CSR if one must, but why the 'S' unless one believes that a company's core occupation is not socially useful?) means providing a product or service in a principled manner, the principles being determined by the values I have cited above.*

> *Stakeholders I see as those who contribute to the success of a company or are affected by its operations. I think I would exclude government from your list. Academics – who too often tend to be academic in the pejorative sense – tend to include NGOs, the media and Uncle Tom Cobbleigh and all so that – as in The Gondoliers – when everyone is somebody, then no one's anybody.[29]*

Thus Sir Geoffrey believes that 'international standards' should be the basis for the interaction with stakeholders. Elsewhere, Sir Geoffrey argues that these standards should come under the auspices of the standards being developed for business by the UN Commission for Human Rights and, in particular, the UN human rights Norms for transnational corporations (TNCs) and other businesses. He writes that: 'The Norms tackled one of the foremost challenges of the 21st century – the need to ensure that companies, now the dominant feature in the post-Cold War economy, reflect the values of society in their behaviour.'[30] But, the choice of which standard to use is a real problem for TNCs, as Sir Geoffrey noted:

> *While human rights today feature in all discussions of corporate responsibility, there are no universally accepted standards against which shareholders, other stakeholders, and, most importantly, the market can judge comparative company performance. The Norms were intended to fill this gap, providing not a legally enforceable framework, but a set of principles which companies could be expected to observe and against which their performance could be judged. They made a significant contribution in distilling from a wide range of internationally agreed instruments the elements relevant to the sphere of influence of companies, something which neither the UN Global Compact nor OECD Guidelines provided. But they suffered from the compromises necessary to obtain unanimous agreement from 26 disparate country experts which led to increasing elaboration and the addition of clauses on monitoring which provided ample fodder for controversy (see Note 29).*

All well and good, but the UN is a collection of over 200 nation states with the UN Commission for Human Rights directly in the sights of the current US administration. It is unlikely that the norms that will eventually emanate from over 200 nation states will be any better than those created

---

[29] Sir Geoffrey Chandler, personal communication, 14 July 2005, reproduced with permission.
[30] *Corporate Responsibility Management* (2005) vol 1, no 6, June/July, www.melcrum.com.

by the OECD which only had 26 nation states with which to reach 'unanimous agreement'. But, as Sir Geoffrey reminded me:

> *These '200 nation states' have outlawed slavery and torture. Sure, they still happen, but they are an international crime. These '200 nation states' have agreed the UDHR and all the subsequent instruments which depend from it. If we want to live in a world dominated by Bush and John Bolton we will dismiss the lot. But at our peril![31]*

But, as Sir Geoffrey worries, what are the limits of a companies' responsibilities on social development? As I argued in Chapter 1, the failure of governments and international organizations to resolve the problem of under-development leaves mainly the private sector to do something about the issue. Obviously, one can argue for improved governance in developing countries and an improved UN and its agencies. However, this latter effort has been ongoing for decades without noticeable improvement. Should, as seems likely, only marginal improvements be seen from these traditional sources, then restricting companies to only those activities directly related to their business means that under-development will continue.

The power and reach of the largest companies in the world have to be put into the service of development much more than ever before. I don't think that this is a 'wild assertion' as Henderson would have it. It is too risky to accept Henderson's conventional view of the firm where anything that is good for business is good for the world. Much more must be expected of companies than hitherto. Continuing under-development is not in the longer-term interests of corporations – those who seek only to service the rich and not the poor will continue to exacerbate the growing divide between rich and poor around the world.[32] This divide will come back and hurt at some point either through a worldwide consumer protest and boycott of those companies who are considered not to 'care' or as targets of worldwide unrest and aggression or a combination of the two.

Sir Geoffrey raises another key problem with my definition of CSR. I state that:

> *CSR is concerned with treating the stakeholders of the firm ethically or in a responsible manner. 'Ethically or responsible' means treating stakeholders in a manner deemed acceptable in civilized societies.*

---

[31] Sir Geoffrey Chandler, personal communication, 8 September 2005.
[32] A UN report – drawn up by the UN's Economic and Social Affairs Department – found that the gap between the rich and the poor is now wider than it was a decade ago, and called for immediate action. http://news.bbc.co.uk/2/hi/americas/4185458.stm.

While Sir Geoffrey remarks:

> *I really have problems with your definition of CSR. Ethical behaviour I do not believe is in the eye of the beholder.*[33]

My statement follows the American 20th-century philosopher Rawls who established universal principles of a just society through a social contract and argued that these principles should be based upon how a 'reasonable' person would act. Obviously, this formulation leads to even further questions, for instance, what is meant by a 'reasonable person'? For more details on this discussion I refer readers to one of the classical books on business ethics by Thomas Donaldson and Pat Werhane.[34] Their book covers philosophical issues of ethics in business, of which the main strands are consequentialism, deontology and human nature ethics. That means, respectively, ethical reasoning concentrating either on the consequences of human actions (consequentialism), or following rules and principles that guide actions (deontological), or a human nature approach that assumes all humans have inherent capacities that constitute the ultimate basis for all ethical claims.[35]

Indeed, as remarked by John Tepper Marlin, Sir Geoffrey is:

> *taking a deontological approach – duty, sacred commandment. The other ethical approach is consequential – what happens if we do x and are we all better off? Some things are universalizable – thou shalt not kill. But seemingly universalizable principles like 'thou shalt not steal' or 'thou shalt not bear false witness' turn out to be parsable under the consequential microscope.*[36]

Who, then, is the beholder? Sir Geoffrey is correct if the beholder is an Adolf, Saddam or a Rumsfeld. So the beholder has to be a 'reasonable' person, that is someone with whom most people would not have a problem. But most people can be wrong. I stop here since it is clear that any definition is going to start running into these philosophical discussions, and there are philosophers such as Rawls who handle these issues better than I.

---

[33] Sir Geoffrey Chandler, personal communication, 5 April 2005.
[34] T. Donaldson and P. Werhane (1999) *Ethical Issues in Business: A Philosophical Approach*, 6th edn, New Jersey, Prentice Hall, pp8–11.
[35] Drawn from Donaldson and Werhane, *ibid.*, pp6–10.
[36] John Tepper Marlin, personal communication, May 2005. John teaches CR and ethics at the Stern School at New York University.

Corporate governance and CSR as a systems approach

Before concluding this chapter, I should like to make a few remarks about the universalism of CSR and why, as I argued in Chapter 1, I see CSR as a systems approach, that is one which, according to Clark et al, states that the problem is defined and the systems boundary delineated so that all important influences on resolving the problem are taken into consideration to the issue of business in society.[37] Many of the criticisms of CSR stem from problems with concepts and definitions.

I believe that the area of corporate governance is also part of the CSR system. Sir Adrian Cadbury defines corporate governance as:

> **Corporate Governance is concerned with holding the balance between economic and social goals and between individual and communal goals. The corporate governance framework is there to encourage the efficient use of resources and equally to require accountability for the stewardship of those resources. The aim is to align as nearly as possible the interests of individuals, corporations and society.[38]**

The basis for recent international work (see, for instance, the World Bank's work in www.gcgF.org) on Corporate Governance is the OECD 'Principles of Corporate Governance' (www.oecd.org) which cover the rights of shareholders, the equitable treatment of shareholders, the role of stakeholders in corporate governance, disclosure and transparency and the responsibilities of the board. The World Bank notes, however, that there is no single model of corporate governance with systems varying by country, sector and even in the same corporation over time. Among the most prominent systems are the US and UK models, which focus on dispersed controls; and the German and Japanese models which reflect a more concentrated ownership structure.

As I noted above, CSR is concerned with treating the stakeholders of the firm ethically or in a socially responsible manner. Stakeholders exist both within a firm and outside. Consequently, behaving in a manner which is socially responsible will increase the human development of stakeholders both within and outside the corporation. This definition is much wider than the stakeholder definition used, to date, by the OECD and the World Bank. For instance, the OECD principles imply that a key role for stake-

---

[37] John Clark, Sam Cole, Michael Hopkins and Ray Curnow (1975) *Global Simulation Models*, published for SPRU, University of Sussex by John Wiley, New York and London.

[38] Sir Adrian Cadbury (2000) 'Global Corporate Governance Forum', World Bank. Cited in www.csd.bg/bg/fileSrc.php?id=461#299,17,A_Broad_Definition, accessed 15 January 2006.

holders is concerned with ensuring the flow of external capital to firms and that stakeholders are protected by law and have access to disclosure. The World Bank have been intrigued by a June 2000 Investor Opinion Survey by McKinsey, which finds that investors say that board governance is as important as financial performance in their investment decisions and that across Latin America, Europe, the US and Asia investors (over 80 per cent of those interviewed) would be willing to pay more for a company with good board governance practices.[39] 'Poor governance' was defined by McKinsey as a company that has:

- a minority of outside directors;
- outside directors who have financial ties with management;
- directors who own little or no stock;
- directors who are compensated only with cash;
- no formal director evaluation process;
- a very unresponsive attitude to investor requests for information on governance issues.

'Good governance' was defined by McKinsey as:

- a majority of outside directors;
- outside directors who are truly independent, with no management ties;
- directors who have significant stockholdings;
- a large proportion of director pay is in stock or options;
- a formal director evaluation in place;
- a very responsive attitude to investor requests for information on governance issues.

Given the questions, it is not surprising that the figure of 80 per cent was reached, but the point is that 'good governance' has a very narrow fit to the OECD principles and an even narrower fit when compared with corporate social responsibility sentiments.

Nevertheless, there is increasing advocacy of a broader and more inclusive concept of corporate governance that extends to corporate responsibility and has a wider concept of 'stakeholder' than that used by the OECD (see Figure 2.1). These ideas are reflected in the King Report for South Africa, the Commonwealth principles of business practice, the UK's Tomorrow's Company and so on.

In conclusion, the notion of corporate governance fits well into current concerns of management structure at the top of corporations and is becoming increasingly better defined thanks to the work of the World Bank and the OECD, but hardly encompasses the concerns of corporate social responsibility notions. On the other hand, notions of corporate social

---

[39] See McKinsey & Co. (2000) 'Investor Opinion Survey on Corporate Governance', http://www.gcgf.org/docs/72CGBrochure.PDF.

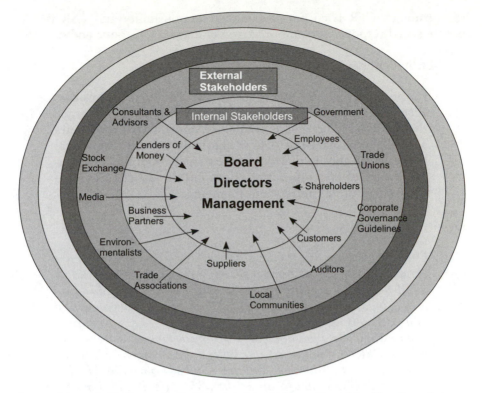

Source: Schematic kindly supplied with permission of Mervyn King of the King Commission, South Africa

Figure 2.1 *Corporate governance framework*

responsibility have not advanced as far as the corporate governance school with its agreed set of principles. There is light on the horizon thanks to work by King and others and also in the Cadbury definition itself that notes that the aim of corporate governance is to align as nearly as possible the interests of individuals, corporations and society.

Corporate responsibility versus CSR

John Tepper Marlin uses corporate responsibility (CR) as a generic term for the responsibility field.[40] Consequently, CER is corporate environmental

---

[40] John kindly sent me his lecture notes from which comes: 'Corporate responsibility as used in this book is the sum of corporate financial responsibility, corporate environmental responsibility and corporate social responsibility, i.e., CR = (CFR+CER+CSR). This follows usage adopted by Chiquita, the Economist Intelligence Unit, and others.'

responsibility, CFR is corporate financial responsibility and CSR is corporate social responsibility, more narrowly defined as labour and community.

Marlin defines CR as:

> **Corporate responsibility (CR) is the conduct of business according to both ethical standards and the law. Some argue that CR is a red herring or even an oxymoron, that companies are simply mechanisms to serve shareholders and that ethical concerns are alien to this idea of the corporation. But a mechanistic view of the corporations does not do justice to the history of corporate charters and financing.**

He also remarks that:

> *Our two definitions (of CR as I use it and CSR as you do) are actually not incompatible, because you refer to all stakeholders and I refer to doing more than the law requires. My objection is to using CSR as meaning only CER and CSR (environmental and narrowly defined social responsibility) – i.e. eliminating responsibility to shareholders (Corporate Financial Responsibility – CFR). Elkington's triple bottom line assigns CSR to the non-financial bottom lines and that is what I object to. Having worked on CSR issues for more than 35 years, I'm looking for the simplest possible definition. But as Lord Melbourne told his Cabinet 'It is not much matter which we say, but mind, we must all say the same.'[41]*

I like John Tepper Marlin's approach, since it more clearly identifies environment and financial responsibilities. However, my sticking point has always been the photo of George W. Bush on the front of many US newspapers in 2001 promoting the concept of corporate responsibility. Frankly, Bush's respect for accuracy has been so doubtful that just about anything associated with him makes me suspicious. But, as John Tepper Marlin remarked:

> *While George W. Bush misused the term CR, Robert Reich [Sec of Labor under Clinton] told me that he objects to the use of CSR as a general term: 'I support CR,' he said, 'but not CSR.' Chiquita now uses CR in their report. The reason Bush misused the term CR is that he was invoking it in the context of introducing Sarbanes-Oxley, which as we all know now was a massive increase in government oversight of corpo-*

---

[41] Personal communication, op cit.

rate finances. Bush was using CR as a distracter. The backdrop
should have said: 'MORE GOVERNMENT REGULATION
OF BUSINESS'.[42]

Concluding remarks on definition

Is the definition I started out with robust enough to withhold the various criticisms that I have outlined in this chapter? In summary, there are three main concerns with my definition:

1   The word 'social' should be dropped and the term 'corporate responsibility' used.
2   Who should be included as the stakeholders.
3   It is too much of a burden for companies to be involved significantly in development.

My response in this chapter has been that first, 'social' must be included in order to emphasize the social aspects of business in society. One cannot leave out the word 'social' without completely changing the notion of CSR.

Second, inside the company it is clear that the key stakeholders are the managers, board of directors and employees. Outside the company the clearly important parties are the customers, shareholders, trade unions, the natural environment and suppliers. But what about the other stakeholders frequently cited, such as the community, government, international bodies (the EU or UN, NGOs and so on)? Certainly, companies need to take account of these stakeholders, but to what extent? Opinion is still divided. There is no consensus here except that companies should obey the law. But in many countries around the world the application of the law is poor and companies can sidestep it relatively easily. Thus, clearly, companies must often be ahead of the law, particularly its application.

Third, it is the responsibility of companies to be involved in development. This widens substantially the notion of a company and their responsibilities. This I tackled in Chapter 1 where I argued that the public sector is doing a poor job and by default there is no one left except for the private sector.

Support for my definition of CSR has come from two authors, Wan and Gully, who, after having reviewed various definitions of CSR, concluded:

Thus, the authors believe that the definition provided by Hop-
kins (2003), that CSR means 'treating the stakeholders of the
firm ethically or in a responsible manner', best depicts the true

---

[42]   Personal communication, op cit.

> *concept of CSR. This definition allows CSR to be seen both as an ethical stance and as a business strategy. It also provides a means of seeing how CSR can or should work in practice. It conforms to the argument that CSR should be an ethical stance of the firm without any expectation of getting rewards or pay-back as this definition does not put any emphasis on reaping benefits to the firm. It also does not reject the notion that CSR should be aimed at enhancing profitability since by serving the needs of all stakeholders, the firm has a better chance to gain their trust, earn an enhanced reputation, and be rewarded by an increased willingness of stakeholders to be involved with the 'ethical organisation'.*[43]

Sir Geoffrey Chandler believes I should shorten my definition to:[44]

> **Corporate responsibility means treating all of a company's stakeholders responsibly, that is in a manner consistent with society's values.**

But I believe my original definition more fully explains what I mean by CSR. So, despite the objections raised, it is not easy to see how the definition could be improved and, to quote one of the reviewers of this chapter:

> *perfection is paralysis.*[45]

Thus I believe my definition is robust enough to convey what I and many others mean by Corporate Social Responsibility, and it is the basis for the rest of this book.

The rise of CSR over the past decade

> *An economist is an expert who will know tomorrow why the things he predicted yesterday didn't happen today. (Evan Esar)*

What has happened to CSR since I started working in the area over ten years ago?

My involvement with CSR was stimulated by the feeling that the public agencies with which we had worked – ILO, UNDP, World Bank and so

---

[43] Wan Saiful Wan and Alan Gully: 'The Definition of CSR', paper submitted to Middlesex University conference on CSR, London, 27 June 2005.
[44] Personal communication, 8 September 2005.
[45] Ivor Hopkins, personal communication.

on – had done many wonderful things in the area of development (and, better publicized, some failures) but their efforts have been little more than a drop in the ocean. After leaving a meeting at the UN HQ in New York, I felt that the UN was getting nowhere fast and that, as the new millennium was five years away, it was clear that the next millennium would be handed to the private sector. Not without challenge nor doubt, but the private sector had, and continues to, show a robustness and vibrancy that, unfortunately, our public sector agencies both nationally and internationally have failed to show.

We have seen both Microsoft and then Google innovate at an amazing pace. The UN has offered us the Global Compact, the MDGs (Millennium Development Goals) and ILO core labour standards: not to be sniffed at, but all proceeding at a snail's pace.

Fifteen key items

There are at least 15 key items on the CSR agenda that we have seen develop over the past ten years:

1 **Corporate scandals**: Certainly CSR was not a new issue in the mid 1990s, for concern over social issues in business had gone back as far as Adam Smith and even before that to the South Sea Bubble. However, the mid 1990s saw an upsurge in interest as the public sector involvement in key industries fell away, particularly after the collapse of the Soviet Union, and as a crop of corporate scandals hit the headlines – the Ken Saro-Wiwa affair that severely affected Shell's international image was perhaps the watershed.

2 **Terminology still unfocused**: We had hoped that there would be a convergence on terminology so that we would, at least, know what we were talking about. However, with the brief dominance of the term CSR in the early 2000s, the terms corporate responsibility (CR) or corporate sustainability (CS) have tended to dominate in corporate circles. And what is meant by CSR has led to some form of convergence – the socially responsible treatment of stakeholders is accepted; environmental concerns are still very prominent but come under the heading of corporate sustainability. Yet issues such as corporate governance have remained firmly in the hard-nosed business camp and are not often treated along with CSR concerns.

3 **The stages of CSR**: In the past ten years we seem to have followed the classical route of the introduction of a new technology – innovation, diffusion (through writings, discussions, seminars and so on) and implementation which is just about starting, particularly in Europe. The US is behind the European trend, as is Japan. There is much interest in CSR in the developing world, especially India and South Africa

even though few major corporations can be found with their HQ in the developing world.

4   **CSR reports** (or similar such as CR or sustainability reports) are now produced regularly by the major corporations in Europe and the US, and there are signs that companies in middle-income developing countries are producing CSR reports. There has also been a move away from printed material into web-based reports.

5   **There are now many newsletters and newsgroups** covering CSR from the very popular Yahoo group CSR-chicks that fostered CSR-blokes and regional newsgroups, to Ethical markets, Csrwire, Ethike, Ethical corporation, Ethical performance, and a whole host of regional newsletters such as CSR Asia, Philippine for Social Progress. Although there is now too much information to read, if one has the time, it is gratifying how much 'good' stuff there is about on companies and their performance, as well as the main actors in the field.

6   **Few new laws** have entered the arena directly related to CSR which was one of the concerns of market capitalists such as *The Economist* and some *Financial Times* correspondents. However, closely related was the Sarbanes-Oxley law covering corporate governance, which has had the unfortunate effects of raising the costs of reporting and reducing the number of new flotations on the New York stock market in favour of slightly more liberal regimes such as London.

7   **Accounting standards:** There has been a growth in 'voluntary' accounting standards for CSR – AccountAbility, for instance, with its AA1000 and then Alice Tepper Marlin's SA8000 standards. Both groups, incidentally, steadfastly refuse to use the term CSR. In the pipeline is a standard (ISO 26000) on Corporate Responsibility coming from the International Standards Organisation (ISO) based in Geneva. Corporations, however, have noticed that observing CSR does not mean just ticking a set of boxes – the approach is more complicated and cannot be covered by legislation.

8   **The Global Reporting Initiative (GRI)** that emerged from the environmental movement **CERES** is still stronger on environmental concerns than social and economic concerns but has had a major impact on the social reporting of companies who try to follow GRI guidelines both for reporting and for the production of very useful indicators. Certainly measurement has improved enormously over 10 years when, in 1995, I had to scrape to find social indicators on companies.

9   **Government** has got into the CSR act, particularly the UK government, which has a lively website promoting CSR and has also appointed a succession of CSR ministers who, unfortunately, do not seem to do very much. Even the US has haltingly produced a report on CSR and what government can contribute after ignoring the field for many years.

10 **International governmental organizations** – the European Union, the World Bank, UNDP, IDB are the most prominent. My previous employer, the ILO, has gained prominence through the application and

citation of its core labour standards but has no policy as such on CSR due to in-house in-fighting between workers, government and employer organizations (most notably the IOE, International Organisation of Employers). The EU, in particular, has done good work in funding CSR initiatives all over Europe although my own personal experience shows that its bureaucracy demands a lot of patience on the part of those trying to work with it.

11 **Non-governmental organizations** have grown in number by leaps and bounds from Tomorrow's Company and SustainAbility in the UK to the Center for Social Markets in India, Ethos in Brazil, Philippine for Social Progress in Manila, Triple Bottom Line in Holland, Business Ethics in US and so on.

12 **Development of currently under-developed parts of the world:** More and more companies are adding development of the under-developed areas to their CSR activities and, as this book points out, Type III development activities are increasing rapidly. In Chapter 1, I noted that there are three main types of development activities – Type I: Development philanthropy, Type II: Assisting developing countries purely through housing local operations there, and Type III: Development assistance as part of reputation building which, in turn, is part of CSR.

13 **Finance centre scepticism:** As CSR has grown in prominence, at least in its various manifestations, the right wing so-called 'think tanks' have been arguing that profit maximization should be the main aim of business while remaining within (more or less) the confines of law. Simply put, they argue that CSR simply adds costs with no immediate benefit to profits. Yet, the business case for increased profits through increased reputation and lower risks that come hand in hand with CSR have been ignored by the right. Despite growing evidence that 'ethical corporations' tend to do better on average in terms of share price, Wall Street commentators and their mirror image in the major financial centres of London, Frankfurt and Tokyo still claim not to understand what CSR is all about as they punch another button flashing money around the world.

14 **Academic courses:** Few, if any universities had courses on CSR, although some had started courses on business ethics 10 years ago. Today, hardly an MBA is taught without at least some discussion of CS or CSR or CR university courses. My own email in-bag points to the popularity of the subject for undergraduate, masters and PhD students – I have two PhD students working with me and have had to turn away others.

15 **Socially Responsible Investment (SRI)** has been the fastest growing financial instrument in US and European financial centres over the past 10 years. The strange contradiction, whereby the subject is ignored in the City but is important to investors will, undoubtedly, change in the coming years. As better educated graduates enter investment houses, and as the investment record of SRIs is better known, the right-wing think tanks and their aficionados in the City and Wall Street will soon be barking up the same tree.

What is the future for CSR?

And what will happen with CSR in the future, at least the next decade?

- **It will become embedded.** There is no doubt that CSR will become embedded in a company's culture and organizational profile to such an extent that it will not be noticed, explicitly, any more. There is also little doubt that the phrase CSR will disappear but the sentiments behind it will be in place. The area of business and society will continue to be one of great debate, and the corporation will certainly change its form. I would hazard a guess that the private sector will still flourish as far as the next 50 years ahead but its power will be very much controlled as our own personal liberties also, unfortunately, become more controlled.
- **No need for an exit strategy.** There will be no need for a CSR exit strategy simply because business will only survive if they can show, and be evaluated to show, a clear social responsibility in their continued treatment of their stakeholders. An exit strategy will not be required simply because social responsibility will just be part and parcel of normal business practice.
- **Major inroads in developing countries.** CSR will continue to make inroads into developing countries, particularly through the main suppliers to the large corporations in the developed world, but also because developing country people will not tolerate corporations that have no connection with local cultures and aspirations.
- **SMEs will have CSR.** CSR will extend to small to medium-sized enterprises (SMEs) through rapid assessment and implementation tools.
- **Companies cannot ignore global concerns.** Companies will grapple with the big issues simply because they see failure as being bad for business. Under-development, labour exploitation, curbs on migration, global warming, trade barriers, global terrorism are all major challenges for governments and corporations. We have already seen signs of these increasing concerns for corporations at the annual World Economic Forum conferences in Davos.
- **UN and third sector cooperation.** As companies cannot easily shape the macro agenda there will be increased cooperation between corporations, the UN and its agencies as well as NGOs, the so-called 'third sector'.
- **Political leadership has been poor.** If the leadership of our nations continues to be poor – there have been very few decent leaders in the last 50 years who have combined decency with social justice (Nelson Mandela, Jimmy Carter, Julius Nyerere, Nye Bevan, Harold Wilson and even Bill Clinton can be named, but even they were not perfect) – then, like it or not, corporations will become even more powerful and influential. But will they be setting a coherent social agenda? Some will, some will not, but their agendas will be examined in ways hardly thought of so far today.

So what is likely to happen next? Hard economics is giving way to softer versions. Culture and ethnicity have dominated recent world events and this trend is likely to continue. Focusing on purely economic growth for countries or profits for companies will, of course, be uppermost in our leaders' minds. But the softer undercurrents of change, such as CSR, will require new, inspired leadership and, as Jem Bendell puts it: 'Understanding power and its responsible use is probably the bedrock question underlying much work on corporate citizenship today.'[46]

And the UN? The UN will remain under-funded as long as it is used as a political football by the major powers to serve their own short-term interests and will not be able to deliver its many excellent development initiatives. Corporations, please note!

---

[46] Jem Bendell (2005) 'Lifeworth Annual Review of Corporate Responsibility', available from www.lifeworth.net.

3

Corporate CSR Development Case Studies: Failures and Success

Introduction

Many, if not all, of the largest corporations are involved in development in some way. Most of these efforts stem from their philanthropic interests with few direct benefits to the company itself except, of course, for PR purposes. What I shall look at in this chapter are some examples of successful development interventions by companies that have also brought them benefits, as well as a number of failures.

In Chapter 1, I covered three main types of development actions by a company – Type I: Charitable or philanthropic donation to a 'good' cause in a developing country, Type II: Development as a direct by-product of company actions, Type III: Activities that promote sustainable development and anti-poverty initiatives that might also be in addition to Type II activities.

Type I development is, in general, what I call 'one-step' thinking, whereas Type III requires 'two-step' thinking. One-step thinking, albeit in a 'good' cause, does not lead to development except, perhaps, at the margins. An example of this is Coca Cola's building of a hospital in Somalia many years ago. Without a proper 'health system' the hospital lacked doctors, nurses, management systems to arrange appointments and security and so on. Within a few days the hospital had been ransacked for any equipment it contained, was quickly used for refugee shelter and today is just a slum. Thus the one-step idea to help health for poor people in Somalia collapsed, not because the goodwill was not there, but because the 'sustainable' implications had not been thought through.

Two-step thinking, inevitably, requires more thought. It must lead to sustainable development and enter into what I call the 'wave of development'. By 'sustainable' I mean more than the environmental implications of sustainable, I mean a development action that, once started, continues into the future without further input from abroad either in terms of additional cash or management expertise. Development is complex. If the wave of development is broken through poorly placed groynes (wave breakers) then, to continue the analogy, eddies are formed that can magnify the destructive effects of the wave and the original purpose can be destroyed. Development must build upon existing structures and try to mould them, if necessary, into more productive and sustainable activities. At its simplest, it means that adding extensions to an existing school will be of little use if there are no teachers or books.

A more complex example comes from the film based upon John Le Carré's book of the same name – 'The Constant Gardener'. The short- versus long-term interests of a fictitious drug company are displayed in a masterly way as the main actors struggle with the ethics of drug trials in the African context. The company believes that short-term pain and failure is preferable to long trials even if recipients of the test drug suffer. By ignoring the wave of development and taking the faster route to 'development', opposition to the drug trials gradually increases. The drug may well have been a success but the short-term profit maximization strategy of the drug company eventually becomes a high-risk strategy that is, eventually, likely to fail. We do not know whether this is eventually the case, since the film does not carry the development story forward. But the film does raise the questions of one-step versus two-step thinking in an interesting way. And one thing is certain about the film, the ending would have been very different if the scriptwriter had gone for a less dramatic effect and thought more about the wave of development. A careful study of the credits at the end of the film, worth waiting for if only for the wonderful African jazz, show no development theorist as an adviser. The film's ending would, undoubtedly, have been different if a development rather than a commercial point had been made.

Normally a successful project will have activities many years later – the setting up of small businesses that grow and provide employment for instance – which is easier said than done. One area that is successful, more or less whatever is undertaken, is education. Years later, as we all know, education received is remembered. I don't want to go into the knotty issue of teaching some subjects that are considered less useful (Latin was an oft-cited shibboleth, but it helped me learn Spanish and French, whereas wood- and metal-working, while frowned upon by many while I was young, have stood with me for many decades to the extent I can still remember how to plane wood, create joints and use a metal lathe!) But here again, one-step thinking that provides only educational buildings or even seemingly cheap $100 computers (relatively expensive when local annual adult earnings are less) are often a waste of effort if there are no teachers or books.

In this chapter I look at a number of case studies on how selected corporations have gone about 'development projects' and classify them into Type I, II or III development activities. The information is, of necessity, incomplete since I have had to rely on secondary sources, not having had the opportunity to visit the projects themselves. There is no substitute for an experienced eye on a project and what, at first sight, may appear to be a successful project can often involve considerable problems. This is because it simply is not easy for a foreign investor or adviser, however well meaning, to capture the necessary 'wave of development' that is so important when developing new activities. This is as true in a corporation's home base as it is overseas, and is particularly so in developing countries.

Disasters and disastrous interventions

To find out whether the corporate responses to three major natural disasters had been successful in terms of 'development' I wrote to Stephen Jordan, the head of the US Chamber of Commerce Center for Corporate Citizenship, who had coordinated much of the US corporate response in 2005. I asked him whether he had done, or knew of, any analysis of the success or failure of corporate interventions after the Tsunami, Katrina or Pakistan disasters in 2005 and, in particular, whether their interventions could be considered 'development' in the sense that they were sustainable and built on existing initiatives. He replied that these are not easy questions to answer. He did note that nine months, post Tsunami, about 10 per cent of the housing and school stock in Aceh had been rebuilt and that the clean-up process post-Katrina was monumental – 3 months after the fact, there were still mountains of debris, and whole neighbourhoods caked in mud.

In one county – Hancock County, Missouri, over which the eyewall of Katrina passed – 800 out of 1400 businesses had not come back by the end of 2005. Between Beaumont, Texas and Mobile, Alabama, Jordan noted that as many as 125,000 businesses were destroyed or disrupted, 60,000 in the greater New Orleans metro area alone. In terms of Pakistan, Jordan further remarked that the response was in line with the historical average, but it looked pale in comparison to the Tsunami and Gulf Coast responses.

There is, in fact, a concern that corporations do not, in fact, always adhere to sound development principles when they assist disaster relief. The concern to do 'something' and to be seen to do 'something' is a natural and decent human response to the misfortune of others. However, rapid support can override more dispassionate analysis of what would be the most useful. The BBC has reported that the rapid response to providing earthquake vicitims in Pakistan with tents had led to a widespread availability of 'summer' but not 'winter' tents.

The BBC reported that tents were 'winterized' after the UN issued a DIY manual on how to add extra layering to canvas-and-parachute tents.[1] But this was mostly done in tent villages in valleys and low-altitude areas. 'Corrugated iron sheets, nails and hammer is all that we need,' said Akhtar Abbassi, a resident of Bambian in the Neelam valley. Like thousands of

---

[1] Aamer Ahmed Khan (2005) 'Dilemma over new quake shelters', BBC News, Karachi, 12 December.

Figure 3.1 *Tents offer little shelter from harsh weather in much of the quake zone*

others, Akhtar was able to pull wooden planks out of the debris but did not have the iron sheets that can be used for a roof or the tools to put the structure together. He was frustrated with the slow response of relief agencies – both public and private. One reason for this, the BBC article said, could be the 'private donors' obsession with prefabricated structures. Manufacturers of prefab structures had moved into Pakistan within days of the 8 October earthquake, with many displaying their wares in exhibits set up in Lahore and Islamabad. By the time they found out that the government had no intention of regulating private housing, prefabrication had ruled itself out as a viable immediate response to the shelter issue'.

The problem of whether emergency relief by the private sector could be better tuned to development needs that do not destroy existing development efforts however fragile is attracting international attention. Provention, a consortium of international agencies and NGOs with the objective to 'support developing countries reduce the risk and social, economic and environmental impacts of natural and technological disasters on the poor in order to reduce poverty and build sustainable economies' has been concerned with this very point. They note, as one of a number of myths about emergency development assistance, the following:

Myth 1: Any kind of material aid is needed, and it is needed now.[2]

---

[2] www.proventionconsortium.org/articles/myths_realities.htm, accessed 20 February 2006.

My experience shows that a hasty response, one that is not based on familiarity with local conditions and that does not complement the national efforts, only contributes to the chaos. It is often better to wait until genuine needs have been assessed. Unsolicited donations of clothing, food and medicines that do not comply with WHO guidelines block the distribution channels. These spontaneous but inappropriate donations place a significant burden on the overtaxed relief workers, monopolize air and ground transportation and occupy costly warehouse space, sometimes for months or years. In most cases, the issue is logistical and financial, as supplies are available nationally or in neighbouring countries. The concerned public far away should be advised to donate cash rather than gather in-kind contributions. With direct financial assistance in the form of vouchers or cash, the affected population may do a better, faster and more cost-effective job in rebuilding their lives.

Thus, it is not just the private sector that has problems in responding to disasters. After Hurricane Mitch devastated much of Honduras in 1998 with a direct hit, the development actors in that country did not respond well. According to an evaluation by UN's development arm, the UNDP, of the US$11.8mn spent by UNDP in the area of environmental protection over 1998–2003, it was not until the year 2000 that even 40 per cent was actually spent on reconstruction.[3] Further, the promise of assistance that quickly came from international governments only led to around 50 per cent being available even several years later.

Large corporations and development – some experiences

An overall study of corporate leaders and development

A study of the indirect economic effects of the 40 'best' companies in the world, selected from those leading the Accountability Rating (AR) 2004 and the Dow Jones Sustainability Index (DJSI), made a number of useful comments on the role of MNEs in development.[4] Similar to the view expressed in this book, the study remarked that 'The public and private sectors are no longer leaving the fight against economic polarization in the hands of governments – instead they are standing beside government and helping to shoulder the responsibility. This type of public support, such as

---

[3] Michael Hopkins and Emilio Klein (2006) 'Country evaluation Honduras – Assessment of development results', UNDP, New York, p45, www.undp.org.eo/documents/ADR/ADR_Reports/ADR_Honduras.pdf, accessed 15 August 2006.
[4] Mark Line and Eric Dickson (2005) 'Speaking indirectly: between the triple bottom line', pp1–2, available in pdf form from www.csrnetwork.com.

the recent commitment of over 200 business leaders to a Business Action Plan for Africa to stimulate the region's failing economies ... shows that business can, and should play an important role in addressing the MDGs, by supporting the Make Poverty History campaign and working towards the economic development of impoverished countries.'[5]

The study also quotes Hewlett Packard who state: 'HP has moved beyond traditional philanthropy and has strengthened the link between our philanthropic investments and our long term business objectives. We are finding ways to use our products, services and skills – not just philanthropic cash contributions – to address social challenges such as poverty and inequality.'

The social reports of the top 40 companies were examined by the study. The main conclusion backed up the findings of this author that companies did present a range of issues pertaining to poverty alleviation (see Chapter 7), but did little to illustrate how their efforts were sustainable in either a 'quantitative or qualitative fashion'.

The study did discover that one exception to this was the Italian oil and gas company ENI, who, although not ranking in the very top of the study, presented some of the most comprehensive reporting on indirect economic impact in Nigeria through their Green River Project. They wrote: 'Although ENI's reporting did stand out among the benchmark group's sustainability publications, many others addressed key issues but largely failed to provide any analysis of the indirect economic benefits. A number of companies, for example, 3M and Diageo, are worthy of note as they identify highly relevant issues and yet fail to develop the broader economic implications of their work. By way of contrast, Novo Nordisk successfully incorporated both good practice in identifying implications and analysis.'

The Green River Project of ENI aimed to encourage the understanding of new techniques among farmers. As I have seen in other countries the setting up of associations and cooperatives was promoted. One may ask why local development efforts have to wait for an outside influence to set up associations and cooperatives. If cooperatives are so obvious and workable why can local people not carry this out themselves without external funds? Sometimes, perhaps often, this is done with the sole intention of prising funds out of the development organization, ENI in this case. On the other hand, the technique of setting up an institution and one that overcomes local rivalries can sometimes be encouraged from an outside influence. ENI claimed that its project did in fact transmit, especially through women, information on the correct utilization of agricultural products, good nutrition, sanitary and hygiene practices and home economics. Fish reproduction and rearing techniques using improved species were also introduced. Machinery to work the land, transport goods and process agricultural products were provided to the communities. ENI claimed that the results

---

[5] www.commissionforafrica.org/english/home/newsstories.html.

were outstanding in that, compared to the traditional agricultural sector, the farmers in the Green River Project almost doubled their production and the family incomes went up by almost 90 per cent.

All well and good, but to 'unpack' this result would require an investigation into whether the inputs from the project led to incomes being increased simply because payments from the project were made. Did ENI return 5 years later and see whether productivity and incomes did, in fact, continue their spectacular first year success or, as I have often seen in developing countries, did rusty equipment abound because there were no funds for maintenance, the cooperative disbanded since the purpose of obtaining funds from a foreign project had disappeared?

Another case study featured a 3M project in Iraq whereby its local partner, 3M Gulf, in coordination with Iraq's Ministry of Health, conducted an intensive three-day train-the-trainer programme on infection prevention practices. Thirty-four Iraqi head nurses and nursing directors attended. Each nurse, it was anticipated, would eventually train 72 others on practices ranging from operating room aseptic techniques and intravenous therapy to wound care management. Readers will already know that I am greatly in favour of training projects simply because something is always left behind. Training once learned is not forgotten, except for details of course and that therefore means there is a need for continual training and education of professional, skilled and semi-skilled people.

A useful example of how sustainable development reporting could be improved comes from the same study. It reports on work by Diageo that is conducted with Diageo's primary stakeholders and not a development project further away from Diageo's radar screen. Diageo's malting company in Kenya buys around £7 million worth of barley each year from farms of all sizes in Kenya and Uganda. On approximately 80 per cent of this business, the company underwrites bank finance that allows smaller farmers without the necessary capital to buy seed and agricultural materials. The report complains that 'Issues that could be addressed in their analysis of this example could include why access to credit is consistently difficult for the poor to obtain, and in turn how Diageo's involvement with underwriting loans has influenced farmers' economic well-being. This would provide a clear portrayal of Diageo's indirect economic impact on specific groups within Kenya and Uganda alone.'

This example poses a general dilemma. Diageo saw an opportunity to assist a small group of farmers and, assuming they followed the basic ground rules of micro-credit, probably did a useful job. But, a development lesson would be whether other farmers could benefit from Diageo's experience. Diageo could easily argue that it is none of their business. However, a small investment in publishing the results of its study as an example of 'best practice' could enable other farmers to be involved in micro-credit or at the very least find out what the main obstacles are. Again, this is the point of this book, MNEs are involved in development whether anyone likes it or not, but it is arguable that if they went the extra mile and reviewed the overall development impact of their projects, they could, helpfully, expand the impact of their project to a wider field.

Wal-Mart

Wal-Mart is, by market capitalization, one of the biggest corporations in the world. It is the largest employer in the US with around 1.3 million employees. It has achieved its success mainly through offering the lowest possible prices for its products. Clearly, to do this, it must be avaricious in its search to find the cheapest producers and lowest production costs. Its effect on its own workers, paid the US minimum wage but struggling to survive, was colourfully displayed by undercover journalist Barbara Ehrenreich in her book *Nickel and Dimed*.[6]

On the other hand, as Mallen Baker noted, its very positive treatment of one stakeholder group – its customers – has led to its rapid expansion.[7] Its approach was not simply based upon making the biggest profit. 'Sam wouldn't let us hedge on a price at all. Say the list price was $1.98 but we had only paid 50 cents. Initially I would say "Well, it's originally $1.98, so why don't we sell it for $1.25?" And he'd say "No. We paid 50 cents for it. Mark it up 30 percent, and that's it. No matter what you pay for it, if we get a great deal, pass it on to the customer" '.[8]

More recently Wal-Mart has started to fall foul of anti-corporate campaigners and, as Mallen Baker documented, has one of the largest number of anti-corporate websites than any other company – www.walmartwatch. com, carries stories and information against the company, www.walmartyrs.com handles employee complaints, www.wal-martlitigation.com is for information sharing by lawyers engaged in suing the retail giant, and so on. But the available information is mixed – Wal-Mart's founder, Sam Walton had strong business ethics and some parts of its empire, such as its UK arm, ASDA, have been able to build a good relationship with its employees. Yet, Barbara Ehrenreich observed, after her experience working for Wal-Mart that 'No one gets paid overtime' and 'Many feel the health insurance isn't worth paying for'.[9]

The conundrum that Wal-Mart faces is at the basis of CSR in the behaviour of corporations both in the developed and the developing world. Wal-Mart pays minimum wages, hardly enough to live on in the US and is roundly criticized by US trade unions for not allowing unions in its

---

[6] B. Ehrenreich (2001) *Nickel and Dimed*, New York, Henry Holt & Co.
[7] M. Baker (2003) 'Corporations and the third world in the first world', *Business Respect*, London, 23 March, p1.
[8] M. Baker, 'Corporations and the third world in the first world', citing Clarence Leis.
[9] M. Baker, 'Corporations and the third world in the first world', p183.

operations.[10] Wal-Mart retorts that if its problems are so grave, why do so many people seek employment in its stores? Yet, its problems, according to American Rights at Work, have led to high turnover rates. 'Turnover among full-time employees increased from between 30–45 per cent in 1995 to almost 56 percent in 2000. And this turnover has a price: the cost of replacing the 600,000–700,000 employees that leave Wal-Mart each year is estimated at $1.4 billion.'

But, perhaps the tide has turned at Wal-Mart, prompted in a large part from the positive publicity it received from its actions after hurricane Katrina. Then it helped thousands of its own employees and other victims of the hurricane with the type of rapid assistance that the Federal Emergency Management Agency (FEMA) found difficult to deliver – despite President Bush's misplaced praise of the FEMA Director who was replaced within days for poor management.

Lee Scott, the chief executive of Wal-Mart, in October 2005 made a series of announcements outlining an apparent paradigm shift in its thinking on a broad range of environmental and operational issues.[11] Wal-Mart will invest $500 million annually in environmental technologies at its more than 5000 stores worldwide. And the company announced it would strive to eliminate the waste it produces and to consume fuels only from renewable resources.

However, these new announcements were not without controversy. Wake-Up Wal-Mart, a group backed by the United Food and Commercial Workers Union and a major Wal-Mart critic, has called the company's efforts 'a publicity stunt meant to repair a faltering public image' and 'empty actions' that shift responsibility to suppliers and others. Then, on the labour front, Wal-Mart announced it would offer new health insurance for its US employees, but quickly lost ground with the initiative when an internal memo surfaced in the *New York Times* indicating that its plan hinged on curbing spending by attracting a 'healthier and more productive workforce', rather than strong improvements in its coverage for existing workers.[12]

What relevance does this story have for developing countries? It illustrates that CSR is not inevitable, at least as far as labour relations go, even in an industrialized nation. Wal-Mart has struggled for some time to stay profitable while minimizing costs. Their actions have led to a round of criticism from NGOs and trade unions. Yet it does seem that Wal-Mart is starting to discover CSR, apparently, very slowly.

As I argued in my book *The Planetary Bargain*, their new approach is inevitable since corporations cannot continue to chase the lowest common denominator in terms of poor wages and conditions since this, if copied worldwide, would lead to a loss in the purchasing power of its consum-

---

[10] See, for instance, American Rights at Work (2005) 'Wal-Mart', Washington DC.
[11] www.ethicalcorp.com/content.asp?ContentID=4009, accessed 23 December 2005.
[12] www.ethicalcorp.com/content.asp?ContentID=4009.

ers.[13] The promotion, and adoption, of CSR both in industrialized and developing countries will eventually raise everyone's standard of living from which all will eventually benefit. The 'bargain' is that corporations will see that global CSR is in their interest and that 'rogue' companies will eventually be hounded out of existence.

Of course, all this will come in stages. One cannot expect developing countries to adopt, overnight, the labour salaries and conditions that currently occur in richer countries. Nor should one expect future developing country 'Wal-Marts' clones to drive down salaries and labour conditions – they may compete for a while but will eventually falter. Indeed, as developing countries become richer, their labour will start to see their salaries and conditions improve much as can be seen today in India, China and Brazil and was certainly seen as the Asian tigers (Hong Kong, Malaysia, Singapore, South Korea, Taiwan) developed rapidly in the 1960s and 1970s.

Unilever

Unilever is a company with a strong belief in development. Its former chief executive, Niall FitzGerald, believes, as many CEOs do, that liberal capitalism will set the world free.[14] FitzGerald, currently chairman of Reuters, was closely involved with Tony Blair's Commission for Africa project. He is also chairman of the British arm of the Nelson Mandela Legacy Trust. The great man personally invited him to take the helm. 'It took a nano-second to say yes,' says FitzGerald. 'That was in 2004 and in the meantime I have helped to set up a fund that will help 10 South African scholars over the next 10 years.' He believes that via Western investment, both sides stand to gain, although he is critical of Western media treatment of the continent. 'It always seems to be about squalor and despair, but there is another side. Countries like Tanzania and Mozambique have pulled themselves up by their bootstraps. In South Africa, instead of the rivers of blood which many predicted as the apartheid regime crumbled, we have a country well on its way to building a true multicultural democracy. In the last five years, two thirds of the countries in sub-Saharan Africa have had elections.'

Following the concern of FitzGerald, Unilever has been active in analysing its impact on development as instanced by a report by Oxfam on Unilever's work in Indonesia to alleviate poverty.[15] The report was unusual in

---

[13] Michael Hopkins (2003) *The Planetary Bargain – CSR Matters*, London, Earthscan.

[14] Richard Wachman (2005) 'Irish knight fights for Africa', *The Observer*, London, 3 July.

[15] Jason Caly (2005) 'Exploring the links between international business and poverty reduction: A case study of Unilever in Indonesia', An Oxfam GB, Novib, Unilever, and Unilever Indonesia joint research project, first published by Oxfam GB, Novib, Oxfam Netherlands and Unilever.

that research on corporate environmental and social impacts often focuses upon a specific aspect of operations, whereas the report examined poor people's interaction with Unilever's business from both the direct and the indirect more informal areas. Indonesia was chosen as a case study since, despite its abundant natural and human resources, Indonesia has high levels of poverty, with more than 50 per cent of its population living on less than US$2 a day. Although not an example of Unilever's direct involvement in development projects, the project was designed to improve understanding about the relationship between a multinational business and poverty, by analysing one example of how business and poverty inter-relate.

As Oxfam noted in the preface to its report, the business activities of multinational companies (MNEs) have an important contribution to make to economic development in developing countries. 'This contribution is particularly significant because the volume of private capital flows exceeds that of development assistance.'

The research focused on Unilever Indonesia (UI), the local operating company of Unilever, one of the world's leading fast-moving consumer-goods (FMCG) companies. UI has been active in Indonesia since 1933, and the majority of its goods are produced for the Indonesian market. By 2003, the company had sales of US$984 million, around 84 per cent of which were home and personal care items such as soap powder, household cleaning products, hand soap and shampoos. Around 16 per cent of sales were accounted for by foods such as tea, margarine and ice cream. Unilever's own estimates put at least 95 per cent of Indonesians using one or more UI products each year, and that 90 per cent of poor people in Indonesia buy UI products in the course of a year. UI was ranked as the 13th largest company by sales in Indonesia in 2005 and the 4th largest company in the FMCG sector. Total taxes paid to the Indonesian government were considerable, averaging about US$130 million per year, or about 19 per cent of company revenues over a five-year period.

UI, the Oxfam report noted, has significant forward and backward linkages into the local economy: for example, forward linkages through distribution networks and retailers, and backward linkages to suppliers (what I call Type II development). The majority of revenues generated by UI remain in Indonesia, through its local sourcing, wages, margins and dividends to local shareholders (15 per cent of total dividends). Following an earlier period of investment by the parent company, inward investment flows from outside Indonesia were nil in recent years: a result of the profitability of the local business. Although that was an important first step, the report explored whether people, through their employment, gained skills and confidence that empowered them to build economic security, accumulate assets and make sustainable improvements in their lives.

UI's business structure consists of a core workforce of about 5000 people, of whom about 60 per cent are employees, most of them permanent, and just under 40 per cent are contract workers, employed directly or through contracting agencies. Beyond this is a well-established network of suppliers, distributors and retailers. UI sets high standards for the treatment of its permanent employees.

It adheres to the Unilever (global) Code of Business Principles. Pay and benefits are above what is required by law, positioning UI in the top quartile of Indonesian companies. In terms of policy and practice, there are high health and safety standards, good retirement and maternity benefits and workplace facilities, and a strong emphasis on training. All UI employees have a written contract, and there are clear procedures for negotiations between workers and management.

The closer and more formally workers are linked with UI's operations, the more they benefit directly from the company. In the period studied (2003/2004), the number of contract workers engaged by UI grew as a proportion of employees, because more workers were needed to cover periods of change at two UI sites. While future trends in contract employment at UI are unclear, there is concern that the number of contract workers functioning within UI is significant, at around 40 per cent of the workforce in 2003. Although contract employment is recognized as an integral part of UI's business strategy, the research indicated two respects in which the application of standards needs improvement, on which UI is committed to take action. One of these is the need to ensure that UI's labour-supply companies observe legal requirements concerning the transfer of temporary employees to permanent employment contracts; the other is the need to respond to the concerns raised by a female contract worker that illness or pregnancy could result in loss of employment. These cases illustrated how contracting out employment may reduce a company's ability to monitor the situation of contract workers or suppliers' employees, and thus result in gaps between corporate policy and practice in respect of these workers.

The report noted that, while it is difficult to use macro-economic indicators to measure the direct impact of UI's activities on people living below the poverty line, indirect positive impacts can be assumed in the contributions to government revenue; the stability of UI's value chain in a turbulent economy, with its attendant employment benefits; and an overall business model that is deeply embedded in the Indonesian economy.

Overall, the research estimated that the full-time equivalent (FTE) of about 300,000 people make their livelihoods from UI's value chain. Strikingly, more than half of this employment is found in UI's distribution and retail chain, with about one third in the supply chain, poorer people working at either end of the value chain, especially primary producers at the supply end.

In concluding the report, both Oxfam and Unilever stated that they were much closer to understanding the limitations and opportunities that determine what companies can and cannot be expected to do to contribute to poverty reduction. UI's wider impact in the community was briefly considered, in terms of both corporate community involvement and UI's influence on government and the business community. UI invests in a wide range of philanthropic activities, often linked to an aspect of its business expertise. Oxfam and Unilever agreed that the greatest potential for pro-poor impacts lay within UI's mainstream operations and value chain. Nonetheless, they said, 'voluntary community involvement could also provide a positive interaction with society, bringing benefits to communities and directly and indirectly to the business itself.'

UI's main influence on other businesses was among its own business partners, which often support similar activities, and which appear to have adopted UI's practices in other respects, such as health and safety standards. One identifiable area of UI's influence in society was in taking a public stand against corruption, for which UI has been cited by other NGOs. Oxfam further concluded that many companies still see their purpose as profit maximization, but 'we have learned from Unilever that in many cases business decisions rarely amount to a strictly profit-based calculation. The notion that "the business of business is business" is outdated, and there are huge opportunities for civil society to engage with companies to explore how they might use their influence to raise performance standards, distribute resources, share knowledge, and innovate for the common good.' What I would call Type III development.

For their part, one of UI's main conclusions of the research was 'the insight that we gained into the extent of the widespread "job" multiplier in UI's total value chain. The findings point to the potential use of value-chain policies as a tool in sustainable poverty reduction. FMCG value chains can offer poor people an opportunity to gain basic skills within a structured learning environment and earn incremental, regular income.'

Shell

Shell has taken a major interest in development. As well as addressing sustainable development issues for their primary stakeholders, they have also embarked through the 'Shell Foundation (SF)' on wider development issues. They directly addressed the issue of poverty alleviation (note that poverty alleviation is just one, albeit one of the most important, aspect of a country's development) in their 2005 publication on 'Enterprise solutions to poverty'.[16]

The Shell Foundation was established by Royal Dutch/Shell Group of Companies as a UK charity in June 2000. Unlike many corporate foundations, the Shell Foundation focuses on social issues aligned to the core characteristics of the company Shell, its founder – 'we address social problems arising from the links between energy and poverty, energy and the environment and the impact of globalisation on vulnerable communities.'[17] Three Type III development case studies are drawn here from the Shell report.

---

[16] Shell (2005) 'Enterprise solutions to poverty: Opportunities and challenges for the international development community and big business', a report by Shell Foundation, London, UK, March.
[17] Shell (2005).

First, using Shell's expertise in energy has been clearly beneficial when working with developing countries. One area has been what SF calls 'catalysing the pro-poor market for solar home systems' as part of its concern to stimulate the use of renewable energy in developing countries. One might question the commitment of Shell, or even oil companies in general, as to why they are investing in alternative energy with, at first sight, a negative business case for themselves. But, clearly, oil companies have realized that they must eventually, as suppliers of energy, start to explore alternative forms of energy creation. What better, then, than to work in developing countries to explore alternative projects and gain experience in how technology, and in this case, solar energy could potentially be used in the future. Shell notes that interventions in developing countries have typically been of the 'technology-forcing and supply-side subsidy variety' which has often been delivered via outside intervention such as those managed, and designed, directly by donors.

There has not been as much success as was hoped, presumably because outside interventions simply delivering technology creates suspicion in local communities as well as not creating a base for continuing maintenance and proper usage.

So in the second case study, an example of what I call 'two-step' thinking, a different approach was taken in a renewable energy initiative in Karnataka State in south India, in which SF has been involved along with UNEP and the United Nations Foundation. The goal of the initiative – called the 'Consumer Financing Programme for Solar Home Systems in Southern India' – was to catalyse the market for solar home systems (SHS) among the under-served rural and peri-urban population in south India. It has two unique features. First, the local private sector was extensively consulted about how the intervention should operate. Second, the initiative is actually being run on a day-to-day basis by Syndicate Bank and Canara Bank – two of India's largest banks with extensive rural operations.

In the $7.6 million programme, donor money is providing a small interest-rate subsidy to this bank-run consumer loan scheme. The banks are administering the scheme much as they do other consumer financing products, but they have received strong training, marketing and other support provided by the approved vendors from whom customers can extract the best deal and system of their choice. The project has catalysed extremely rapid growth in the SHS market (80 per cent between the start of 2003 and the end of 2004 with 10,000 systems installed) and now accounts for an average of 60 per cent of new business being secured by the four participating vendors. Over time the interest rate subsidy to the banks has been reduced but the success of the programme in catalysing market growth will probably lead SHS consumer finance to be greatly expanded by the India banking sector, yet on an entirely commercial basis and involving no further donor contribution.

Much of the development assistance has, quite rightly, been in the area of helping SMEs and, in particular, helping SMEs gain better access to credit. In the third case study, SF has created what they call a number of 'Investment Partnerships' in Uganda and South Africa, soon to be extended elsewhere in Africa and beyond. The issue – lack of energy access by poor rural households and producers – is the same as in India only more extreme. Key features of the SF SME financing case study are business development assistance and non-collateralized finance. African SMEs are typically unable to secure commercial finance because local banks are reluctant to take on the 'risks' represented by lending to entrepreneurs who lack both business experience and collateral. Over 2003–2004, in partnership with local banks, SF set up the $5 million Uganda Energy Fund and the $8 million Empowerment through Energy Fund in South Africa.

A total of 345 pro-poor enterprises received business development assistance (BDA) – finance and ongoing mentoring. SF estimated that the two funds created almost a thousand new jobs in addition to generating a variety of other pro-poor outcomes. Again as in India, African banks view lending to SMEs as high risk because their view is that entrepreneurs lack business experience and acumen and have little or nothing in the way of collateral or assets to secure against a loan. But the main problem is that banks simply find it too costly to service small loans of the $1–5000 level and prefer larger credits where they are more comfortable and where they have tried and tested procedures. Competition, of course, would drive the price of credit down and force banks to look for new business. However, many if not most African countries are highly regulated and/or corrupt, making it very difficult for new entrants to enter the market. As a result, local and international finance, even if earmarked, for the SME sector in Africa goes unused or is invested elsewhere.

SF, taking account of this reality with its local partner, developed an approach based upon four key items in Uganda and South Africa. First, to look for local sources of finance and business know-how as partners. Second, to organize the provision of financing and business development activities (BDA) around the needs of the entrepreneur. Third, to design initial forays into the sector in ways that would provide robust evidence, learning opportunities and a strong demonstration effect. Fourth, to choose areas where there was a fair chance that local capital would eventually be willing to undertake subsequent scale-up activities.

The approach, according to SF, delivered close to commercial returns from investments in the 'risky SME sector'. Having decided in Africa not to partner with non-profit-making groups, Shell Uganda and Shell South Africa's local knowledge helped the Foundation to identify the most promising partner candidates from among the local financial institutions (FIs). But it was the commercial credibility and convening power of Shell that subsequently persuaded these FIs to meet the Foundation to discuss the model. Then, having got the banks' attention, it was the packaging of the Foundation's funding and a sound business plan that helped secure commitments from local banks to join SF at equal risk in launching the funds.

In Uganda, DFCU Bank agreed to match the Foundation's $2m investment capital and agreed to set up the $4m Uganda Energy Fund (UEF). In South Africa, ABSA Bank and the Industrial Development Corporation each contributed investment capital of $3.5m alongside $1m by the Shell Foundation to create the $8m Empowerment through Energy Fund (ETEF). Because of the small size of these pilot funds, the Foundation also provided a limited amount of grant funding to cover start-up and ongoing business development costs. Another feature of the business plan that attracted both sets of banks was that the funds were to be commercially managed to achieve, as a prime objective, financial viability of the funded enterprises and the funds themselves. This was very different from the developmental goals the banks had previously been offered (and rejected) to get involved with other SME funding opportunities. Moreover, funded enterprises were to be charged full commercial finance rates while the banks were offered funds with a familiar seven-year, closed-end structure but with net returns of 5 per cent.

Such returns were clearly below normal commercial expectations, but were attractive to SF's banking partners for two reasons. First, they were perceived as realistic and attainable based on the size of the market and risk conditions (compared with the international rates of return some African venture funds propose). Second, they were acceptable to banks with a long-term view of investing in the SME sector in order to grow their own business.

Having helped bring about a marriage between the banks and the Foundation, Shell's local knowledge was brought further into play by introducing the banks to the realities of SME energy sector financing. This was achieved by providing the banks with technical assistance relating to both the supply and demand sides of the small scale and rural energy sector. In Uganda, this took the form of advising loan officers about the financial risks related to various energy technologies. And for ETEF in South Africa, Shell became a useful source of client referrals – a critical input to portfolio funds reliant on adequate deal flow – while in both countries fund governance and marketing was strengthened with Shell support.

Another feature of the business model that proved attractive to the banks and subsequently critical to the success of the funds was the remit given to loan officers on how, and for what purposes, the funds could be used. Their broad specification was to support SMEs that require energy-related inputs to boost production or that sell pro-poor energy services. Few restrictions were put on the funds beyond that, aiming to ensure they were flexible enough to allow sufficient deal flow to make their portfolio finance structure work. Hence the deal range was broad: there were no restrictions on type of energy, meaning all sources of energy could be financed rather than just renewables; and non-energy assets could be funded as well if they facilitated the productive use of energy. These criteria thus allowed the funds to support a very broad range of SME activity. So, for example, financing was provided that allowed small farmers in eastern Uganda to acquire solar-powered agricultural crop driers.

BP (British Petroleum) and the Equator Principles

BP has initiated financing projects similar to those of Shell. In Azerbaijan, for instance, it has set up a financing initiative to service SMEs, in particular those related to the Baku-Tbilisi-Ceyhan (BTC) oil and gas pipeline project. Operational as of 2005, the pipeline will carry up to a million barrels of oil a day over 1000 miles across Azerbaijan, Georgia and Turkey. The remarkable scope of the project has raised many questions regarding how oil companies can best integrate human rights protections in their operations.[18] The pipeline, because of its size, its importance to Western oil consumers and the fact that it runs through Russia's former backyard, has focused attention on all sorts of development problems and issues – ranging from the displacement of populations along its route to how to involve local SMEs, who lack 'pipeline' skills, into its construction and maintenance.

It is also a test of the Equator Principles (EP), according to Jane Monahan.[19] She noted that two-thirds of the project's cost – $2.6 billion – was financed by public and private institutions, including the International Finance Corporation (IFC), the UK's Export Credits Guarantee Department (ECGD) and nine EP banks: ABN AMRO, Citigroup, Mizhuo, Dexia, HVB, ING, KBC, Royal Bank of Scotland and West LB.

But, according to BankTrack – an international network of NGOs that monitors banks' investments – adopting the Equator Principles 'ought to lead to banks financing projects that are positive for the environment, such as renewable energy. And banks should be expected to reject projects such as oil and gas pipelines and coal mining, which all contribute to global climate change.' However, for the EP banks, adopting the Principles is mainly about managing social, environmental and reputational risk, and avoiding potentially costly litigation that could damage their bottom line when financing projects of all kinds, including those in traditional areas such as fossil fuels.

Yet, BankTrack and many other NGOs have singled out the BTC pipeline as an example of how EP banks are continuing to finance unsustainable projects. The report said that EP banks backed the project in spite of accusations by NGOs that it violated dozens of the Principles, not to mention World Bank human rights, legal, ethical and environmental standards. For instance, NGOs allege that the BP-led consortium did not provide sufficient consultation or compensation for Azeri, Georgian and Kurdish locals along the pipeline route. The pipeline has also been hit by construction issues.

Felicia Swanson, an IFC investment officer on the BTC project, said, according to Monahan's article, that 'the BP-led consortium did not inform the IFC and other lenders about these problems before they approved its

---

[18] See for instance the WBCSD discussion on www.wbcsd.org/includes/getTarget. asp?type=DocDet&id=16742, accessed 3 November 2005.

[19] Jane Monahan (2005) 'Principles in question', *The Banker*, 7 March, p60.

loans'. This led to hearings last November by a special committee in the UK parliament on the circumstances of the ECGD's BTC funding. However, Mrs Swanson says that the 'IFC and some other lenders' are 'now satisfied' with the 'corrective actions' on the pipeline taken by BP.

Microsoft

Microsoft has never been very popular because, as *The Economist* noted, of the 'quality more than the quantity of its critics'.[20] Internet users, who tend to have higher than average educational levels, are continually frustrated with Microsoft because of its dominance of the way most personal computers are run.

Nevertheless, Microsoft is concerned with development. For instance, it launched a technology skills partnership for unemployed textile workers in Portugal in conjunction with the Technological Centre for the Textile and Clothing Industries of Portugal (CITEVE). The Technology, Innovation and Initiative (TII) programme will provide unemployed workers in Portugal's textiles industry with new skills and qualifications to improve their long-term employment prospects. Supported by Microsoft through its Unlimited Potential programme, it aims to train at least 3000 unemployed people in the sector, which is being significantly affected by increasing global competition. Both partners in the programme, together with the Instituto do Emprego e Formação Profissional, will also work with local companies and unions to help trainees find jobs or start new businesses. The venture has been welcomed by the European Commissioner for Employment, Social Affairs and Equal Opportunities, Dr Vladimir Spidla, who hailed it as an 'important contribution' to the European Jobs and Growth Partnership Initiative launched by the EC last year.[21]

Remarkable, too, has been the goodwill generated by Microsoft's founder, Bill Gates, through the Gates Foundation. Bill Gates has, to date, donated $258 million to battle against malaria. The fact that neither the rich countries nor the UN's health agency WHO, have done very much to curb this major killer of poor people is little short of scandalous. As Bill Gates noted, 'the rich world's efforts in tackling the disease is "a disgrace"'. The grant was equivalent to more than three-quarters of global spending on research into the disease in 2004.

But good works can quickly be negated by crass actions that illustrate the dividing line between doing good for its own sake and doing good when it is good for business. In December 2005, Microsoft acceded to a Chinese government request to shut down a blog carried on its MSN service and

---

[20] *The Economist* (2005) Christmas edition, p96.
[21] For more information about the TII programme see: www.microsoft.com/emea/presscentre/pressreleases/CITEVEPR_16012006.mspx, accessed 10 January 2006.

written by an outspoken government critic, Zhao Jing, who also goes by the pen name An Ti.[22]

Similarly, in another case, the Chinese government asked for and received from Yahoo!, the internet company, the information it needed to trace the identity of a Chinese internet user, Shi Tao. Mr Shi was arrested in late 2004 and sentenced in April 2005 to ten years in prison on charges of revealing secrets by e-mail. Microsoft and Yahoo! have both reaped withering criticism for cooperating in these cases.

But what is business to do when the Chinese market is so large and is dominated by the government? Their business would obviously have been severely negatively affected if neither Microsoft nor Yahoo! had acceded to the Chinese request. On the other hand, providing information that leads to long years in prison for those critical of the Chinese regime is hard to accept. That the George W. Bush administration has also tried to subpoena Google records to find instances of wrongdoing does not make acceding to Chinese requests acceptable.

As well as the legal issues involved, these questions test the wit of ethicists, such as Roger Steare, who would regard this as a 'social conscience' (also known as a utilitarian or consequentialist) decision. His book on 'ethicability' presents how an ethicist would tackle such a problem.[23] I am against the reduction of human rights and consequent reduction in civil liberty that ensues. Business, too, must take a stand in defence of human rights as so many have agreed to, including companies, in the Universal Declaration of Human Rights. Companies must work with other companies to form a united face to any government, whether it be the Chinese government or the US government – the basis for my 'planetary bargain' – and resist any chiselling away at human rights.

British American Tobacco (BAT)

British American Tobacco (BAT) is a curious company to include as an example of close links between a company and development.[24] A hugely profitable concern based upon selling tobacco products is not everyone's idea of an ethical organization. Certainly tobacco contributes to reduced life expectancy through enhanced cancer risk. But should we ban every company that contributes to the reduction of life expectancy? If that were the case then there would be no more Toyota or Rolls-Royce (cars kill people), Moët and Chandon or Georges Duboeuf (alcohol causes liver disease), Lockheed (weapons kill people), and so on. Where does one draw the line? Better to let the buyer beware – 'caveat emptor' – as is currently being

---

[22] *The Economist*, 13 January 2005.
[23] Roger Steare (2006) *Ethicability*, London, self-published.
[24] This section is drawn from www.bat.com, accessed 28 December 2005.

Table 3.1 *International issues map*

International Issues Map

The International Issues Map gives an indication of the types of issues raised by stakeholders in dialogue in the countries where our companies had published Social Reports up to 1 June 2005.

Principle groupings across the country columns:
- *The Principle of Mutual Benefit*
- *The Principle of Responsible Product Stewardship*
- *The Principle of Good Corporate Conduct*

CORE BELIEFS	ISSUE TYPES	UK	Argentina	Australia	Bangladesh	Brazil	Chile	Colombia	Costa Rica	Cyprus	Fiji	France	Germany	Hong Kong	Hungary	Japan	Kenya	Korea	Malaysia	Mauritius	Mexico	New Zealand	Nigeria	Pakistan	Poland	Russia	South Africa	Sri Lanka	Trinidad	Uganda	Uzbekistan	Venezuela	Zimbabwe
We believe in creating long-term shareholder value	Corporate communications; not diversifying out of tobacco	•	•	•	•		•	•	•	•	•	•				•	•	•		•	•	•					•	•	•	•	•	•	
We believe in engaging constructively with our stakeholders	Retailer engagement; stakeholder engagement	•	•	•	•		•	•	•	•	•	•		•		•	•	•		•	•	•					•	•	•	•	•	•	
We believe in creating inspiring working environments for our people	Occupational health and safety management; workplace HIV/AIDS; employee communication; welfare; empowerment; security; equal opportunity; training & development; workplace smoking policies	•	•	•	•		•	•	•	•	•	•				•	•	•		•	•	•					•	•	•	•	•	•	•

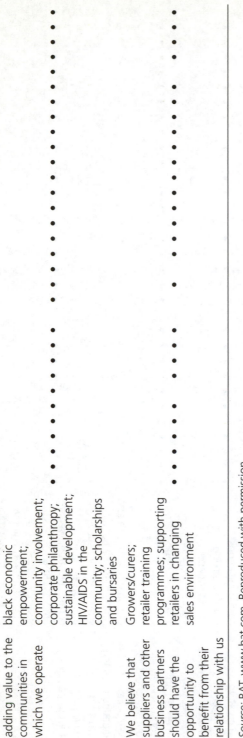

| We believe in adding value to the communities in which we operate | Selection of suppliers; black economic empowerment; community involvement; corporate philanthropy; sustainable development; HIV/AIDS in the community; scholarships and bursaries |
| We believe that suppliers and other business partners should have the opportunity to benefit from their relationship with us | Growers/curers; retailer training programmes; supporting retailers in changing sales environment |

Source: BAT, www.bat.com. Reproduced with permission.

done in the area of drug consumption – research on the negative effects of marijuana, banned in some countries such as the US, has led to increased warnings of the negative health effects of a drug that many of my generation once thought was harmless.

BAT is aware of these issues and claims to only supply those who request their products. Cynics might sigh at this point, but the author believes this claim is true. From the point of view of this book, what is intriguing is the lengths that BAT has gone to in the area of development.

It notes in its social report, that 'we believe that companies should be prepared to "think long", recognizing that their investments are part of a country's development goals. Indeed we see a fundamental link between acting responsibly and generating sustainable profits.'

The direct, Type II, effects of the tobacco industry are impressive. It contributes substantially to the economies of over 100 countries. It provides employment globally for more than 100 million people and major revenues for governments. BAT's global sales and operations enable governments worldwide to gather over £14 billion a year in taxes, while its companies employ over 85,000 people.

BAT has also been a leader in the Eliminating Child Labour in Tobacco Growing (ECLT) Foundation. The initiative began in October 2000 in Nairobi, Kenya, at an international conference hosted by BAT and attended by farmers, trades unionists, NGOs, government officials, the media and manufacturers from three continents. In the last few years, the Foundation has supported several projects and research initiatives to tackle child labour and has worked directly with ILO's anti-child labour programme. The Foundation is based in Geneva under its Director, Marc Hofstetter, a former senior Red Cross executive, with the mission to: 'Contribute to the elimination of the use of child labour in the tobacco growing sector and to provide children with an upbringing that gives them the best chance to succeed in all aspects of life.' In addition to BAT, members now include Altadis, Philip Morris, Japan Tobacco, Scandinavian Tobacco, Imperial Tobacco, Gallaher Group, and the world's leading tobacco dealers Universal Leaf Tobacco Co., Standard Commercial Corporation and DIMON Incorporated.

For instance, in Brazil, family labour is an essential part of life on the 160,000 small landholdings in southern Brazil where tobacco is grown. But for children under the age of 16, BAT insists they need to be educated first. With the support of Souza Cruz, the BAT subsidiary in Brazil, an unprecedented agreement was signed in 1998 between the Union of Tobacco Industries (Sindifumo) and the Association of Brazilian Tobacco Growers (Afubra) aimed at keeping children in schools. So far, almost 30,000 farmers have joined the company's Future is Now programme, working to end child labour. The programme is run in partnership with key stakeholders such as the ILO, the Abrinq Foundation for Children's Rights, and the National and State Council on the Rights of Children and Youth.

There has been child labour in the Mexican tobacco growing industry for centuries. Traditionally, farmers in Nayarit, the tobacco growing region, have employed indigenous people from the highlands to harvest the leaf. Families migrate to the tobacco fields for four months to work on the harvest and adults and children, some as young as five years old, work and live in the fields. The children suffer interrupted schooling and potential exposure to health and safety risks.

Cigarrera La Moderna, the BAT subsidiary in Mexico, saw that a purely business-led initiative would be of limited effect in addressing the issue, so it developed partnerships with key stakeholders including government and civil society organizations, the Mexican Tobacco Growers Association, competitors and suppliers. The partnership commissioned a study by the Nayarit State University whose findings concluded that the children are mainly involved in cutting and wrapping tobacco leaf, that growers overwhelmingly admit that the children are not paid for this and also that most migrant workers live in poor conditions during the harvesting season.

In 2001, Cigarrera La Moderna initiated Project Blossom to eliminate the use of child labour in the tobacco fields, to improve the children's quality of life during their families' time in the fields, to raise family awareness and to promote cultural change. Working with its partners, the company's programme covers education for the children with the help of the Ministry of Education and the National Institute for Indigenous People. With the Health Ministry, health follow-ups, dental care and basic sanitary education are provided. And, with social workers from the Mexican Institute of Social Security, the children are provided with two to three nutritious meals each day. Initially two centres were built providing these facilities for 40 children and by the harvesting season (January to May) 2002, the programme had expanded to four centres helping 400 children. The final goal is systematic implementation of similar programmes, led by appropriate authorities, to achieve a shift in understanding and attitudes.

Of course, many would argue that BAT carries out these development tasks purely to encourage children to smoke when they get older. However, there is no getting away from the fact that better educated people will, anyway, shy away from tobacco consumption. What can be seen, too, is that BAT has tried to institutionalize its development assistance through working with partners in NGOs and the government and, where an institution does not exist, it assists in creating one – the ECLT Foundation.

MDG case studies

The Millennium Development Goals (MDGs) are the UN's current major initiative to promote development through announcing a number of targets that must be achieved by the year 2015 (see Chapter 10 on whether the MDGs are stimulating business involvement in development and their relation with another UN initiative, the UN's Global Compact).

The eight MDGs are:

1   Eradicate extreme poverty and hunger
2   Achieve universal primary education
3   Promote gender equality and empower women
4   Reduce child mortality
5   Improve maternal health
6   Combat HIV/AIDS, malaria and other diseases
7   Ensure environmental sustainability
8   Develop a global partnership for development.

I illustrate this section with a number of short case studies, the many development initiatives that have been stimulated by the World Bank for business to be involved in the UN's MDGs.[25] A list is given in Box 3.1, together with a website address where more details can be found. Each company initiative is briefly introduced, followed by my observation in italics on whether, indeed, these initiatives are sustainable under a CSR strategy. Most, as can be seen, are either Type II or Type III initiatives.

AMD personal Internet communicator – MDG Goal 8

AMD's President and CEO Dr Hector Ruiz is passionate about the pivotal role that technology can play as an instrument for social change, growth and economic development. At the 2004 World Economic Forum in Davos, he announced AMD's ambitious 50X15 initiative, a global commitment to empower 50 per cent of the world's population with basic internet service and computing access by the year 2015. The success of the 50X15 initiative which Ruiz calls a 'global necessity' will be determined by the alliances across multiple industry sectors and their ability to create economic opportunities for businesses and entrepreneurs in emerging markets. The Personal Internet Communicator (PIC) is an affordable consumer device designed to provide internet access for people in developing markets to enhance communications, entertainment and education opportunities. The PIC includes a monitor, keyboard, mouse and pre-installed software including a suite of communications, entertainment and education applications that give users improved communications and opportunities for furthering education. (*A nice dream but no matter how cheap for those living on $2 a day and then often on subsistence income, i.e. non-monetary income, the other 50 per cent will mainly be the poor and under-privileged. Type II.*)

---

[25] Drawn, with some editing and except where marked (*), from a number of case studies on a World Bank website www.businessandmdgs.org, accessed 5 January 2006.

Box 3.1 MDG case studies

Akshaya Patra Foundation School Feeding Program
AMD Personal Internet Computer
BASF/UNIDO/UNEP Eco-Efficiency Program for Small and Medium-Sized Enterprises
The Business of Development Video Awards and Ethical Markets (*)
Center for Science, Technology, and Society and the Global Social Benefit Incubator
ChevronTexaco Nigeria YES Alliance
Coca-Cola Africa Foundation Employee HIV/AIDS Program
Fairtrade Movement (*)
Freeplay Foundation
GlaxoSmithKline
Global Alliance for Illumination for Education
Global Learning Portal Network
Global Review of Private Sector Participation in Water Supply and Sanitation
Guidelines for private sector participation in water supply and sanitation services
Global Student Leadership
Hasbro Afghan Women's Development Center
Henkel's Make an Impact on Tomorrow
HSBC Promotes CSR to Board Level
JUNJI Corporation Learning Together Program
MTN Village Phone
Microsoft, IBM, Hewlett Packard, Aerolíneas Tampa, ANDI, Sun Microsystems, and
Saferbo Computers to Educate Program
Mindset Network Alliance
Nicaragua Model School Reform Alliance
Novo Nordisk
ResponsAbility Global Microfinance Fund
Royal Dutch Shell Group (*)
Sister Cities International
Swiss–South African Co-operation Initiative
Tata Group (*)
Teddy Trust HIV/AIDS Education Program
Television Education for the Advancement of Muslim Mindanao Alliance
Tetra Pak Integrated Dairy Development Project
TIME Magazine Special Advertising Series
Unilever's Novella Edible Oilseeds Project
World Business Awards in Support of the MDGs
WWF and ABB Access to Electricity Program

Akshaya Patra Foundation School Feeding Program – MDG Goal 4

The Akshaya Patra Foundation School Feeding Program is a private sector-led programme to address two of the most pressing problems facing India: hunger and education. The Akshaya Patra Foundation provides free meals everyday to poverty-stricken school children in and around Bangalore, Hubli, Mysore, Hassan and Mangalore in southern India, Vrindavan in Uttar Pradesh and Jaipur in Rajasthan. Since 2001, the programme has been scaled up to provide over 85,000 hygienic and nutritious meals every day. Akshaya Patra seeks to serve over 100,000 children per day by 2010 for replication by other organizations across India. For many children, the Akshaya Patra meal is the only healthy meal they will have, thus producing dramatic improvements in enrolment, attendance and attention span at schools. (*This is not a sustainable project, since once the aid stops so do the meals. Type I.*)

BASF/UNIDO/UNEP Eco-Efficiency Program for Small and Medium-Sized Enterprises – all MDGS

The Eco-Efficiency Program for Small and Medium-Sized Enterprises is a joint project in collaboration with the German chemical group BASF, the United Nations Industrial Development Organization, and the UNEP. The main objective of the initiative is to help small businesses produce and manufacture not only competitively, but in an environmentally sustainable manner, adhering at the same time to standards of safe working conditions. The programme was started in 2003 in Morocco in the textile sector where the dyeing sector plays a vital role, providing significant employment by many SMEs. Their eco-efficiency analysis seeks to achieve a balance between environmental and economic factors in production processes: to manufacture cost-effective products with the smallest possible amount of raw material and energy use, and to minimize emissions. Based on the exclusive know-how of BASF, the programme is made available for the first time to SMEs in a developing country which otherwise would not be able to obtain and absorb cutting-edge international know-how. Today, the service is available to UNIDO/UNEP's network of Cleaner Production Centres in 35 countries. (*My previous experience of an UNIDO project was that a lot of money was pumped into SMEs but the projects were not sustainable in the sense that, once the injection of funds stopped, so did the S or ME. There is a danger, too, that by supporting certain SMEs other SMEs will suffer through not being competitive, simply because they do not have the assets which have been offered either in-kind through training, such as BDA, or through a grant or subsidized credit. Possible Type III.*)

Ethical markets and The Business of Development Video Awards – all MDGs

'The Business of Development' is one of the world's first television series dedicated to profiling the links between the business world and global development issues. Another, US-based TV series, is known as 'Ethical

Markets'.[26] Set up by author Hazel Henderson, its mission is to foster the evolution of capitalism beyond current models 'based on materialism, maximizing self-interest and profit, competition and fear of scarcity'. Its founders believe that 'capitalism combined with humanity's growing knowledge of the interdependence of all life on Planet Earth can evolve to serve today's new needs and our common future – beyond maximizing profits for shareholders and management, to benefiting all stakeholders'. (*Although these initiatives seem esoteric, in fact spreading the word about good sustainable projects through high-level media broadcasts can be very cost-effective. Type III.*)

Center for Science, Technology, and Society and the Global Social Benefit Incubator – all MDGs

The Center for Science, Technology, and Society promotes the common good of an increasingly technological world. Through its signature programme, the Global Social Benefit Incubator (GSBI), it works with the private sector and non-profit initiatives from around the world – with a particular emphasis on those from developing countries which seek to address the issues of poverty. The GSBI brings together private sector Silicon Valley expertise in scaling technology innovations to support social entrepreneurs. Its partner organizations include The Tech Museum of Innovation, Global Junior Challenge, World Bank Development Marketplace, Schwab Foundation Fellows, and Silicon Valley sponsoring organizations. (*An excellent initiative but care has to be taken that it does not solely address the rich, rather than the poor, poor. Type III.*)

ChevronTexaco Nigeria YES Alliance – MDG Goal 2

The Nigeria YES Alliance utilizes corporate experience and expertise to emphasize business skills training among Nigerian in-school youth. The alliance helps teenage secondary school youth build literacy and maths proficiency while introducing real world business skills and problem-based learning through community service. By linking traditional formal education with business and entrepreneurship, the alliance is structured to create greater youth leadership and community ownership in Nigeria while fostering social and economic development. The programme is divided into three learning cycles: introduction to business and entrepreneurship; community service; and design and development of community ventures. Nigeria YES training is currently conducted only with youth who attend school, ChevronTexaco is now bidding to extend the programme to out-of-school

---

[26] www.ethicalmarkets.com – the author is on the Advisory Board.

youth. ChevronTexaco is the primary resource partner, and also plays a role in implementation through linking education with employment. (*Linking practical and experienced businessmen and women with students in a training environment always gets very high marks from me. All the usual problems of education exist, however, such as whether the young people can afford to be at school rather than helping their parents, whether the training is carefully designed to ensure maximum impact, whether the training is carefully monitored to ensure the students get jobs afterwards, and so on Type III.*)

Coca-Cola Africa Foundation employee HIV/AIDS Program – MDG Goal 6

In 2001, the Coca-Cola Africa Foundation established a programme to offer anti-retroviral drugs to employees, spouses and children with UNAIDS and to cultivate local partnerships and community involvement for Coke's 60,000 employees (and 40 independent African-based bottlers). Project goals include encouraging behavioural change using television, radio, printed materials and lectures. (*An excellent initiative although a bit hard for extended families, friends and others in the community, and it will dolittle to alleviate poverty since those employed by Coca Cola will already be reasonably well-off. Type II.*)

The Fairtrade movement – MDG Goal 8

At the global level, the media is awash with advocates for the need to accept free trade of developing country agricultural and textile exports. The reluctance of countries such as France to open their agricultural markets is a sore point in the European Union and among consumers who must pay up to three times the world price for their milk, butter, beef, and so on. One way around trade restrictions and one that takes advantage of the trend to healthier living in the industrialized world is 'fair trade'. According to Roger Cowe, the Fairtrade movement has helped many small farmers.[27] It guarantees medium-term deals at a minimum price, plus a special premium to be invested in the community. Sales of brands such as Cafédirect have grown rapidly, and the Fairtrade Foundation claims 18 per cent of the UK ground coffee market.

Nevertheless, Cowe notes, all the Fairtrade coffee in the world adds up to barely 1 per cent of the annual crop. The US NGO, the Rainforest Alliance, which campaigns to protect ecosystems such as the El Sal-

---

[27] Roger Cowe (2005) 'Brewing up a better deal for coffee farmers', *The Observer*, London, UK, 5 June.

vador forests, has developed standards for sustainable agriculture, which apply to bananas, cocoa, citrus fruit and flowers as well as coffee. These include community relations and labour conditions as well as environmental aspects such as agrochemical use, water conservation and waste management. It wants to reverse the trend towards monoculture which has seen the destruction of many forests, with repercussions for wildlife, soil and water systems as well as communities. One of the key buyers is Kraft, the US multinational that owns Maxwell House and Kenco. Two years ago, Kraft signed a deal with the Rainforest Alliance to buy thousands of tonnes of certified beans. It still amounts to only 2 per cent of Kraft's annual purchase, but Chris Wille, chief of sustainable agriculture for the alliance, says it is significant. (*A small, but rapidly growing area, Fairtrade shows that CSR of production can lead to new markets. One can see in the supermarket chains in Europe, even Wal-Mart's subsidiary Asda, shelves now lined with clearly marked fairtrade and organic produce from around the world. Shoppers must still pay a premium, but prices are converging between the old and the new. Type II.*)

Freeplay Foundation – MDG Goal 2

The Freeplay Foundation provides wind-up and solar powered radios and life-saving information for some of the poorest people in Africa sourced from the private sector in Silicon Valley. (*Low-cost products aimed at poor people is a worthwhile endeavour; however, like my criticisms of Prahalad and Hart in Chapter 7, a supply-orientated solution has limited reach. Type II.*)

GlaxoSmithKline and TB Alliance – MDG Goal 6

GlaxoSmithKline's Drugs for the Developing World centre are participants in pioneering public–private partnerships with pharmaceutical companies, philanthropists and governments. Since its creation in 2000, the TB Alliance, a non-profit group in New York, has helped to mobilize more than a dozen projects for new treatments. It is working with GSK, has signed a letter of intent with Novartis, and is in discussions with AstraZeneca. A similar model has worked for the Medicines for Malaria Venture (MMV), which, since 1999, has cooperated with companies such as GSK, Novartis, Roche and Ranbaxy of India, forging links between them and academic institutions. And Sanofi-Aventis has agreed to produce an affordable new combination malaria therapy with DNDi (Drugs for Neglected Diseases Initiative; see www.dndi.org/newsletters/10/partnership.htm). One reason for such recent activity is a change of heart towards corporate social responsibility by the drug companies. 'It has a lot to do with our Swedish shareholders, who have a strong sense of social commitment and ask questions at the annual general meeting,' says Aileen Allsop, from the Discovery division of AstraZeneca, formed by the merger of Astra, of Sweden, and Zeneca, of the UK, in 1999. Philanthropy, above all from the Bill and Melinda Gates Foundation, has made a big difference, allowing beneficiaries to approach pharmaceutical groups with money and ideas instead of simply pleas for funding. Two such recipients, MMV and the TB Alliance, jointly fund half of Tres Cantos' 100 scientists, with GSK paying the rest. (*Philanthropic activities that lead to sustainability get my vote and research leading to an increase in the amount of widespread realistically available drugs aimed at poor countries' main health problems can have a major impact on reducing disease. Type III.*)

Global Alliance for Illumination for Education – MDG Goal 2

The Global Alliance for Illumination for Education promotes adult literacy and primary education in Mali, where 75 per cent of the population is illiterate. Through the introduction of a technology to allow for adult educational activities at night, the alliance enhances the learning of the 1500 adults currently participating in community-based literacy classes in Mali. The enabling technology, the Kinkajou Projector, is a low-cost, easy to use and durable projector that runs on multiple energy sources and has low energy requirements. This alliance increases access to education by allowing educators to teach at night – the only time available to adults due to work requirements – and will enhance the educational experience since students will no longer be required to huddle around a shared book by lamp or candle light. The implementing partner is World Education, an NGO with more than 10 years experience in Mali. MIT-based Design that Matters is a non-profit organization that takes private sector technologies to improve quality of life in poor communities. (*An excellent initiative that takes into account poor people and their children's work habits and, of course, the availability of power at affordable prices is particularly problematic in many developing countries especially Mali. Type III.*)

Global Learning Portal Network – MDG Goal 2

Addressing the need to replace an estimated 68,000 teachers by the end of the decade, the Global Learning Portal Network (GLPNet) is a global web portal offering education and a meeting space for teachers to discuss, share instructional materials and information on good teaching practices, and network with colleagues on a transnational scale. GLPNet has implemented pilot activities with education professionals, schools and NGOs in Brazil, Ethiopia, Nicaragua, South Africa and Uganda, with recent expansion to the Philippines and Egypt. GLPNet continually fosters partnerships with private sector content providers to deliver targeted content to education professionals around the world. Sun Microsystems is the corporate partner and distributes free software to every new registrant. Academy for Educational Development is the implementing partner. (*Promoting the exchange of ideas between teachers is an excellent initiative, since they rarely get together in developing countries because of the cost of transport. Unfortunately, as so often is the case, it is the richer teachers with adequate power supplies and computer equipment who will benefit, thereby eventually worsening the distribution of income as the 'richer' students benefit from increased up-to-date human capital. Type III.*)

Global Review of Private Sector Participation in water supply and sanitation – MDG Goal 7

Issues such as privatization, commodification, conditionalities and prepaid water meters have sparked protests and demonstrations throughout the world for many years. In Bolivia, for example, months of civil protest against private sector participation (PSP) in water services led to the imposition of a state of emergency in 2000. Yet the private sector does make a significant contribution to reducing the large number of people in developing countries who lack access to safe water and effective sanitation. The Global Water Scoping Process found that more than 90 per cent of the over 300 stakeholders agreed that a global review of the impact of private sector participation is needed to help meet the UN's MDGs in water and sanitation.

In response, a stakeholder workshop was held in 2004 to review findings. The 60 workshop participants came from government, regulatory groups and agencies; public utilities; representatives of poor communities with PSP experience; private sector stakeholders, from small-scale independent producers to large companies; labour unions; NGOs; international financial institutions; and bilateral donors.

By promoting broad-based discussion at national and local levels on appropriate roles for the private sector, through multi-stakeholder assessment, the Global Review of Private Sector Participation aims to remove barriers and allow for accelerated access to water and sanitation services for the poor. The 2005 United Nations Millennium Project Report 'Health, Dignity and Development: What will it take?' identifies the need for greater constructive engagement on private sector participation. (*Any initiative to promote dialogue and better understanding gets my vote. One of the problems of these types of meetings is that the participants gain greatly but the information flow to others, who cannot afford to attend, is buried under too much work or lack of access to information. Each meeting of this type should try to engage the services of professionals in local media to publicize the results of the event and any insights learned in appropriate media. Type III.*)

Guidelines for private sector participation in water supply and sanitation services – MDG Goal 7

The initiative 'Policy Principles and Implementation Guidelines for Private Sector Participation in Sustainable Water Supply and Sanitation Services' is a multi-stakeholder initiative comprising the Swiss Government, with the Swiss Agency for Development and Cooperation (SDC) and the State Secretariat for Economic Affairs (seco), and the reinsurance company Swiss Re. The initiative facilitates public–private partnerships in water supply and sanitation services in development and transition countries in order to promote water sector development worldwide. For this purpose, it has developed a range of policy principles and implementation guidelines as well as a toolbox for practitioners. (*The Swiss generally have an excellent reputation for well thought out development projects and Swiss Re is one of the leaders of CSR thinking in the corporate field, so one can expect very interesting results from this initiative. Type III.*)

Global Student Leadership – MDG Goal 3

Global Student Leadership (GSL) was started by Michaela Walsh, former private sector banker and founder of Women's World Banking, to allow young people in developing countries to start projects in the private sector. Each participant to GSL is sponsored by a local individual or organization including school, non-profit organizations, United Nations Development Program, United Nations Association, United States Agency for International Development, International Finance Corporation, Women's World Banking, and so on. After weeks of intensive training in leadership and communication, English language, management and computer networking skills, students return home with her or his Action Plan (business plan) to implement for one year with private sector sponsor supervision and support. (*At least these projects will have a good start but most fail simply because of the enormous administrative, bureaucratic and wheeling and dealing hurdles that need to be surmounted once the student returns home. But, as any businessman or woman knows, success normally comes only after a fair amount of failure that, one way or other, creates experience for dealing with future problems. Type III.*)

Hasbro Afghan Women's Development Centers – MDG Goals 3, 4, 5, 8

In collaboration with Hasbro, Inc. and the Hassenfeld Foundation, the Afghan Women's Development Centers (AWDCs) increase women's literacy, the health of women and their families, awareness and participation in politics, and also strengthen the network of women's NGOs in Afghanistan. In collaboration with Relief International (RI), the two organizations have been closely involved with monitoring the project, providing further input, and ensuring that resources provided are used to benefit the greatest number and most needy of Afghan women. By delivering AWDC services through community-based organizations and establishing satellite locations for the AWDCs in less accessible districts, RI, Hasbro and the Hassenfeld Foundation work toward achieving the Millennium Development Goals of promoting gender equality and empowering women, reducing child mortality, improving maternal health, and developing a global partnership for development between the public and private sector, as well as the governments of developing countries. So far, the programme has empowered over 8000 women in several sectors. (*Projects such as these address crucial issues and normally handle them very well. However, the effects of Taleban-type thinking will take generations to change even if there is a will to do this and, unfortunately for women, the will is generally lacking by the powerful male-dominated structures that exist in Afghanistan. Poor women, too, often don't work in their own best interest since they want to preserve their culture which they believe will enhance stability (true) and create better conditions for their family (depends what is meant by 'better'. Increasing life expectancy is the best development indicator, but is not enhanced by Taleban-type thinking). Type III.*)

Henkel's Make an Impact on Tomorrow – MDG Goal 7

In the past five years, Germany-based Henkel, which makes personal and homecare products for over 125 countries, has increased its operating profit by 27 per cent and its sales by 18 per cent, while cutting carbon dioxide emissions per metric ton of output by 12 per cent and its water use by 28 per cent over the same period. Other key social and environmental performance indicators also showed improvement, among them the occupational accident rate, which has fallen by 56 per cent since 2000. The data can be found in Henkel's Sustainability Report which includes an overview of the firm's support for non-profit projects around the world through its Make an Impact on Tomorrow initiative, and features comment from five sustainability specialists from Brazil, Germany, India, Russia and the US on the challenges they believe the company faces in their countries and regions. (*The impact of CSR thinking is changing the way companies do business and leading them down new paths. But why only support non-profit projects? They might not necessarily be sustainable without external support whereas for profit projects may be able to create the conditions for increased income and well-being. Type II.*)

HSBC promotes CSR to board level – MDG Goal 8

HSBC has created a new department working solely on the sustainable development sector, a sign of the bank's high-profile focus on environmental and corporate social responsibility issues. The job of the Sustainable Development unit will be to expand sustainability into HSBC's mainstream operations, both from a risk and a business development perspective. It will report directly to Alan Jebson, group chief operating officer, bringing board-level responsibility for managing HSBC's environmental impact.[28] (*An example of a major bank not only investing in developing countries, something they have always done, but one that is bringing CSR to the core of its operations. Of course, only a full analysis of intentions and results will really tell us how far along the road of CSR and development HSBC has gone, but this shows encouraging signs nonetheless. Type II.*)

JUNJI Corporation Learning Together Program – MDG Goals 2 and 3

JUNJI is a private company launched in 1970 to create, plan, promote, stimulate and supervise the organization and operation of kindergarten classrooms in partnership with the Chilean government via the Department of Education. The project contributes to achievement and improvement in children's education – specifically girls under six through the strategic use of radio, in-person training, distance education and educational booklets. (*Chile is developing rapidly and its education system is widely admired. Former ILO official and ex-President of Chile, Ricardo Lagos, implemented many social projects that had been thwarted by General Pinochet and his regime. Type III.*)

MTN Village Phone – MDG Goal 8

One of the greatest success stories in international development has been Grameen's Village Phone Program in Bangladesh. In rural villages, where no telecommunications service has previously existed, cellular phones are provided to very poor women who use the phone to operate a business providing communications services to her community. Grameen Foundation along with MTN Uganda launched MTN Village Phone Uganda in November 2003. There are now over 1000 rural Village Phone Operators throughout Uganda, each earning enough money to repay their microfinance loan and put money aside for the welfare of their families: food, education, health needs. Grameen Foundation along with MTN is look-

---

28 Bank Marketing International, London, October 2005, p4.

ing to launch Village Phone in Rwanda. (*Telecommunication costs are still high in developing countries having been considered to be used only by the 'elite' who can therefore be taxed heavily, there being many difficulties in collecting taxes on incomes, which is why consumer taxation is preferred. However, the costs of telecommunications for poor and/or SME entrepreneurs is often prohibitive, thereby greatly reducing marketing opportunities. Therefore any initiative aimed at reducing the costs of telecommunications will help oil the wheels of development which, in turn, will outweigh any short-term advantage in tax revenues. Type III.*)

Microsoft, IBM, Hewlett Packard, Aerolíneas Tampa, ANDI, Sun Microsystems, and Saferbo Computers to Educate Program – MDG Goal 8

Since 2000, Colombia's Department of Communications and Education, private enterprise and the Canadian Government collect computers for reconditioning and delivery without cost to schools throughout Colombia. The goals are to improve education in Colombia, facilitate access to new information and communication technology, contribute to the formation of a cadre of youth prepared to face the challenges of the present world, and diminish the gap between those with access to resources and technological benefits and those without. (*Despite Colombia's poor international reputation stemming from violence and drugs, Colombia actually has very progressive and well thought out social programmes. The sophistication of its information technology would surprise many outsiders. Nevertheless, re-conditioned computers can provide the first step for many young people to enhance their computer knowledge. There is always some concern that rich countries send their unwanted technology to developing countries and thereby keep them technologically poor and unable to compete with the rich countries' brain intensive technologies. However, without allowing many under-privileged youths access to, at least, get on the first step on the technology rung, development is hindered, thereby reducing the markets for rich countries and allowing the violent movements in Colombia to continue their havoc. Type III.*)

Mindset Network Alliance – MDG Goal 2

One of the legacies of apartheid is a substandard South African schooling system, where only 65 per cent of children reach grade five and many educators lack adequate qualifications. The Mindset Network Alliance supports basic education in the schooling system and professional development of teachers in South Africa through developing, packaging and distributing effective educational content via broadcast satellite networks and supporting multimedia. By developing free video content, the alliance can potentially reach all students in the 22,000 primary schools in South Africa. Mindset was launched by Nelson Mandela in 2003 with the help of a variety of partners including the Department of Education that assists with content and access; PanAmSat, a private sector contributor of bandwidth and channel setup; and the Liberty Foundation, Telkom Foundation, Multichoice Foundation and Synergos. (*Nelson Mandela has rarely put a foot wrong in recent years; with a few more leaders like him there would be less need for books like this! However, I don't see how a few free videos is going to take the figure of 65 per cent much higher. Poor literacy has as much to do with the willingness to read and write and the complicity of parents as well as the quality of teaching and teaching tools. Type III in intent at least.*)

Nicaragua Model School Reform Alliance – MDG Goal 2

The *Escuela Modelo* programme, an educational model practised in Nicaragua and other Latin American countries, is being expanded through the Nicaragua Model School Reform Alliance. The objectives of the programme are to engage local communities in school management, introduce model school reforms, and decentralize the education system. *Escuela Modelo* has been successfully implemented during the last four years in over 200 schools in Nicaragua, with participation rates as high as 90 per cent. Operationally, the programme focuses on encouraging active parent and community participation, the introduction of interactive learning, retraining teachers to serve as learning facilitators rather than traditional lecturers, individually paced and self-managed learning, small-group and peer-directed study, classroom learning centres by subject area, teacher-quality circles to exchange best practices, and student government in each school. The programme expansion has toughened requirements for schools. Quality assurance must be assured, not just passive participation, and frequent follow-ups monitor compliance. The American Chamber of Commerce of Nicaragua is a resource partner whose efforts have enlisted the support of over 50 companies, including DHL Worldwide Express, Continental Airlines and Intercontinental Hotels and Resorts. The American Nicaraguan Foundation is both a resource and implementing partner. Both private sector partners are supporting schools and are providing furniture, books, equipment, supplies, infrastructure improvements, libraries, construction and repairs, computers and the Internet, and health and nutrition services. (*Education, almost however delivered, is a good in its own right. The advantage of involving communities in education cannot be over-emphasized to the extent that I have always felt that educating the grandmothers was a successful educational policy simply because grandmothers are role models in most societies. The impetus given to children and their parents to see their grandmothers being educated is marvellous. There is a tendency to ignore elders in Western society which other cultures do not do. Literate elders provide motivation and incentives to be like 'grandmother' and should not, as Western society tends to do, be ignored. Type III.)*

Novo Nordisk – MDG Goal 4

By posing the question in its 2004 annual report, 'Can diabetes really be defeated?' the Danish pharmaceuticals firm, Novo Nordisk, describes its fight against diabetes, particularly in the developing world where diabetes is growing fastest. In 2004, Novo amended its articles of association to specify that the company will 'strive to conduct its activities in a financially, environmentally and socially responsible way'. It also sold insulin at 20 per cent of the average price to 33 less-developed countries (LDCs); reached an estimated 21 million people through its National Diabetes Program and Diabetes, Attitudes, Wishes and Needs (DAWN) programme; made increased investments in new markets such as Brazil, China and the US; developed a climate change strategy to achieve an absolute reduction in carbon dioxide emissions by 2014; began 'roadtesting' the United Nations Norms on the Responsibilities of Transnational Corporations, with a view to developing human rights standards; and established a bonus scheme for its 26 senior executives that includes performance on key sustainability-driven projects. (*A small step in development by Novo Nordisk can reduce the misery of thousands. The UN would like to obtain cheaper drugs, and can do this through buying in bulk, but cannot get lower prices without the complicity of the powerful, and rich, drug companies. Type III.)*

ResponsAbility Global Microfinance Fund – MDG Goal 8

The ResponsAbility Global Microfinance Fund is a social investment fund founded by Swiss banks and a social venture capital fund. It aims at building bridges between social investors in Switzerland and neighbouring countries seeking a combination of financial and social returns, and microfinance in developing and transition countries seeking private and institutional capital. The Swiss Agency for Development and Cooperation (SDC) gave technical assistance and the State Secretariat for Economic Affairs (seco) gave financial assistance in the start-up phase and both agencies continue a policy dialogue on a regular basis. The total fund volume in early 2005 was $9 million. The Fund's main investment focus is microfinance with an emphasis on fair trade. The portfolio is highly diversified across regions and countries, and consists of direct loans to microfinance institutions and indirect investments through partners. (*Small amounts are involved to begin with but, as experience shows, this is a useful initiative to enhance the access of poor people to finance. Type III.)*

Royal Dutch/Shell Group – MDG Goals 1, 7, 8

The aim of the Royal Dutch/Shell Group is to meet the energy needs of society in ways that are economically, socially and environmentally viable, now and in the future. One major initiative is Shell's six-step initiative against corruption. The first step spells out its general business principles and articulates the company's stance on business conduct. It explicitly states that any violations of these principles by employees will not be accepted. On business integrity, it states that direct or indirect offer, payment, soliciting and acceptance of bribes in any form are unacceptable practices. The second step involves internal communication and training where staff are made aware of the policies and principles in staff contracts, new staff induction programmes, guidelines on gifts, political contributions and potential conflicts of interest. The company's 'Management Primer' spells out exactly what bribery and corruption entail and the various strategies to deal with the problem. It also highlights these through the 'Dilemma's Supplement' which details case study examples. The third step promotes its anti-corruption culture, for which Shell appoints 'Country Chairs' in each country of its operations. The country chairs develop their own specific guidelines to reflect local traditions and cultures and draft precise rules and staff exercises. Its internal and external assurance process has staff involvement through the widely praised 'Tell Shell' facility. The remaining steps include the internal and external assurance process that involves staff through the 'People Survey' and a 'whistle-blowing scheme' called the 'Business Principles Helpline'. The Shell Report that is published is an example of the external reporting while close links with NGOs, industrial organizations and international bodies form a part of its external engagement. This also includes the company's active role in signing up various international agreements and adhering to Transparency International's Business Principles. Shell has structured its values, mindset and engagement in support of the UN Global Compact principles. This engages people – suppliers, contractors, customers of the company – and policies at various levels including employee rights, health and safety, equal opportunity, diversity and inclusiveness, training, local HSE quality, social equality, national rights and social equity, among other ideas. Shell also promotes advocacy by engaging stakeholders for identifying and sharing issues. (*Most of these words have been taken from Shell's own publicity material. Nevertheless, shaken by criticism of its lack of involvement in human rights' issues in Nigeria in the mid 1990s, Shell has tried to move away from being the international pariah it once was. It has become one of the leaders in CSR and has also, through its Shell Foundation, noted above, moved into being both a Type II and Type III development actor.*)

Sister Cities International – All Goals

The Millennium Development Goals City-to-City Challenge Pilot Program mobilizes city-to-city relationships to focus on MDGs as part of membership in the Sister Cities Network for Sustainable Development. In cooperation with the World Bank Institute (WBI), Sister Cities International selected task forces in each community to undertake the following steps:

1   participate in WBI learning activities about MDGs;
2   select an MDG and specific target(s), and indicator(s) using a participatory process;
3   conduct a diagnostic assessment of present conditions;
4   prepare an action plan to raise awareness and improve conditions;
5   implement the first steps of the action plan;
6   monitor progress and compare results with initial conditions.

The goal of the pilot programme is to demonstrate the effectiveness of city-to-city cooperation in addressing the Millennium Development Goals. The pilot programme will give communities the skills to build development capacity, enrich their communities, and strengthen international bonds of cooperation and friendship. (*Frequently, these city-to-city partnerships serve to bring the leaders of communities together at not inconsiderable expense to the cities themselves. It would be valuable to see the results of the monitoring programme on 'progress' and to see what is meant by progress. On the other hand, any initiative that brings citizens together through cross-cultural exchanges reduces ignorance and adds to ethnic and racial harmony. Possible Type III.*)

Swiss–South African Co-operation Initiative – MDG Goal 2

In February 2001, the Swiss Agency for Development and Cooperation (SDC) – together with ten Swiss private corporations – launched the Swiss–South African Co-operation Initiative (SSACI) as a long-term project designed to help improve educational and vocational skills of youths aged 16–25 years old in South Africa. SSACI was established as a common trust fund, sponsored equally by SDC and the participating Swiss companies. The Board is equally composed of representatives of the Swiss Government, corporate sponsors and South African civil society. Annual disbursement of the fund is 2 million Swiss francs. By mid 2004, SSACI had granted $6 million to 40 youth development projects. A total of 2417 unemployed young women and men were enrolled for training, and 80 per cent found a job at the end of the programme. A key factor for SSACI's success is its focus on *outcome* in terms of employment rather than *supply* in terms of training. (*It is good to see a focus on 'outcome' which vocational specialists track either through using 'backward' tracer studies where the employed are asked where they received their training, or through 'forward' tracer studies where graduates are tracked through to their first job. However, this tracking is easier in theory than it is to do. Most institutions do not have the resources to keep in touch with their graduates, while backward tracer studies tend to be expensive to carry out. Type III.)*

The Tata Group – all MDGs

The Tata Group was one of the first to promote CSR (what it calls corporate citizenship) in India. The Group believes, as does the author, that a real contribution comes when communities are enabled in a manner that has a sustained developmental impact. Approximately 30 per cent of profits after tax (PAT) of the Tata Group as a whole is invested in community development programmes across India. The group has a centrally administered agency – Tata Council for Community Initiatives – that helps its companies through specific processes in social development, environment management, biodiversity restoration and employee volunteering. The Tata Group's corporate citizenship initiatives range from health and education to livelihoods and women–children welfare, from tribal hamlets to disadvantaged villages – a multitude of initiatives that have touched the lives of thousands of people across the nation. The Group has also created cities and towns around some of their industrial facilities – Jamshedpur, Mithapur, Babrala, Mathigiri – which are tangible manifestations of a commitment to employees that stretches much further than any formal or mandated contract.

Tata Steel caters to over 600 villages and several company towns in the states of Orissa and Jharkhand. It has created Town Services, a Community Development and Social Welfare Department and an Energy and Environment Cell. Tata Steel has promoted rural economy through natural resource management, micro financing and credit and training for gainful employment. It has created a ripple effect across towns and villages, and its services have grown to cover 700,000 beneficiaries. Today, Tata Steel is also responsible for environment management, family initiatives, medical services, emergency fire services, airport, mobile medical services, sports facilities, libraries and education centres. In Jamshedpur, Tata Steel takes care of public utilities including road maintenance, water and electricity supply, street lights, sanitation and more. The company also runs eight primary schools, nine high schools and a college, while supporting many more schools indirectly. Community initiatives are as high on the Tata agenda as education and this has spawned a wide variety of programmes, most notably on AIDS awareness and drug abuse. Tata Steel has also utilized a web of income generation, empowerment and health and hygiene schemes in its rural development programmes for the tribal communities in the state of Jharkhand. This integrated programme employs the company's best practices while drawing on the experience and expertise of independent development agencies. It also takes management learning and skills to the grassroots population. In its huge plantation holding in Munnar in south India, Tata Tea has initiated three projects to equip mentally and physically disabled children to secure a better future. Through its micro insurance schemes for villagers, Tata AIG has been providing security cover to the weaker sections of society. Tata Consultancy Services works to promote literacy to adults who cannot read or write. This special computer-based programme has lifted more than 46,000 people out of illiteracy and has the potential to deliver to millions more. Tata Chemical's initiatives to empower village women, run a 'biodiversity reserve plantation project' driven by employee volunteers to create a botanical reserve for endangered plant species, Tata Motors' anti-leprosy crusade are further examples of the Tata creed of community work. Environment is another focus area within the Tata Group's overall corporate responsibility matrix. A host of the Tata companies adhere to the environmental procedures drawn up by the GRI. (*The Tata Group follows the classical tradition of companies such as Bourneville in the UK (the forerunner of Cadbury) which believed in cradle-to-grave care for its workers. Tata, of course, goes beyond its own workers. There are quibbles that the Tata social ventures are done to consolidate its many monopolistic business activities in India. Only time will tell whether these activities will continue in the new, less paternalistic, India. Type III.*)

Teddy Trust HIV/AIDS Education Program – MDG Goal 6

Teddy Exports, through its Teddy Trust, developed an HIV/AIDS workplace and local community education programme in Tirumangalam, India and Madurai district. The programme seeks to educate high-risk, largely illiterate groups. Their AIDS Awareness Project uses street theatre and puppetry as a way of communicating the message to a largely illiterate audience. Their Healthy Highway Project houses two 'truckers' booths' on the main highway to southern India and one at an oil refinery unit at Manila to provide information on HIV/AIDS and prevention to over 80,000 truck drivers through street plays, slide shows, leaflets, stickers and condom distribution. And their Women in Prostitution Project uses peer mentors to provide HIV/AIDS awareness, medical assistance and counselling for commercial sex workers. The all-female project team works with a network of commercial sex workers, pimps and their clients to promote condom use through education and innovative strategies for condom carrying by the commercial sex workers. (*One would think, given its international exposure, that HIV/AIDS awareness would be as well known as the importance of clean drinking water. That many techniques must be used to propagate information illustrates the failure of information access in many developing countries. Clearly the situation is not helped by the Catholic church banning the use of contraceptives and head-in-the sand attitudes of such 'luminaries' as President Mbeki of South Africa, who has only recently, and reluctantly, acknowledged the importance of blood exchanges as a major cause of transmission of HIV/AIDS. Type III.)*

Television Education for the Advancement of Muslim Mindanao Alliance – MDG Goal 2

The Television Education for the Advancement of Muslim Mindanao (TEAM) Alliance seeks to provide educational opportunities to children in the Autonomous Region of Muslim Mindanao (ARMM) in the Philippines. The Alliance provides access to education for 40,000 students from 70 public schools in ARMM through the Knowledge Channel, the only curriculum-based educational channel available for free to public schools in the Philippines. Knowledge Channel content is also used to improve the teaching capacity of teachers. The programme aims to raise the maths, science and English competencies among at least 50 per cent of the elementary school beneficiaries in Maguindanao by the end of one school year. In addition, 350 public school teachers will be trained in using educational TV to teach maths, science and English. The programme will also equip girls with life-skills and knowledge of their rights through educational TV modules. Indirect beneficiaries include 2.4 million public school children and 6 million cable TV subscribers. Partners include the Knowledge Channel Foundation, Philippine Department of Education, private corporations such as Central CATV and ABS-CBN Broadcasting Corporation, local governments and community organizations. Alliance partners comprising TEAM Mindanao will contribute cash and their expertise in communications technology, broadcast media, education, electrification and educational television to deliver services to the target beneficiaries. (*Using the media, and media companies, to promote educational activities particularly in areas such as Mindanao, which is beset with religious conflicts, can only be a plus. Type III.*)

Tetra Pak Integrated Dairy Development Project – MDG goal 4

In 1997, Tetra Pak started its own school milk programme in Indonesia serving 10,000 children. Through cooperation with the US Trade Office, a model for financing based on food aid donations was developed. The US Government, through the US Department of Agriculture, have for many years donated surplus commodities to developing countries, often through the UN's World Food Program. Some of these donations are used for the School Feeding Programs. At the G8 meeting in Japan in 2000, the US launched the Global Food for Education Initiative. This and other initiatives have so far resulted in a number of school feeding programmes based on Tetra Pak technologies and knowledge (Vietnam – 300,000 children; Bangladesh – 200,000 children; Indonesia – 800,000 children; and a new programme will begin in the Philippines). All these programmes are managed by the International Development Office of the US cooperative Land O'Lakes with whom Tetra Pak has established a close co-operation. (*NGOs such as Land O'Lakes have good experience at ground level that they can share with multinationals such as Tetra Pak. However, one drawback of bringing in free food from abroad is that local cultures and markets can be negatively affected. Milk is not a staple part of diets in tropical developing countries simply because there are no cows. It would be better to use local products such as mangoes, bananas, rice, and so on that are in keeping with local cultures and, when bought locally, help to promote local agriculture. The US, and other well-meaning countries such as Canada, have often been accused of dumping their surplus wheat or canned luncheon meat or pilchards in the name of development. Could be a Type I.*)

TIME magazine special advertising series – MDG Goal 8

TIME magazine has embarked on a four-part special advertising series that puts the UN Millennium Development Goals in the spotlight. This special advertising series will be read by 21 million readers around the globe. Highlights of the campaign include 'calls to actions' in which business, religious and entertainment leaders explain why we must participate in the achievement of the MDGs. (*It is no good having good ideas that are meant to mobilize people, which is what the MDGs are, if the popular mass media cannot be used. However, TIME should ask itself whether there would be a business case for running their adverts in the absence of purely philanthropic notions. Further, proponents of the MDGs should work to make their ideals popular enough that the media would run the story anyway. Type I with possible Type III.*)

Unilever's Novella edible oilseeds project – MDG Goal 7

The Novella initiative aims to develop a sustainable supply chain of a non-wood forest product – the seed of the Allablackia tree – and establish a new industry of plant oil production in West Africa. The partnership originated as a result of research conducted in Ghana by Unilever, who then reached out to local environmental NGOs and local authorities in Southern Nigeria. Unilever is guaranteeing long-term demand and fair prices for the products, while local environmental NGOs are ensuring that the partnership operates in a participatory, transparent and equitable manner. (*The Novella initiative is clearly a Type II development initiative.*)

World Business Awards in support of the MDGs – MDG Goal 8

Selected from 64 nominations in 27 countries, ten projects have been presented with World Business Awards representing the 'tip of the iceberg' of businesses around the world that are making a significant contribution to the Millennium Development Goals. The following are the winners of the International Chamber of Commerce, United Nations Development Program, and Prince of Wales International Business Leaders Forum World Business Awards in support of the MDGs:

- Amerindians on Barima, Waini, Kumaka rivers. Amazon Caribbean Ltd
- Commercial beekeeping for poverty alleviation in Kenya. Honey Care Africa
- Community Benefit – Clean Water. Georg Fischer Bicentenary Foundation
- De Beers HIV/AIDS Program. De Beers Consolidated Mines, Ltd
- ITC eChoupal Information Technology Centers. ITC Ltd
- Microfinance in Ecuador. Federcasse and Italian Co-operative Credit Banks Association
- Mogalakwena HP i-community. Hewlett-Packard Company
- PHASE – Personal Hygiene and Sanitation Education. GlaxoSmith-Kline
- PuR – Purifier of Water. Procter & Gamble
- Water for All. SUEZ Environment.

(*This is an excellent initiative to draw company attention to the sorts of development activities they can engage in. Type III.*)

WWF and ABB Access to Electricity program – MDG Goals 1, 7 and 8

ABB's Access to Electricity program, designed to promote sustainable economic, environmental and social development in poor communities, is yielding its first concrete results – in a remote village in southern Tanzania. The 1800-strong village of Ngarambe, on the edge of the Selous National Park, has received electricity under the programme. Changes and improvements – in such areas as small businesses, education and health care – are already noticeable. ABB and WWF, the global conservation organization, have teamed up to ensure the sustainable development of the village. The project is serving as a model for further, larger Access to Electricity projects aimed at easing poverty in other rural or semi-urban parts of Africa and Asia.

The programme is much more than a rural electrification project. ABB works with other stakeholders – governments, companies, NGOs, aid agencies, civil society – with each partner bringing its complementary skills to the project. In Ngarambe, power from a diesel-fired generator is lighting up the school, dispensary, local government office, mosque, small businesses on the main road and a number of homes. The electricity – which is cheaper than the kerosene used until now – is on for four hours a day after dusk.

The benefits are tangible: The local school holds classes and stays open at night. 'They can study more for their exams, and it will be beneficial to society,' says a teacher. The number of pupils has risen from 250 to 350 since the arrival of electricity in mid 2004. At the dispensary, the doctor can now also treat his patients at night. He is intending to install a refrigerator for medicines. The measures will save some of his patients from the lengthy journey to the nearest hospital 70 kilometres – or two hours ride – from Ngarambe. Local stores and a teashop are also feeling the benefit from being able to stay open longer and provide cold drinks.

ABB supplied the generator, installed underground cables and low-voltage equipment, and trained local people to run the power supply. WWF provided guidance on issues ranging from reducing deforestation to health care and environmental education. (*No doubt ABB are looking into how the project could be of wider, and more profitable, application. ABB were once one of the leaders in sustainable development, but a change of management reduced its interest. It will be interesting to see whether that negatively affects their share price in the longer term – its 2005 performance, on the other hand, was excellent. Type II.*)

UNDP and the Business Centre – A model?

Clearly, there are many areas where business cannot be involved in development activities. This is particularly the case for macro level involvement such as tax planning, improved governance, anti-corruption, investment planning, fiscal policy, and so on. Partnering with a government or international governmental organization can provide a useful platform. There is more on this in Chapter 10 where I discuss the role of the UN. Here I report on a personal experience with the UN where the UN believed it had a 'model' which could be used to work with the business sector and wanted to know, given that the 'model' appeared very successful, whether it could have widespread applicability. During 2004, I was invited to lead a team to evaluate all the UNDP's activities in Honduras and one of my roles was to evaluate the 'business model' implemented there.[29]

The team was briefed in New York that the Business Centre (BC) 'model' of Honduras appeared attractive and perhaps worthy of replication elsewhere. Core UN resources for Honduras were few, less than $1 million in 2003, particularly since funds for UNDP as a whole are limited (less than

---

[29] See my report on www.undp.org/eo.documents/ADR/ADR_Reports/ADR-Honduras.pdf.

$1 billion per year – see Chapter 10) and, quite correctly, UNDP decided to consolidate resources into priority low-income countries while, at the same time, not losing its omnipresence in all developing countries. Clearly, for UNDP to continue its development efforts, it needs alternative forms of financing. The approach adopted in its BC in Honduras allowed UNDP to act as an intermediary between government and recipients in a transparent and non-corrupt manner. In 2003, about 7–8 per cent of government expenditure passed through UNDP hands. From these sums, the UNDP takes between 3.5–11 per cent that can be used for programme and office support. But controversy lurks here, as will be examined in this section.

On the basis of an aggressive marketing of UNDP's value added, it entered into a strategic alliance with the government's Presidential Office for Project Follow-Up (OPSP – Oficina Presidencial de Seguimiento a Proyectos). Further, on the basis of UNDP strategic support to the Honduran government in its efforts against corruption at all levels, the Government officially instructed every government ministry that all major procurements were to be made through UNDP. The Office's total execution for 2002 reached $53.4 million, of which almost $40 million was spent through the BC.

This procurement process was planned to continue for the foreseeable future but, eventually, would be phased out as confidence returned to government bidding processes. The World Bank, the Inter-American Development Bank (IDB) and the Tegucigalpa Chamber of Commerce all had deep reservations about the BC. The former two institutions felt that competitive bidding should eventually replace the BC while the third felt that business was being drained away from the private sector. Given the high level of corruption and inefficiency seen when government had handled the bidding process, the criticism could well have been one of 'sour grapes'. Indeed, the director of the BC claimed much success and noted that the BC had:

- 'allowed the purchase of equipment for neonatal care that led to the fall in morbidity among neonatals from 12 per 1000 to 6 per 1000 births in 2003;
- reduced the percentage of deaths in neonatal intensive care from 18.5 per cent in 2002 to 12 per cent by 2003;
- helped IHSS (Instituto Hondureño de Seguridad Social) to acquire technical equipment that allowed the intensive care centre in Tegucigalpa to be the best in Central America;
- acquired specialized laboratory services that helped to bring all hospitals to the national level.'[30]

Further, the impact on UNDP operations had been substantial – while the UNDP country office had suffered resource cutbacks from core funds allocated from UNDP HQ in New York, the office actually marshalled growth of over 10 per cent per annum in portfolio management, while establishing

---

[30] Personal interview, August 2004.

leadership in the policy arena. By 2002, Honduras had become the fifth largest disbursing country in Latin America, with over $50 million in actual delivery.

My own evaluation of the BC showed that there were both advantages and disadvantages. The main advantages were fourfold:

1   Money earned was used to increase UNDP Honduras reserves in considerable excess of core funding received from New York.
2   Earnings were used to focus on specific UNDP development programmes in Honduras.
3   The transparency of public bidding processes were enhanced and efficiency increased – for instance, delivery times in telecommunication equipment and medical supplies and so on improved considerably.
4   UNDP became a major player in the country with its increase in resources leading to increased visibility and a major influence on Honduras – inter alia improving democratic governance, reducing corruption, improving response to natural disasters and so on.

However, there were also three main disadvantages:

1   Support to some entities, such as the telecommunications firm Hondutel (the biggest component of the BC activities) made them more efficient but, thereby, diminished competition, since the costs of Hondutel's competitors, for instance, were not reduced through benefiting from efficient UNDP assistance.
2   The BC could be seen to be too close to businesses that have major influences on the government, i.e. UNDP independence was threatened.
3   By carrying out its own operations, neither the capacity of the government nor the private sector was enhanced; for instance, it did not lead to improved transparency of government bidding procedures.

Although the advantages greatly outweighed the disadvantages, it is doubtful that the BC Model of Honduras, as the UNDP had hoped, could be transferred to other countries, since Honduras is a special case – the government (or at least some in the government) had realized that corruption was hampering its ability to deliver its programmes and wanted to use a less 'tainted' organization. Few other governments accept this.

Nevertheless, the BC 'model' could have more widespread appeal if it could be transformed to a model of 'business partnership' between the UN and the private sector using CSR as the basis. The intention would be to begin a process of introducing CSR into each business (actually this 'model' could also apply to public institutions as well as NGOs) with which the UN deals. CSR, as defined in this book, is a system-wide approach to business that is beneficial to business over time. Many corporations around the world are now adopting this new model of conducting business. CSR is not charitable giving, it aims to bring about responsibility among all the stakeholders of a company or institution – from the shareholders, owners, managers, employees to external stakeholders – such as respect for consumers, human rights, communities and suppliers. If successful in introducing CSR thinking into business in Honduras, UNDP would be one of the first international organizations in Latin America to do so. Having CSR as the main goal of its BC would help UNDP to introduce more transparency and better governance among companies and institutions.

Thus, the BC as currently constituted in Honduras is unlikely to be a model for use in other countries. If it were, this would mean UNDP being transformed into more of a deliverer of services for government than a development agency. But, building upon the BC's success in working with companies could well become a model, especially if developed within a CSR (or similar) framework.

Corruption and responses

It has been gradually accepted that corruption places a severe damper on development. For instance, when a government offers a tender to construct a bridge, road or building and the winner is not the one with the best record and/or most competitive price but the one who has greased the right palms, trouble occurs right across the board. First, the 'winner' has paid off one or more government officials. Second, the project then gets implemented poorly using inferior materials. Third, the project is evaluated by the government, who produce an excellent evaluation report. The project ends but the consequences start. Maintenance costs rise sharply as the project's poor quality becomes apparent. Who will pay for this? The local population pays through a costly and badly prepared project and then continues to pay through more expensive than necessary maintenance and a poor quality product. These results can be observed in nearly every developing country, often in abundance. They may not all be the result of corruption, but sadly many are.

I remember some years ago evaluating Egypt's social fund for development. In Aswan, I was walking along the top of a cemetery wall with an engineer on my team. The wall was large enough to stop a tank and snaked for miles into the distance. This was meant to be a community-led development project, the Governor of Aswan province assured us. The engineer told me, and this was the first time I knew about this issue, that perhaps as many as 50 per cent of construction projects in the world were corrupt simply because it was so easy to cheat – inferior concrete, less reinforcement, poor quality sand, and so on. Whether this was the case with the cemetery wall I do not know, except that I had never seen walls around cemeteries in Egypt before, although the Governor of Aswan told me that the Egyptian people required this as a basic need.

Curiously our discussion was picked up by long-range microphones and our team was recalled to Cairo where I was accused of not having the interests of Egypt at heart, the UNDP Resident Representative (RR) at that time told me to forget about my report and to go and visit the pyramids with my team. Our mission was abandoned, but I did submit a report to the UNDP. Years later, a good friend of mine, Osman Osman, published a report on the Social Fund highlighting a number of deficiencies that turned out to be very similar to my own report. Osman eventually became the Minister of Planning in Egypt. The UNDP RR relocated to Jordan, where our paths crossed again. After what I thought was a very successful project that I had undertaken to set up social statistics in Jordan, my UNDP file ended up with a black mark. Happily I continued to work with UNDP, as people with integrity ignored the black mark and, incidentally, eased the RR out of his post in Jordan.

These two examples show the additional costs placed upon society because of corruption and help to explain continuing under-development in many countries. These days this issue is being increasingly documented thanks to the sterling work of Transparency International that ranks countries in terms of a Corruption Perception Index – Egypt, by the way, stands at No 70 in a list headed by Chad and Bangladesh (the most corrupt) to Iceland the least corrupt.[31] In both the UN's Human Development rankings, and Transparency International's Corruption Perception rankings, these countries are three times more likely to be at the bottom of the rankings than they are at the top. A lack of transparency and accountability for those revenues drives this poverty and corruption.

Anti-corruption, of course, is a key plank of CSR. Stakeholders cannot be treated responsibly if they are subject to corrupt practices. The oil and gas industry, where some of the world's largest companies work profitably – Shell, BP, ChevronTexaco, Exxon, and so on – have made some strides in recent years to reduce the level of corruption in their dealings with developing countries. A major initiative to this end is the Extractive Industries Transparency Initiative (EITI) launched by Tony Blair at the World Summit on Sustainable Development in September 2002. It seeks to increase the transparency of payments by oil, gas and mining companies to governments, as well as the transparency of revenues received by governments. The aim is to ensure that revenues from the extractive industries fulfil their potential as an important engine for economic growth in developing countries, instead of leading to conflict, corruption and poverty. In 2005, the founder of Transparency International, Peter Eigen, became head of the EITI technical secretariat.[32]

The oil companies, and I featured Shell above, have been the leaders in CSR around the world and, most notably, have also been heavily involved in development efforts. This, of course, is due to the fragile nature of the countries where they drill and produce oil, as exemplified by the well-known battering Shell received over the execution of Ken Sara-Wiwa, Leader of the

---

[31] www.infoplease.com/ipa/A0781359.html, accessed 21 February 2006.
[32] See www.eitransparency.org/iag.htm, accessed 27 December 2005.

Nigerian Ogoni tribe. More recently, the oil bonanza due to the rapid rise in oil prices and concomitant rapid rise in oil profits has turned the world's attention to the oil companies once again. Even more worrying for them is that, as *The Economist* (2005) has argued, big oil is the number one target for future public hostility, particularly in the US.[33] Because, in Europe, taxes count for so much of the final cost of oil, criticism is more muted than in the US where the magnitude of oil price rises are immediately reflected in gas (petrol) and heating oil prices. A Gallup poll, cited by *The Economist*, showed that, in May 2004, 22 per cent of the US public felt that the price of gas had been rising because of price gouging by oil companies and refiners; while only 8 per cent assessed what was perhaps the main reason, the economics of supply and demand. In August 2005, 42 per cent of Americans disliked the oil industry, including 35 per cent who disliked it very much.

It must be worrying, therefore, for the oil companies that even EITI is not without its critics. Global Witness argues that if EITI is to be credible then it must do more to ensure companies and countries are held to account and says 'At present there is no way for EITI stakeholders to tell who is truly implementing the EITI in letter and spirit, and who is merely going through the motions. As a result, countries and companies which are genuinely implementing EITI may not get the credit they deserve for improved governance, while freeriders will be able to claim participation in EITI as a way of evading international pressure to curb corruption.'[34] Richard Murphy, an independent chartered accountant, analysed the EITI Reporting Guidelines and the EITI Source Book and found that they had 'major flaws, inconsistencies and opt-outs which could allow a country or company to claim to be implementing EITI without providing anything like a clear picture of revenue flows.'[35]

An interesting snippet, available on the EITI website, is a table illustrating the long-term benefits to companies and countries when they sign up to the EITI.[36] This is particularly important when it is considered that more than 50 countries are dependent on oil and mining, yet they are consistently among the poorest and most corrupt countries in the world.

Ms Nedadi Usman, Minister of State for Finance for Nigeria, has emphasized the waste of oil resources in Nigeria, a country which is rich in both oil and agricultural resources.[37] Indeed, it is not just Nigeria that has failed but many other single resource countries have also failed – Sierra Leone,

---

[33] 'America's most hated companies', *The Economist*, 24 December 2005, p97.
[34] Global Witness (2005) 'A constructive critique of the EITI Reporting Guidelines and Source Book', London, UK, p1.
[35] Global Witness (2005) 'A constructive critique of the EITI Reporting Guidelines and Source Book', London, UK, p1, www.globalwitness.org/reports/show.php/en.00068.html, accessed 15 January 2006.
[36] www.eitransparency.org, accessed 27 December 2005.
[37] Jonathan Power (2004) 'Nigeria and perils of African oil', *Arab News*, London, UK, 6 February.

Iraq, Venezuela, Libya, Angola, Chad, Iran, Maldives, Saudi Arabia. The list could go on and on, and transitional economies have not yet escaped the blight – although it is early days, neither Kazakhstan nor Turkmenistan seem to be using their oil wealth wisely.[38]

But not all is gloom and doom. Some currently very rich countries have used their single resource wisely. Norway's oil boom revenues have been invested back into its people and, despite problems, it has managed to keep unemployment low – at 4.2 per cent at the time of writing. Dubai has few oil resources left, although it is part of the oil-rich United Arab Emirates. Yet, Dubai has massively invested in its human resources, allowed immigrant labour and is currently diversifying its economy into trade, information technology, financial services and tourism with outstanding success. Switzerland, too, was only 100 years ago a resource-poor economy with only its lakes and mountains to look at. Yet, through careful management of its resources and massive investment into human capital, it today boasts thriving banking, tourism and innovative light industries. It worries about an unemployment rate that is also 4.2 per cent at this time.

So, corruption is not the only reason that single resource countries fare badly in terms of development. An oil bonanza can lead to a rise in the real exchange rate, thereby leaving the non-oil sectors such as agriculture and industry non-competitive in terms of price. This leads to a collapse in non-oil production, since imports become much cheaper than domestic production – known in the economics literature as the 'Dutch Disease' after the same phenomena devastated the Dutch economy as oil and gas flowed in from the North Sea.

It is possible to avoid this collapse with foresight and careful policy making – the author is engaged in such a project in Azerbaijan, which he has called 'converting black to human gold'.[39] Essentially the project seeks to raise, as rapidly as possible, human capital in the country in order to compensate the rise in prices stemming from the oil boom.[40]

---

[38] Drawn from Michael Hopkins (2004) 'Main challenges for Azerbaijan', speech given by the author at the 'Tenth Anniversary of Humanitarian Intervention' held in Baku on 18 February.

[39] Details of the implementation of EITI in Azerbaijan are available on the State Oil Fund EITI website www.oilfund.az/search.php?get=EITI and on the EITI NGO Coalition website www.eiti-az.org/ts_gen/eng/index.htm.

[40] More details on the project can be found in UNDP's website dedicated to the idea, see www.un-az.org/blackgold/index.php. The theory behind the approach can be found in Michael Hopkins (2003) 'Structural employment problems with a focus on wages', Geneva, ILO, (in an edited volume by Eugenie Date-Bah, ILO, 2003).

Endnote

The many examples given here, and these are only a subset of the enormous efforts going on worldwide, show that large private corporations are heavily involved in development. Not perfectly, as my comments show, but it can be concluded that although profits need to be made, companies have realized that economies must be encouraged to develop and it is this need that is prompting companies to be realistic about how pro-poor their policies are.

But there are other questions to consider. Should, for instance, our Type II model 'indirect economic impact' really refer to a company's role in economic development? Should companies incorporate the MDGs into their annual reporting in order to link their work to true 'global citizenship' or is membership of the UN Global Compact sufficient? In other words, where do we go from here? My proposal is that companies produce a development vision and associated report that shows their understanding of indirect economic impact and how these link to wider issues of development. There is further discussion of this point in my conclusions in Chapter 12.

4

Failures of Development: A Global View

In the last 40 years, the west has spent $450bn on foreign aid to Africa. However, experience and research shows that aid has often failed to achieve many of its objectives. (Richard Laing, *The Guardian*, 22 February, 2006)

Introduction

Has world development failed? This is a big question for a small chapter. I write this chapter as I sit in the US and therefore currently have a US perspective. It is the day after the State of the Union speech by the President; I cannot write his name, I am so appalled at what he and his band have done in the past few years. It seems only blindingly obvious truths are uttered by the leader of the US, long after their sell-by date. In his speech, he finally proffered the need for the US to reduce its oil dependence on volatile states!

The US is now clearly in decline from the period when it was much admired as a promoter of opportunity, freedom and democracy helping, on the one hand, its allies to defeat fascism, resisting communist Russia and yet, on the other hand, supporting any dictator who allegedly opposed communism and thereby interfering in many countries on the planet with its anti-communist views, and relying on the fact that the dollar was very strong – not a great moment in history: just ask the new President of Chile who was tortured by US-supported Pinochet, or the Vietnamese who suffered the effects of Agent Orange.

Today, the US is highly dependent on its energy supplies from volatile nations, its dollar can change in value based on a whisper from the Central Bank of China, its fiscal deficit continues to widen as taxes are reduced for the rich which, in turn, has led to the need to finance its external trade gap by borrowing $2 billion a day, and its international relations are at their lowest ebb with anti-Americanism growing daily. Even poverty is rising; as I noted in Chapter 2, there are around 37 million poor in the US, which is something around one in 10 citizens, and the gap between the 'haves' and 'have-nots' is widening. This number of people below the poverty line comprises 12.7 per cent of the population – the highest percentage in the developed world. Under President George W. Bush an extra 5.4 million US inhabitants have slipped below the poverty line.

The short-sightedness of the US Government has fed back to the short-term perspective of some of its major companies. Both General Motors and the Ford Motor Company have announced plans to cut tens of thousands of jobs. They are suffering severely from the competition of Japanese imports, manufactured by companies that have invested in the technology of quality and in customer needs that have been ignored by the US major players. The roads of the US are packed with gas-guzzling SUVs (sports utility vehicles), some as large as a tank, normally with only single person occupancy. The uses these vehicles are put to rarely seem to justify their size and fuel consumption figures. Gas (petrol) prices are around $2.40 a gallon – up to a third the price of gas in Europe. Energy prices, in general, are low in the US compared with Europe. With their high taxes on energy, the Europeans have innovated and are now the leaders in alternative energy – a brand new market for them. The US is far behind.

Short-term thinking is encouraged through the incentive systems set by governments and the accepted way of life. Who wants to invest for the longer term when Wall Street is only interested in short-term profits? Investments in training, technology and CSR are treated as costs (in general, although there is some leeway on tax relief) and therefore feed negatively on the bottom line in the short-term.

So how does all this affect world development? There are both positive and negative effects. The main positive effect has been that the US current account deficit has helped many nations to increase their own exports – most notably India and China.

The main negative effects have been threefold, at least. First, the US has been consistently hostile to the UN, an acceleration typified by the appointment in 2005 of John Bolton as US ambassador to the UN – a man whose record suggests he is actually hostile to the UN. Second, the US has engaged in wars to preserve its oil imports which, in turn, has led to world terrorism to the extent that its symbols, such as Bin Laden, command more international media attention than anyone else alive today on the planet. Third, the US, while preaching the need for good governance and democracy, has, since the Second World War, supported a number of national leaders whose rule could be described as despotic – Pinochet in Chile, the Shah of Iran, Mubarak in Egypt, King Saud in Saudi Arabia, Saddam Hussein in Iraq (until his eyes wandered toward the oil fields of Kuwait with Saudi Arabia on the horizon), Guatemala, Nicaragua, Somalia, Uzbekistan … the list goes on and on.

This one-step thinking – supporting a despot to conserve your source of oil – leads to other, even more serious, problems once the despot falls as, indeed, they all do eventually. Thomas Friedman neatly summarizes these effects for the Middle East when he writes:

once you sweep away the dictator or king at the top of any Middle East state, you go into free fall until you hit the mosque – as the US discovered in Iraq. There is nothing between the ruling palace and the mosque. The secular autocratic regimes, like those in Egypt, Libya, Syria and Iraq, never allowed anything to grow under their feet. They never allowed the emergence of any truly independent judiciary, media, progressive secular parties or civil society groups – from women's organizations to trade associations. It is not this way everywhere. In East Asia, when the military regimes in countries like Taiwan and South Korea broke up, these countries quickly moved toward civilian democracies. Why? Because they had vibrant free markets, with independent economic centres of power, and no oil. Whoever ruled had to nurture a society that would empower its men and women to get educated and start companies to compete globally, because that was the only way they could thrive. In the Middle East, oil and democracy do not mix. It's not an accident that the Arab world's first and only true democracy – Lebanon – never had a drop of oil.[1]

As will be seen in this chapter and has been blazed across the newsreels, the main development laggard has been Africa. The world's attention had drifted far from Africa for so long that it, also, had become a haven for despots and poor governance, driving nation after nation into the ground. For instance, why the world cannot intervene in the disaster that is Zimbabwe today is a mystery. Mugabe has done what no economist could possibly do and that is to ruin a successful economy in no time at all. But before returning to some of the reasons behind development failures, I shall take a broad overview of trends in development in the world today.

Development trends

Economic growth

According to the UN (Table 4.1), the first few years of the new millennium have seen slower growth than in the 1990s, following the overall slowdown experienced by the global economy. These trends have been influenced by a marked deceleration in the growth of international trade as well as unfavourable non-oil commodity prices. Latin America, the Caribbean and Western Asia have suffered a decline in per capita output after experiencing improved average growth in the 1990s. Eastern and Southern Asia have

---

[1] Thomas Friedman (2006) 'Addicted to oil', *The New York Times*, New York, 1 February.

continued to grow faster than other regions, although more slowly than in the previous two decades. Clearly the region has benefited from the high growth that has been consistently achieved by China, and, more recently, India.

Africa, and sub-Saharan Africa in particular, has been the worst performer over the past two decades although there has been a slight improvement in this century. However, as will be seen below, average income per capita growth of a half per cent in sub-Saharan Africa could not reduce poverty in a significant way. Sustained growth of at least 3 per cent in real GDP per capita is deemed necessary, according to the UN report cited in Table 4.1, for meaningful poverty reduction in these regions within any useful time period.

Table 4.1 *Developing countries: growth of per capita GDP (annual average percentage change)*

	1981–1990	1991–2000	2001–2003
All developing countries	0.8	2.8	1.6
Latin America and the Caribbean	−0.6	1.4	−1
Africa	−0.7	−0.2	0.5
Sub-Saharan Africa	−1.2	−0.3	0.7
Western Asia		0.4	−1.4
Eastern and Southern Asia	4.7	5.0	3.8
Eastern and Southern Asia excluding China	3.9	3.5	2.4
Least developed countries	−0.5	0.5	2.2

Source: Department of Economic and Social Affairs.[2]

Poverty

Poverty trend

Has poverty increased over the past two decades? It all depends what is meant by poverty and how it is defined. Clearly, in order to compare across time and between countries and regions, the same reference poverty line has to be used, and expressed in a common unit across these countries. Here I follow the well-known work by the World Bank that uses poverty lines set at $1 and $2 per day (more precisely $1.08 and $2.15 in 1993 Purchasing Power Parity terms). These figures themselves are controversial, since they

---

[2] United Nations (2003) 'Progress towards and challenges and constraints to the achievement of the major development goals and objectives adopted by the United Nations during the past decade', Report of the Secretary-General, August, New York, Ref: A/58/327, p4.

imply that all poverty is income related and that the amount is sufficient to clear poverty for the people affected.

The World Bank is, of course, very aware of these deficiencies and aware that much of poverty is related to a lack of access to food, water and shelter as well as publicly provided services.[3] Furthermore, many people who are poor (Table 4.3 illustrates this) live in rural areas where money is a rarity and people live what is called a subsistence lifestyle, that is they live on their own produce and barter with others what they don't need for what they do.

Curiously, there is no objective measure to identify what is a poverty line, although many have tried referring back to the celebrated work of Rowntree in 19th-century England. Poverty is a little like beauty, you know it when you see it but find it hard to define.

Even worse for poverty estimates is the fact that the data themselves are very suspect. They depend on regular household consumption surveys that, in turn, depend upon the respondent to estimate accurately how much food has been consumed in the past week. Some surveys even go as far as weighing the food that people eat and must therefore stay with the household for at least a week. Other surveys depend on households making accurate records in a daily diary. This is difficult, of course, if you are illiterate, which many poor people are.

Another key poverty issue is the fact that poverty lines measure absolute poverty but not the more important issue, to most people, of relative poverty. If you are poor and desperate, there is some comfort in knowing that your neighbour is in the same situation. However, if you are poor and the distribution of income is uneven, that is to say that the rich live like kings, then discontent is much higher.

As Isabel Ortiz of the Asian Development Bank wrote, 'The definition and measurement of poverty is a highly political issue. Countries tend to hide the existence of large pockets of poverty as it makes them look underdeveloped and shows up public policy failures.'[4] She also wrote that 'poverty is not only income poverty. Poverty also has non-economic dimensions, like discrimination, exploitation or fear. Other aspects should be considered, such as lack of control of resources, vulnerability to shocks, helplessness to violence and corruption, lack of voice in decision-making, powerlessness and social exclusion.'

The World Bank figures are all that we have to go on, but this is an improvement on the situation compared with only a few years ago, when there was very little data available on poverty in developing countries. The

---

[3] The World Bank, under tremendous pressure to improve its poor performance, has, nevertheless, done superb technical work on mapping the extent of poverty and working on policy approaches – see its huge database on poverty on www.worldbank.org

[4] Isabel Ortiz (2005) 'Backgrounder: Poverty reduction – Poverty trends and measurements', Manila, Asian Development Bank.

World Bank estimated that, in 2001, 1.1 billion people had consumption levels below $1 a day and 2.65 billion lived on less than $2 a day. The former figure is lower than the 1990 estimate of 1.2 billion, while the latter figure was slightly higher at 2.74 billion. These figures indicate that very little progress has taken place in reducing poverty over the past decade. Poverty still remains too high in terms of human suffering, and the fact that it may be increasing shows that very much more remains to be done.

That there are fewer people living below $1 in 2001 compared with 1990 but more below $2 shows that extreme poverty is reducing slightly but that poverty, in general, has increased. As many as 2.65 billion, or nearly half the people on the planet, live on less than $2 a day. This is a massive failure on the part of our global institutions and governments who have genuinely been battling to reduce poverty for many decades, dating as far back as the founding of the UN in 1945!

Regional poverty trends

The global picture is bad enough. However, as the picture is dismantled to look at the various regions of the world, the picture worsens. Serious headway is being made in a number of regions, while some have experienced (Table 4.3) major setbacks. From 1990 to 2002, for example, the heavily indebted poor countries saw their incomes rise only from $298 per capita to $337 in 1995 dollars (World Bank estimates).

What progress has been made toward poverty reduction in the last decade has been driven by advances in East Asia and South Asia, home to China and India. In all these areas the private sector has been the prime mover, not necessarily from overseas, but through major investment in human capital and allowing local markets to flourish.

The African region, and sub-Saharan Africa in particular, has been, and continues to be, a major failure. The Sachs-authored UN Millennium Development Goals (MDG) report shows Africa falling behind in meeting the MDGs on almost every dimension of poverty (Table 4.3). Between 1990 and 2001 the number of people living on less than $1 a day in sub-Saharan Africa rose from 227 million to 316 million, and the poverty rate rose from 45 per cent of the population to 46 per cent (Table 4.2: Chen and Ravallion, 2004).[5] In the 33 countries in tropical sub-Saharan Africa, the average GDP per person is only $270 a year, a mere 71 cents a day (World Bank 2004).[6] If we raise the poverty line to $2 per day then we can see that

---

[5] Shaohua Chen and Martin Ravallion (2005) 'How have the world's poorest fared since the early 1980s?' Development Research Group, World Bank, New York, p29, www.worldbank.org.research/povmonitor/MartinPapers/How_have_the_poorest_fared_since_the_early_1980s.pdf.
[6] World Bank (2004) *World Development Indicators 2004*, Washington DC, World Bank.

516 million or 77 per cent of sub-Saharan Africans live in poverty, up from 75 per cent in 1990!

The picture is a little brighter in the Middle East and North Africa, although one in four people live on less than $2 per day in a region rich with oil resources. It is depressing that the numbers in poverty in the Middle East are increasing – 23 million people in 2001 compared with 21 million in 1990.

The movement to the political left in Latin America and the Caribbean (Venezuela, Bolivia in recent times) is hardly surprising given that 128 million or 25 per cent of the population live on less than $2 per day – a figure that hardly changed in the 1990s.

Eastern Europe and Central Asia, appallingly left to their own devices by the West after the fall of the USSR, saw a stark increase in poverty over the period under discussion. Note that measurements that use a $1 a day standard understate the real extent of poverty in regions where the cost of living is higher. For example, a $2 a day standard is more appropriate in Latin America, the Caribbean and the transition countries of Europe.

Table 4.2 *Measures of average progress in the developing world, 1990–2002 (population-weighted)*

GDP per capita (1995 US$)	1071	1299
Headcount poverty (%)[a]	28	21
Undernourishment prevalence (%)[b]	20	17
Under-five mortality (per 1000 live births)	103	88
Life expectancy at birth (years)	63	65
HIV prevalence (%)	0.5	1.6
Access to improved drinking water supply (%)	71	79
Access to improved sanitation facilities (%)	34	49

Notes: [a] The poverty headcount percentage is the proportion of the national population with incomes below $1.08 a day. 2002 data unavailable; 2001 data used as a proxy.
[b] Does not include CIS countries in 1990.

Source: UN Millennium Project (2005) 'Investing in Development: A Practical Plan to Achieve the Millennium Development Goals (MDGs)', London, Earthscan, p14.

The socio-economic picture

Some parts of the social and economic conditions that people live under are obscured by poverty figures. Perhaps the ultimate indicator of well-being is the average life expectancy that one can expect at birth. For the developing world as a whole, the picture improved slowly over 1990–2001, as life expectancy rose from 63 years to nearly 65 years (Table 4.2). In addition the rate of undernourishment declined slightly by 3 percentage points, and the under-five mortality rate dropped impressively from 103 deaths

Table 4.3 *Population living below the poverty line, by developing region*

$1.08 a day poverty line[a]

	Millions of people		Share of total population (%)		Share of poor people living in rural areas[b] (%)	Rural population as share of total (%)
	1990	2001	1990	2001	2001[c]	2001
East Asia	472	271	30	15	80	63
Eastern Europe and Central Asia	2	17	1	4	53	37
Latin America and Caribbean	49	50	11	10	42	24
Middle East and North Africa	6	7	2	2	63	42
South Asia	462	431	41	31	77	72
Sub-Saharan Africa	227	313	45	46	73	67
Total	1218	1089				

$2.15 a day poverty line[a]

	Millions of people		Share of total population (%)	
	1990	2001	1990	2001
East Asia	1116	865	70	47
Eastern Europe and Central Asia	23	93	5	20
Latin America and Caribbean	125	128	28	25
Middle East and North Africa	51	70	21	23
South Asia	958	1064	86	77
Sub-Saharan Africa	382	516	75	77
Total	2655	2736		

[a] Poverty lines set in 1993 US$ adjusted for purchasing power parity.
[b] Calculated as rural poverty rate × (100 − urbanization rate)/national poverty rate. Note that published poverty rates often underreport urban poverty.
[c] Where 2001 data are not available, uses most recent year available.

Source: World Bank. Cited in UN Millennium Project (2005) 'Investing in Development: A Practical Plan to Achieve the Millennium Development Goals (MDGs)', London, Earthscan, p16.

per 1000 births to 88. An additional 8 per cent of the developing world's population gained access to improved drinking water supply, and 15 per cent more to basic sanitation services.

Another area to consider is the relative situations of men and women. Progress on gender equality targets, according to the MDG Report, has been limited and uneven.[7] For instance, the basis of the future for any country and individual is education. Yet the ratio of girls to boys in secondary education was just 0.77 in South Asia and 0.79 in West Asia and sub-Saharan Africa in 2001. But, as seen next in the section on HIV/AIDS, aggregate figures obscure some nasty news, again, especially in Africa.

Focus on sub-Saharan Africa

It is not surprising that the world's attention has focused on Africa – from the War on Poverty to Live Aid to much publicity garnered by harnessing the photogenic power of actors and pop singers. This is because it was in sub-Saharan Africa that GDP per capita shrank by 14 per cent, poverty rose from 41 per cent in 1981 to 46 per cent in 2001, and an additional 150 million people were living in extreme poverty.

Table 4.4 shows some recent data from which it can be seen that life expectancy for over 700 million people is a mere 46 years (data for 2003). One in ten children die at childbirth and HIV/AIDS captures at least one in ten young women aged 15–24.

And, at the time of writing, sub-Saharan Africa is suffering from yet another food crisis and requires urgent food assistance.[8] The UN's Food and Agriculture Organization (FAO) is warning that 27 sub-Saharan countries now need help. These problems, of course, are not new and stem from years of under-investment. Curiously, the African continent was more than self-sufficient in food at independence 50 years ago, but is now a massive food importer. In less than 40 years the sub-continent went from being a net exporter of basic food staples to relying on imports and food aid.

Much of the problem in Africa has been self-inflicted, although the debate still rages whether, or not, it was decades of colonial misrule that left the continent in such a mess. But, 50 years later, it is hard to believe that colonial misrule has led to such continuing mismanagement. The FAO, for instance, notes that there are political problems such as civil strife, refugee movements and returnees in 15 of the 27 countries it declares in need of urgent assistance. By comparison, drought is only cited in 12 out of 27 countries. The implication is clear – Africa's years of wars, coups and civil strife are responsible for more hunger than the natural problems that befall it. In 2004 the chairman of the African Union Commission, Alpha Oumar Konare, reminded an African Union (AU) summit that the continent had suffered from 186 coups and 26 major wars in the past 50 years. It is estimated that there are more than 16 million refugees and displaced persons in Africa.

---

[7] UN Millennium Project (2005) 'Investing in development: A practical plan to achieve the Millennium Development Goals (MDGs)', London, Earthscan, p23.
[8] This section is drawn from Martin Plaut (2006) 'Africa's hunger – a systemic crisis', BBC, www.bbc.co.uk, accessed 31 January 2006.

Table 4.4 *HNP group data*

HNP group data: sub-Saharan Africa	Most recent year	Data
Socio-economic context		
Total population (000s)	2003	704,684
GNI per capita, Atlas Method (US$)	2003	510
Expected years of schooling	—	—
Adult literacy rate (% of population ages 15+)	—	—
Demographic indicators		
Average annual population growth rate (%)	1990–2003	2.5
Age dependency ratio (dependants as a proportion of working-age population)	2003	0.9
Total fertility rate (births per woman)	2003	5.2
Adolescent fertility rate (births per 1000 women ages 15–19)	2003	127
Contraceptive prevalence rate (% of women ages 15–49), any method	—	—
Health status indicators		
Life expectancy at birth (years)	2003	46
Infant mortality rate (per 1000 live births)	2003	101
Under-5 mortality rate (per 1000)	2003	171
Maternal mortality ratio (per 100,000 live births), modelled estimates	2000	917
Prevalence of child malnutrition – underweight (% of children under age 5)	—	—
Health care indicators		
Child immunization rate, measles (% of ages 12–23 months)	2003	61
Child immunization rate, DPT3 (% of ages 12–23 months)	2003	59
Births attended by skilled health staff (% of total)	—	—
Physicians (per 1000 people)	—	—
Hospital beds (per 1000 people)	1990	1.2
Tuberculosis treatment success rate (% of registered cases)	—	—
DOTS detection rate (% of estimated cases)	—	—
Health finance indicators		
Health expenditure, total (% of GDP)	2002	6.4
Health expenditure, public (% of GDP)	2002	2.6
Health expenditure, public (% of total health expenditure)	2002	40.4

Health expenditure per capita ($)	2002	31.9
Risk factors and future challenges		
Prevalence of HIV, total (% of population ages 15–49)	2003	6.70
Prevalence of HIV, female (% of population ages 15–24)	2001	9.40
Tuberculosis incidence (per 100,000 people)	2003	353
Tuberculosis death rate (per 100,000 people)	—	—

HNP group data: World

Socio-economic context

Total population (000s)	2003	6,273,584
GNI per capita, Atlas Method (US$)	2003	5,520
Expected years of schooling	2002	12
Adult literacy rate (% of population ages 15+)	—	—

Demographic indicators

Average annual population growth rate (%)	1990–2003	1.4
Age dependency ratio (dependants as a proportion of working-age population)	2003	0.6
Total fertility rate (births per woman)	2003	2.6
Adolescent fertility rate (births per 1000 women ages 15–19)	2003	62
Contraceptive prevalence rate (% of women ages 15–49), any method	—	—

Health status indicators

Life expectancy at birth (years)	2003	67
Infant mortality rate (per 1000 live births)	2003	57
Under-5 mortality rate (per 1000)	2003	86
Maternal mortality ratio (per 100,000 live births), modelled estimates	2000	411
Prevalence of child malnutrition – underweight (% of children under age 5)	—	—

Health care indicators

Child immunization rate, measles (% of ages 12–23 months)	2003	77
Child immunization rate, DPT3 (% of ages 12–23 months)	2003	78
Births attended by skilled health staff (% of total)	—	—
Physicians (per 1000 people)	1998	1.7
Hospital beds (per 1000 people)	1991	3.9
Tuberculosis treatment success rate (% of registered cases)	—	—
DOTS detection rate (% of estimated cases)	—	—

Health finance indicators

Health expenditure, total (% of GDP)	2002	10.0
Health expenditure, public (% of GDP)	2002	5.8
Health expenditure, public (% of total health expenditure)	2002	60.0
Health expenditure per capita ($)	2002	523.7
Risk factors and future challenges		
Prevalence of HIV, total (% of population ages 15–49)	2003	1.00
Prevalence of HIV, female (% of population ages 15–24)	2001	1.60
Tuberculosis incidence (per 100,000 people)	2003	140
Tuberculosis death rate (per 100,000 people)	—	—

Note: HNP = Health, Nutrition and Population; DOTS = direct observed treatment short course.

Source: World Bank Development Statistics

As Martin Plaut observed, there are (at least) four issues which are critical:

1 Decades of under-investment in rural areas because they have little political weight. Africa's elites respond to political pressure, which is mainly exercised in towns and cities.
2 Corruption and mismanagement stemming from poor governance. Clearly, farmers need stability and certainty before they can succeed in producing the food their families and societies need.
3 HIV/AIDS depriving families of their most productive labour. This is particularly a problem in southern Africa, where over 30 per cent of sexually active adults are HIV positive. According to aid agency Oxfam, when a family member becomes infected, food production can fall by up to 60 per cent, as women are not only expected to be carers, but also provide much of the agricultural labour.
4 High rates of population growth (2.5 per cent per annum as shown in Table 4.4 – and this would be higher if the AIDS pandemic did not exist), are both a result of poverty (as couples rear as many children as they can to get a few survivors for security and to help them in their old age) and a contribution to poverty. Between 1975 and 2005, the population more than doubled, rising from 335 to 751 million. In some parts of Africa land is plentiful, and this is not a problem. But in others it has had severe consequences. It has forced farming families to subdivide their land time and time again, leading to tiny plots or families moving onto unsuitable, overworked land. In sub-Saharan Africa soil quality is classified as degraded in roughly 72 per cent of arable land and 31 per cent of pasture land.

HIV/AIDS

More than 20 million lives have been lost worldwide since the first case of HIV/AIDS was detected in 1981 and the number of people infected has doubled over the 1990s to 2001.[9]

According to a UN report, average life expectancy in sub-Saharan Africa is now only 47 years, whereas it would have been 62 years without AIDS.[10] In Botswana, life expectancy has dropped by 33 years to levels not seen since 1950. Asia and the Caribbean are experiencing a similar phenomenon, albeit to a lesser degree. Under-five mortality rates have increased by as much as 40 per cent in some countries. HIV/AIDS is not solely a health problem. The scale of the pandemic in many developing countries means that it is also a major impediment to economic and social development because it shrinks the labour force and lowers its productivity.

Millennium Development Goals (MDGs)

The public sector is trying to do something about these problems. A re-invigorated effort at the turn of the century led the governments of the world to join together to resolve the problem of poverty and under-development. In September 2000, 189 countries signed the Millennium Declaration, which led to the adoption of the Millennium Development Goals (MDGs). The MDGs are a set of eight goals for which 18 numerical targets have been set and over 40 quantifiable indicators have been identified. The goals, as noted in Chapter 2, are as follows:

1   Eradicate extreme poverty and hunger
2   Achieve universal primary education
3   Promote gender equality and empower women
4   Reduce child mortality
5   Improve maternal health
6   Combat HIV/AIDS, malaria and other diseases
7   Ensure environmental sustainability
8   Develop a global partnership for development.

Projections in meeting the MDG poverty goal are given in Figure 4.1.[11] One measurable goal has been halving the proportion of people living in

---

[9] UN Millennium Project, 'Investing in Development', p13.
[10] United Nations (2003) 'Progress towards and challenges and constraints', p11.
[11] For an assessment of progress towards the MDGs see IMG and World Bank (2004) 'Global Monitoring Report 2004 – Policies and actions for achieving the Millennium Development Goals and related outcomes', Development Committee (Joint Ministerial Committee of the Board of Governors of the Bank and the Fund on the Transfer of Real Resources to Developing Countries), 16 April.

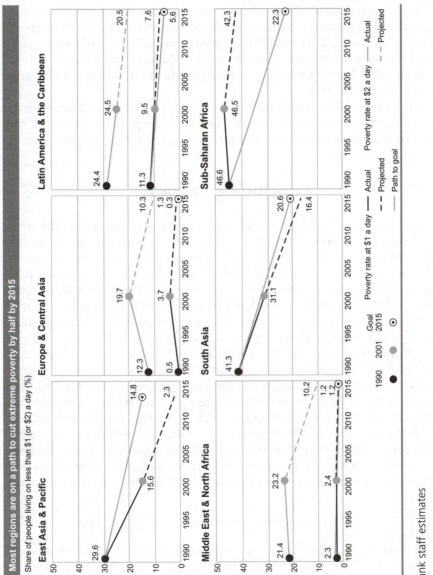

Figure 4.1 *Share of people living on less than $1 (or $2) per day (%)*

Source: World Bank staff estimates

extreme poverty – and those suffering from hunger – between 1990 and 2015. According to these projections by the World Bank, poverty rates will fall fastest in East Asia and the Pacific outside China, but the huge reduction in the number of people below the $1 a day line in China will dominate global totals.[12] In Europe and Central Asia and in the Middle East and North Africa, where poverty rates measured at $1 a day are low, a continuation of current trends will cut poverty rates to half their current levels. South Asia, led by continuing growth in India, is likely to reach or exceed the target. But growth and poverty reduction are proceeding more slowly in Latin America and the Caribbean, which will not reach the target unless growth improves.

But, as emphasized here, the most difficult case is sub-Saharan Africa, where poverty has increased since 1990 and will, on present trends, fall very slowly in the next 11 years, unless there is a major change in prospects.

Concluding remark

The evidence presented here shows that, despite some progress, the problem of developing world poverty continues to be a serious problem. The serious effort by UN in the MDGs is to be welcomed. However, the current US Government has been critical of its targets through its continual petulance in its relations with the UN (see Chapter 10). The MDGs, serious and crucial as they are, will nevertheless fail in achieving the goal of reducing poverty – the graphs given in Figures 4.2–4.4, are optimistic but, on a close reading, show that the MDGs remain a distant goal.

Thus my thesis that the UN and individual governments' efforts must be supplemented by something completely new, that is a major effort by the private sector, in particular by the large MNEs, rings true. But, can the private sector be mobilized to emulate the Asian miracle countries and China? The thesis of this book is that much more, very much more, mileage can be obtained through harnessing the power and wealth of the world's major corporations. The slide back to the anti-liberalism of several Latin American countries will, it is likely, repeat the sad story of so many left-leaning governments of the latter half of the 20th century.[13] The power and

---

[12] World Bank (2004) *World Development Indicators Report*, Washington DC, World Bank.

[13] This deserves a comment. There is no doubt that left-leaning governments do help the poor – Cuba, Allende's Chile and Chavez's Venezuelan Government are examples. However, at some point markets must be allowed to flourish since governments are notoriously poor at creating economic growth. It is instructive to see an Allende supporter, Ricardo Lagos, Chile's democratically elected President, whose term has just ended, encouraging markets to improve Chile's economic position. However, he did 'little, if anything at all, on social issues' (according to Emilio Klein, personal communication, July 2006).

wealth of the MNEs can be involved in ways never seen before. It is simply not in the best interests of the major corporations that the world becomes a sorrier place.

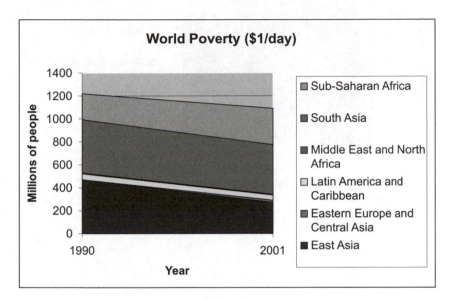

Figure 4.2 *World poverty ($1/day)*

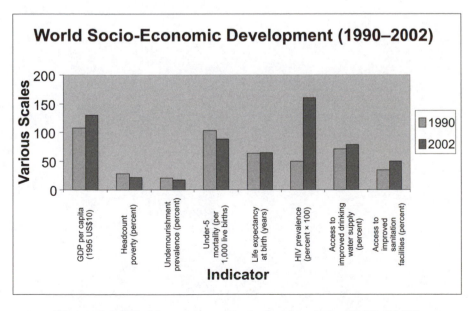

Figure 4.3 *World socio-economic development (1990–2002)*

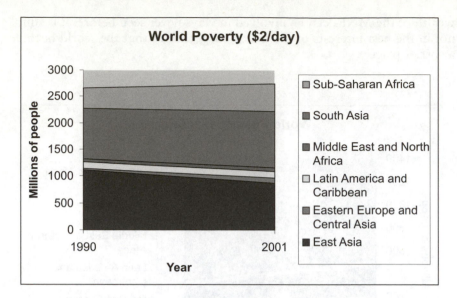

Figure 4.4 *World poverty ($2/day)*

5

Corporations Should Abandon Philanthropy and Concentrate on CSR

Business is the key to beating global poverty, but we're talking so much more than handouts. (Simon Caulkin, business journalist, *The Observer*, 13 March, 2005)

...philanthropy will have to shed the amateurism that still pervades much of it and become a modern, efficient, global industry. (*The Economist* (2006) 'Survey of wealth and philanthropy', 25 February, p4)

Introduction

It is hard to state that corporations should abandon philanthropy. What I really mean is that philanthropy that does not lead to sustainable development should be abandoned. CSR, as this chapter argues, can help in assessing the merits of philanthropy.

CSR is not philanthropy

Some people equate philanthropy with CSR. For instance, Michael Porter wrote:

Corporate philanthropy – or corporate social responsibility – is becoming an ever more important field for business. Today's companies ought to invest in corporate social responsibility as part of their business strategy to become more competitive.[1]

So Michael Porter has got it wrong. When even an internationally respected management guru mentions philanthropy and corporate social responsibility

---

[1] Michael Porter, www.ebfonline.com/debate/debate.asp.

as being the same, it is hardly surprising that business leaders, academics and politicians confuse them. CSR is not the same as corporate philanthropy as I shall explain.

I argued in Chapter 2 that CSR is a system-wide concept that touches all the stakeholders of a corporation. CSR does not concentrate on only one stakeholder but philanthropy, 'the practice of performing charitable or benevolent actions' does, in general. Most, if not all, philanthropy is devoted to items that governments should be doing – health grants to developing countries, help to the handicapped, drugs for HIV/AIDS for example. And their failure should not be the preserve of corporations. However since government is one of the stakeholders of a corporation, there is nothing to stop corporations offering their management and technical skills to government to improve or introduce programmes to help vulnerable groups. Corporations exist to make profits. There is nothing wrong with that, only the *way* profits are made is the concern of CSR practitioners. Philanthropy does little or nothing to help companies make profits, while *all* CSR activities are linked to improving a company's bottom line.

CSR is before profit

One of the confusions over defining and acting upon CSR, according to Young-Chul Kang and Donna Wood (1995) is that results and interpretation come from a flawed assumption that CSR is an *after-profit* obligation.[2] This could mean that if companies are not profitable they do not have to behave responsibly! They say 'in the extreme, if all firms are affected by severe economic turmoil or are run by lazy, short-sighted managers, then societies would have no choice but to accept pollution, discrimination, dangerous working conditions, child labour etc.'

Embedding socially responsible principles in corporate management is what these two authors call a '*before-profit*' obligation. They cite corporations which embody these ideas and see the trend accelerating. For instance, in 1950 Sears' CEO listed four parties to any business in order of importance as: 'customers, employees, community and stockholders'. For him, profit was a 'by-product of success in satisfying responsibly the legitimate needs and expectations of the corporations' primary stakeholder group'. By the 1980s, Levi's even repurchased its stock in the public market under the rationale that stockholder's interests might limit the firm's effort to be a socially responsible organization. And, Migros of Switzerland funds its cultural and social programmes not by profits, but by gross sales, so that profitability does not influence the firm's level of involvement.

---

[2] Young-Chul Kang and Donna J. Wood (1995) *Before-Profit Social Responsibility: Turning the Economic Paradigm Upside Down*, Proceedings of the Sixth Annual Meeting of the International Association of Business and Society, Vienna, pp408–418.

CSR is sustainable, philanthropy is not

We should stop kidding ourselves that charity and philanthropy do much to help the poor. (Rob Reich, cited in *The Economist*, 25 February 2006)

CSR is sustainable in that CSR actions become part and parcel of the way in which a company carries out its business. Its links to the bottom line of a company must be clearly laid out because, if it does not contribute to the bottom line, it will eventually be rejected by hard-nosed directors and shareholders.

Philanthropy has an inclination to be whimsical. It simply depends on the whims of the company directors at a particular time. Many NGOs receive their funds from corporations and carry out excellent work. Others, of course, willingly admit that the major stimulus to funding and membership is 'outing of corporations' which is sometimes more potent than helping corporates to fix things, but nevertheless often serves the public interest!

Rather like the advertisements for Heineken beer, most NGOs involved in development carry out programmes that other programmes (mainly government ones) can't reach. But NGO interventions are based on a scatter-gun approach and are *spotty*. They can intervene wherever they like. Governments, on the other hand, have to intervene everywhere or nowhere. It is better, much better, for a corporation (including non-profit ones such as NGOs) to assist a government in making its contributions either nationally, or internationally, more efficient and appropriate. This then ensures widespread and even coverage.

As the above-mentioned *Economist* article stated, there are some useful social investment actions that have been carried out by more far-sighted organizations – The Rockefeller Foundation found a cure for yellow fever, the Gates Foundation has donated billions to tackle the health problems of the world's poor and Carnegie built thousands of public libraries. However, this long-term investment ethos, *The Economist* argues, has proved to be 'the exception, not the rule'.

Should sponsorship be stopped too?

Corporate sponsorship is different from corporate philanthropy. Sponsorship is a business tool used by companies as part of their communication, advertising or PR budgets to associate the corporation's products and services with dynamic images for their customers' consumption. Sponsorship usually requires a service, or action, in return for financial support, so this frequently has clear marketing benefits and is therefore directly linked to a company's bottom line.

Sometimes, this may indeed be for good causes such as supporting UNI-CEF to associate the company's products with reducing child labour around the world. Philanthropy does not necessarily ask for a definite service or action in return and it is certainly not usually based on a business relationship or partnership. On a personal level, this is like responding favourably to the postal requests made by the major charities. Yet the line between philanthropy and sponsorship is difficult to draw and there are many grey areas – but it is preferable to have a clear sponsorship potential than a fuzzy charitable action that may well be unsustainable.

But what about all those good causes?

I can see that my words will irk many readers who may accuse me of undermining good people and good causes. But this is not my point, I want sustainable actions that do not depend on the whims of albeit good-natured people. But what about all those charities that depend on companies for financial support? Should these be stopped? Obviously this is unreasonable and many hundreds of millions would suffer if corporations suddenly stopped contributing to charitable organizations.

Yet, there is a structural problem here. Governments mainly encourage charitable giving, often through tax breaks, since it takes the responsibility away from them. Governments are also corporations and must act in a socially responsible manner. My suggestion is that charitable giving is phased out over a long period, say 10 years, so that both existing charitable organizations and governments can adjust. Corporations can help in this transition period not only with managerial and technical advice but with cash as well.

In conclusion, here are a number of actions that could be considered:

1   Companies should abandon all philanthropy which is outside a CSR framework.
2   Companies should work hand-in-hand with governments to promote economic and social development.
3   The performance of social investment under a CSR framework should be measured and monitored to ensure it is sustainable.
4   Government should help those people who cannot be helped to help themselves through a subsidy. Government should look after vulnerable groups and not just await the whim of corporate philanthropy: if a charity fails because a company fails then this is a disaster for all the vulnerable groups and people concerned.

In the end, a company that is philanthropically generous but is not aware of, or engaged in, its broader CSR role will not be in business for very long. In this I agree fully with one point made by Michael Porter:

If companies are just being good and donating a lot of money to social initiatives then they will be wasting shareholders' money. That is not sustainable in the long-run, and shareholders will quickly lose interest. (See note 1.)

6

A Critique of CSR and Development

Introduction

As a proponent of CSR for many years, one finds that those who criticize the concept appear to make more headway than those who propose. It is, of course, easier to criticize than to propose, which leads to this chapter on some of the common criticisms of the concept and a response.[1]

Many are sceptical about the potential for MNEs to have positive impacts on poverty. They note that companies can reach people living in poverty as consumers (at the so-called 'bottom of the pyramid') – what I call Type II development assistance – and as producers of primary agricultural products; but they expect companies' pursuit of profits to be damaging to poor communities.

Some more radical critics argue that MNEs marginalize local entrepreneurs and small-scale competitors, thereby undermining local economies and traditional employment.[2] They argue that MNEs rarely support local entrepreneurs to generate income and jobs. For the even more critical, selling branded products to the poor is little more than an attempt by MNEs to capture the income of the poor without giving anything in return.

At the other end of the spectrum, many investors and corporate executives believe that foreign direct investment will automatically benefit the host country. They argue that all jobs related to the company's activities are additional jobs created, and that technology, skills and expertise will be transferred to local workers and companies. They believe that investment by MNEs will help the country to be better integrated into the global economy

---

[1] Parts of this chapter first appeared in Michael Hopkins (2005) 'Criticisms of CSR', published as a chapter in Ramon Mullerat (ed.) (2005) *CSR: The Corporate Governance of the 21st Century*, The Netherlands, Kluivert Publishers.
[2] Drawn from a report by Jason Caly (2005) 'Exploring the links between international business and poverty reduction: A case study of Unilever in Indonesia', an Oxfam GB, Novib, Unilever and Unilever Indonesia joint research project, first published by Oxfam GB, Novib, Oxfam Netherlands and Unilever in 2005.

and so, directly or indirectly, will help to reduce poverty. They argue, there-fore, that host countries should welcome such investment, no matter how much or how little of the wealth that it generates is retained within the country. There are examples around the world of poor countries and com-munities that have suffered many of the negative impacts described above, while others have benefited significantly from the positive impacts.

Conservative think tanks such as the Institute for Economic Affairs in the UK are very wary of any attempt to drive MNEs away from pure profit maximization. Its Director General, John Blundell, wrote:

> *when it comes to issues vital to business, such as deregulation or liberalization, CSR advocates are uniformly silent, leaving one with the sense that the concept is nothing other than the ashes of the debunked and defunct view that the state should direct the economy.*[3]

CSR does not necessarily imply more regulation and less liberalization, in fact a closer examination of what CSR proponents are saying will reveal that the key point is not the pursuit of profits per se but how profits are made. Therefore, in some cases further liberalization makes sense as does de-regulation if both are carried out in a socially responsible way.

Many of the criticisms, as will be seen, stem from problems with con-cepts and definitions, as discussed in Chapters 1 and 2, where we saw that a proliferation of concepts has grown up relating to the area of business in society – corporate sustainability, corporate citizenship, corporate respon-sibility, business responsibility, business social responsibility, business repu-tation, the ethical corporation, and so on. In this chapter some of the many criticisms of CSR are channelled into seven essentially different statements. In brief they are:

1   CSR lacks a universal definition, everyone seems to have their own con-cept or definition.
2   CSR is just part of a public relations plan to bamboozle an increasingly sceptical public.
3   CSR is just another word for corporate philanthropy and the contri-bution that a business directly makes to the welfare of society (or 'the planet') is to be viewed as largely independent of its profitability.
4   CSR is misleading as it diverts attention from key issues; it is a curse rather than a cure.
5   CSR ignores development economics and its concerns with capitalism and neo-liberalism and it is just a way to introduce socialism through the back door.

---

[3] John Blundell (2004) *Corporate Social Responsibility Poisons Market*, London, IEA.

6   The social responsibility of business begins and ends with increasing profits; CSR is an unnecessary distraction.
7   CSR is a sham because companies cannot be left to self-regulate.

This chapter will look at each of these concerns in more detail.

Lack of definition, everyone seems to have their own concept or definition

I covered at length in Chapter 2 many of the issues and problems with a definition of CSR and shall not repeat them here. Clearly, there is a wide variety of concepts and definitions associated with the term *corporate social responsibility*. However, there is no general agreement on terms and one well-known CSR manager told this author that it was all a question of 'semantics' and therefore definitions were not important.

But without a common language we don't really know whether our dialogue with companies is being heard and interpreted in a consistent way. These flaws lead some companies to consider CSR as pure corporate philanthropy while others dismiss the notion entirely. But there are others such as Shell, BP-Amoco, Co-operative Bank who see CSR as a new corporate strategic framework.

CSR is just part of a public relations plan to bamboozle an increasingly sceptical public

Is CSR just fodder for a company's PR department? Tim Wright thinks so. In a prize winning essay he states:

> *The number of public relations companies adding CSR practices or strengthening existing offerings endorses the assertion that corporations desire to seize and dictate the agenda through savvy media management. For example Edelman Public Relations, which has hired non-profit veteran Steven Voien to launch First&42nd, its first national CSR practice and management consultancy. Similarly WPP Group's BursonMarsteller brought Bennett Freeman aboard as managing director for corporate responsibility, based in Washington, D.C., and Hill & Knowlton Canada created a global CSR practice.[4]*

---

[4] Tim Wright (2003) 'Plus ça change, plus c'est la même chose: The grand illusion of corporate social responsibility', Leicester University Management Centre, winner, Guardian/Ashridge MBA Essay Competition.

These concerns were also voiced in a World Bank-sponsored internet conference on CSR and the media. Rachel Olivier, a journalist from Hong Kong who jointly moderated the conference with the current author, made the following remark about CSR information from companies in Asia:

> It is all very well to promote easy access to sources of information, but the public relations industry would have you believe that is what they already do. And their very existence more often than not hampers the development of a story instead of encouraging it. One of the key problems I have faced (as have many, many others) is the institutionalization of spin which gives the appearance of increased access to information through heavily staffed internal and external PR offices, but the reality often means these individuals serve more to control the flow of their own messages as opposed to facilitating deeper relationships between the media and those in the know. That then puts them in the position of gatekeeper. Unfortunately, for non-listed companies, there is little incentive for the dissemination of information to the public – why would they do something they are not legally required to do? (personal communication, April 2004)

So, there seems to be no doubt that companies use CSR in their PR to promote their reputation. But is there no more to CSR than just that? Evidence I have produced elsewhere using sources such as the Dow Jones Sustainability Indices led me to conclude that the top companies are becoming more socially responsible over time.[5] This does not mean that all is well with the corporate world but it might suggest that all the actions, protests, analysis and so on of disparate groups all over the world might be having a positive effect. In fact, my article showed that, on balance, companies are becoming more and more responsible on *average*. In fact the word *average* is the key to unlock what is going on. For example, it is always easy to start to get better CSR rankings in the beginning than as time goes on: cleaning up a leaking pipeline, producing a code of ethics that nobody reads, producing a glossy CSR report, making extra sure that your product does not kill your customers, closing down a supplier in Bangladesh that uses child labour and so on. So, on *average* it is relatively easy to make progress on CSR. But the problem becomes how to embed these ideas throughout the organization? That is the problem and that is why scandals will continue to erupt in supposedly 'clean' organizations such as Shell or BP and that did erupt in Enron, Parmalat and World Com.

---

[5] Michael Hopkins (2004) *Measurement and Progress of Corporate Social Responsibility*, March, www.mhcinternational.com and Michael Hopkins (2005) 'Measurement of CS', *International Journal of Management and Decision Making*, vol 6, nos 3/4, pp213–231, available from www.mhcinternational.com/monthly_feature. html#Measurement_and_CSR.

CSR is just another word for corporate philanthropy

I covered this, at length, in the previous chapter but it remains a popular view. For instance, *The Economist* in an article entitled 'Two Faced Capitalism' stated: 'CSR is philanthropy with a few bits added on. CEOs should ignore this and go back to doing their jobs'.[6]

Thus, *The Economist* seems to imply that a company that pays starvation wages, pollutes, treats employees as slaves, ignores customer complaints, bribes governments, leaves human rights issues to Bush, and makes glorious profits is fine. Anyone who opposes that model is anti-capitalist.

An alternative view to that of *The Economist* is that CSR is not anti-capitalist since it questions not profit-making in itself but *how* profits are made. Long-staying companies have focused on values as well as their social responsibilities – work at Boston and Yale Universities based upon the book *Built to Last*[7] found that visionary companies achieved their extraordinary performance by working productively and positively with other primary stakeholders such as customers, employees, communities and the environment. Identifying key stakeholders, evaluating what works better, while keeping an eye on costs is what CSR is all about.

CSR is misleading since it diverts attention from key issues, it is a curse rather than a cure

The curse, as elaborated in an article by Geoffrey Chandler, is that with 'the absence of a clear definition ... CSR is likely to delay the introduction of a regulatory framework ... the shirt of Nessus poisoned those who wore it'.[8] He continues: '... the prevalent interpretation is that "CSR" is simply a voluntary add-on'. This is not the total concept of corporate responsibility which he believes, as I do, to be the necessary basis for corporate success and survival in the 21st century. The curse, Chandler says, 'has yet to run itself out: the misinterpretation of "CSR" is a continuing diversion for companies from the reality that regulation has throughout corporate history been necessary to get the corporate world to fulfil its non-monetary responsibilities. "CSR" is giving employment to many and has raised the profile of debate. Its impact in practice has been to divert attention from what is fundamentally required.'[9]

---

[6] *The Economist*, 24 January 2004.
[7] James C. Collins and Jerry I Porras (2002) *Built to Last: Successful Habits of Visionary Companies*, HarperBusiness, New York.
[8] Geoffrey Chandler (2003) 'The curse of CSR', *New Academy Review*, vol 2, no 1, Spring.
[9] Personal communication, spring 2004.

Unfortunately, Chandler's flowing words are likely to harm his vision of CSR as a total concept. Using strong words such as 'curse' misleads companies and provides them with ammunition to avoid CSR – not something that either of us wants.

CSR ignores development economics and its concerns with capitalism and neo-liberalism

Michael Bryane writes that within the literature focusing on CSR's role in development, 'three "schools of practice" appear to be emerging: the neo-liberal school (focused on self-regulation by industry according to the risks and rewards of CSR activity), the state-led school (focused on national and international regulation and co-operation), and the "third way" school (focused on the role of for profit and not-for-profit organisations). Yet, each of these schools of practice may be critiqued using theories applicable to the broader field of development. Namely, the neo-liberal school fails to address the resource misallocations caused by CSR. The state-led school fails to address the underlying politics behind government encouraged CSR. The "third way" school fails to address the self-interest involved in CSR.'[10]

Michael continues:

> the CSR discourse appears to signal a new form of co-operation between government, business, and civil society in the promotion of social objectives. Yet, left out of the discourse are all the difficulties and complexities which development theory has been debating for a century. The neo-liberal school stresses the adequacy of the incentives versus insurance model – yet fails to address important resource misallocations. The state-led school emphasises the balance between co-operation versus control exercised by the state – yet ignores important contestation of political power by international organisations, national governments, and business interests. The "third sector" school notes the new potential for public engagement in policymaking – but ignores the highly politicised and conflictual nature of that engagement. CSR is part of a larger transformation in the relations between government, business and civil society.[11]

---

[10] Michael Bryane (2003) 'Corporate social responsibility in international development: An overview and critique', *Corporate Social Responsibility and Environmental Management*, vol 10, no 3, pp115–128.

[11] Michael Bryane (2003) *ibid*.

Michael's points are useful and he is correct to note that there is a tendency for CSR practitioners to ignore history as well as theory. But Michael's three models are not necessarily discrete. Academics often use stylized facts to conceptualize difficult issues. CSR is no exception to this trend. Moreover, transposing into the current CSR debate as: (1) legislate for CSR (state school); (2) no legislation (voluntary or self-regulation school); and (3) some legislation to ensure a level playing field (third way) actually captures the debate about whether to legislate or not quite well.[12]

The social responsibility of business begins and ends with increasing profits. CSR is an unnecessary distraction

Milton Friedman's oft-cited pronouncement that the 'social responsibility of business begins and ends with increasing profits' implies that social issues are best left for anyone but business. But, as the pressure increases on governments to spend less and less to rectify social problems these problems refuse to go away – developing world under-development and unemployment also refuse to go away. HIV/AIDS has defeated many Governments especially in Africa. It is logical, therefore, in the absence of public funds, or even in partnership with existing institutions, that business must play a larger part in human development issues than ever before.[13] In the longer term richer consumers and an improved worldwide income distribution is obviously good for business. But should business be directly involved in these issues or simply pay their taxes and rely upon governments and public organizations to use these taxes wisely? That is to say, is it simply enough for business to maximize profits in the anticipation that this is in the best interest of human development?

On 16 May 2001, Martin Wolf of the *Financial Times* wrote a provocative article criticizing CSR where he argued, based on a pamphlet by David Henderson, former Chief Economist of the OECD, that social responsibility distorts the market by deflecting business from its primary role of profit generation.[14]

---

[12] See my evolving views on this debate in Michael Hopkins (2002) 'CSR and Legislation', Monthly Feature, www.mhcinternational.com, July.

[13] It is noteworthy that the World Bank has an evolving programme on partnership with the private sector and corporate social responsibility called 'Business Partners for Development', and the UN has embarked on a Global Partnership that requires business partners to sign up for good practice in labour, human rights and the environment.

[14] See Martin Wolf (2001) 'Sleep-walking with the enemy', *Financial Times*, 16 May, www.ft.com.

Wolf's main concern was that CSR is conducted by activist groups, who are 'with few exceptions ... hostile to, or highly critical of, multinational enterprises, capitalism, freedom of cross-border trade and capital flows and the idea of a market economy. One might expect, and indeed hope, that the business community would effectively contest such anti-business views. But ... the emphasis is on concessions and accommodation.'[15]

Henderson, unlike Wolf, realized that CSR was not confined to so-called 'anti-capitalists' and set up a number of more reasonable assertions. Henderson's view is that businesses should 'act responsibly, and should be seen to do so' but not that 'responsible behaviour today need mean endorsing the current doctrine of CSR'.[16] Henderson did not define what he meant by 'responsible behaviour' although he listed eleven points that he thought were unwise for corporations to accept. His main points are listed in *italics* next followed by my response:

> *i. That the objective of 'sustainable development', and the means to achieving it, are well defined and generally agreed.*

The term sustainable development originally emanated from the environment movement. Even there the term 'sustainable' had been criticized as ambiguous and open to a wide range of interpretations many of which were contradictory.[17] Confusion arose because 'sustainable development', 'sustainable growth' and 'sustainable use' were used interchangeably as if their meanings were the same. The IUCN (International Union for the Conservation of Nature) rejected this and argued that 'sustainable growth' is a contradiction in terms since nothing can grow indefinitely. While 'sustainable use' was applicable only to natural resources so that they may be used at rates within their capacity for renewal. Sustainable development means improving the quality of human life while living within the carrying capacity of supporting ecosystems. We increasingly hear of the term corporate sustainability and no one is against their own corporation being sustainable, that is continuing for ever. Hence Henderson's complaint is well founded in this case.

> *ii. That the contribution that a business directly makes to the welfare of society (or 'the planet') is to be viewed as largely independent of its profitability.*

The implication is that so-called 'activists' require corporations to be philanthropic even when they are unprofitable. Few are as silly as this.

---

[15] Martin Wolf (2001) 'Sleep-walking with the enemy', *Financial Times*, 16 May, www.ft.com.

[16] David Henderson (2001) *False Notions of Corporate Social Responsibility*, London, Institute of Economic Affairs (IEA).

[17] World Commission on Environment and Development (1987) *Our Common Future*, Oxford, Oxford University Press.

> *iii. That 'corporate citizenship', which is now to be endorsed, carries with it an obligation to redefine the goals of businesses, in terms of 'meeting the triple bottom line' and pursuing 'social justice'.*

There is a worrying unconcern with definitions and concepts – when challenged on this, one CSR manager stated that her 'corporation was more interested in the issues than worrying about semantics'. But the definition cited in Chapter 2 that 'corporate citizenship implies a strategy that moves from a focus on short-term transaction to longer-term, values-based relationships with these stakeholders and that loyalty will be based on a company's ability to build a sense of shared values and mission with key stakeholders' is sensible and hardly requires corporations to meet 'triple bottom line (TBL)' considerations. It is true that TBL has become prominent and stems from John Elkington's book *Cannibals with Forks*,[18] which itself arose from the NGO environmental movement. CSR itself, as defined in Chapter 2, carries no such obligation.

> *iv. That new planning, monitoring and review systems should be introduced into businesses to ensure that they meet a range of often questionable environmental and 'social' targets.*

This point is similar to the previous point and it is true that environmentalists wish to reduce polluting emissions and so on, but there is widespread agreement on the need to do this. To date CSR implies treating stakeholders in an ethical manner, but no 'social targets' have been set except for the need to open this dialogue.

> *v. That an array of 'stakeholders' should now be closely and formally involved in the conduct and oversight of businesses.*

Stakeholders include internal parties such as owners, shareholders, management including the board of directors and also external stakeholders such as Government, local communities and consumers.[19] Clearly, internal stakeholders need to be 'closely and formally involved in the conduct and oversight' of their own business. External stakeholders will have different perceptions but, in each case, legislation does have a role to play in how business is conducted so as to protect the externals – consumer safety, ethically produced products and so on.

> *vi. That society has conferred on businesses special privileges and benefits, in return for which each of them must obtain*

---

[18] John Elkington (1997) *Cannibals with Forks*, Oxford, Capstone.
[19] The seminal work on stakeholder involvement in corporations is R. Edward Freeman (1984) *Strategic Management: A Stakeholder Approach*, Boston, Pitman.

from it an informal 'licence to operate', by engaging in good
works that are not directly related to profitability.

Much has been written about the phrase 'licence to operate' but, in fact,
no business actually requires a licence to operate in the sense of a driving or pilot's licence. Therefore to link a 'licence' to operate with a 'must'
obligation for good works does not characterize the main players. There
continues to be much discussion on which aspects of CSR should lead to
regulation and which to voluntary measures to ensure a 'level playing field'
for companies to operate in.

> *vii. That 'society's expectations', which are not to be ques-*
> *tioned and which have to be met if businesses are to earn and*
> *keep their 'licence to operate', can be largely identified with the*
> *current demands made by NGOs, 'ethical' investment funds,*
> *and other radical critics of the market economy.*

Ethical (and social) investment funds are rapidly gaining ground (see below)
but work within the market economy can hardly be associated with 'radical
critics of the market economy'.

> *viii. That grave environmental damage has been done, and is*
> *being done, as a result of economic activity in general and the*
> *profit-directed operations of companies in particular.*

The concern for these issues stands by itself and is not easy to dismiss.
Clearly, Henderson falls into the radical camp of free marketers so characterized by the Bush administration's rejection of international treaties on
the environment such as Kyoto.

> *ix. That recent globalization has brought with it (1) dispropor-*
> *tionate gains to multinational enterprises, (2) 'social exclusion'*
> *everywhere, (3) 'marginalization' of poor countries, and (4) a*
> *transfer of the power to act and decide from governments to*
> *multinational enterprises, so that the role and responsibilities of*
> *these latter now have to be conceived in more ambitious terms.*

There is truth to each of these concerns stemming from the so-called anti-
globalization lobby. However, not everyone who supports CSR is necessarily against globalization.

> *x. That progress within national economies, and in the world*
> *as a whole, is to be largely identified with the adoption and*
> *enforcement of ever more stringent and more uniform norms*
> *and standards, environmental and social, both within and*
> *across national frontiers.*

The discussion on norms and standards has been a regular feature of international organizations such as the ILO, OECD (where Henderson used to work) and EU. Some proponents of CSR are very hesitant to suggest ever more stringent standards and are aware that business should not be enveloped in a fog of new rules and regulations.

> *xi. That it has become the duty of businesses to work with governments, moderate NGOs and international agencies, in the name of improved 'global governance' and 'global corporate citizenship', to realize such standards internationally.*

There is increasing agreement that improved corporate governance is necessary to prevent abuse not only by the rich and powerful but also by large corporations in countries in the developing world which, hitherto, have been powers in themselves – the OECD corporate governance principles are contemporary examples of this process.

In summary, Henderson's views can be easily situated within the school of radical market capitalism where any hint of regulation is seen as an attack on the market economy. Nevertheless, CSR cannot be considered completely in isolation from the business case. It is, therefore, more appropriate to revise Friedman's aphorism from one of social responsibility *or* profits to one of social responsibility *and* profits!

CSR is a sham because companies cannot be left to self-regulate

This is the argument pursued by Oxfam in their report *Behind the mask: the Real Face of CSR*.[20] Citing among others the case of Shell, Oxfam argue that Shell's fall from grace in early 2005 over the misreporting of its oil reserves showed that its CSR policy was not working. If CSR is going to have any teeth then there must be legislation that forces companies to adhere to its precepts. In response, David Vidal has argued (see previous footnote) that it is dangerous to make the 'perfect the enemy of the good. Holding companies to a standard of perfection in CSR performance is a false promise'.

As discussed in Chapter 2, CSR still has some way to go from a few statements at the top of the company and from a few in-house activists to being embedded in a company's ethos. On average a company may seem to be following CSR policies but the average, as we know from statistics,

---

20 Oxfam (2004) *Behind the Mask: the Real Face of CSR*, Oxford, Oxfam 2004 and argued by Andrew Pendleton, the author of the report, and David Vidal of the Conference Board in New York in 'Beyond the bottom line', *The Guardian*, London, p18, 12 June 2004.

covers a variety of sins. Further, no one is particularly against legislation that moves toward a level playing field for all companies. Indeed, some corporate leaders of the CSR movement welcome legislation that would bring their competitors in line with their own best practice. But the story on legislation is not one of allowing voluntary action versus legislating for action. There is a continuum between purely voluntary and total legislation. The current pointer is probably nearer the former than the latter and will, over time, gradually move toward the latter.

Concluding remarks

CSR is not a new concept, but has rapidly come to prominence in the past few years with hardly a day going past without a new report on CSR by a leading company, international organization, NGO or journalist. But, given the criticisms, is CSR here to stay? Or will CSR disappear into the mists of time as just another fad?

More likely is that CSR will transform into different concepts but not disappear entirely. Since the realm of business in society is so crucial, CSR and its entrails will eventually become embedded in all organizations rather like the concern with the environment right now. Consequently, in the future there will be less talk about CSR simply because it will become just part of routine daily operations.

7

CSR and Poverty

The private sector is sometimes seen as the enemy of the poor. However, it plays an important role in the economic growth that is essential to reducing world poverty. As well as driving economic growth, the private sector can have a direct effect on poverty through its own policies and practices. More and more businesses and governments recognise its critical role in international development. (UK, DfID)[1]

What the poorest developing countries need absolutely in order to make poverty history is the growth of pro-poor enterprise. (Shell Foundation)[2]

Introduction

Is there a role for large-scale corporations in alleviating poverty in developing countries?[3] To date, of course, the need to address questions of low living standards, exploitation, poverty, unemployment and how to promote human development in general has been almost entirely the preserve of Governments.

Yet, to date, over the last 50 years, the international community has spent more than a trillion US dollars, and many times that amount in effort, exhortation and emotion, to relieve human suffering and create the start-

---

[1] Department for International Development (DfID) (2003) 'DFID and corporate social responsibility: An issues paper', London, UK.

[2] Kurt Hoffman, Chris West, Karen Westley and Sharna Jarvis (2005) 'Enterprise solutions to poverty: Opportunities and challenges for the international development community and big business', A report by Shell Foundation, London, March.

[3] A version of this chapter was originally presented at a Corporate Social Responsibility Working Group, Development Studies Association (DSA), University of Manchester, 11 September 2001.

ing conditions for poor people to escape poverty.[4] Is it therefore possible to harness the value-creating assets of multinational corporations?

As more and more companies adopt socially responsible policies, take on board codes of ethics, and struggle with recommendations from Cadbury, Greenbury, Hampel and now Turnbull (all in the UK) on corporate governance, does this mean that corporations must now also take on board a major concern for poverty? If so what can corporations do in the poverty area given that their main experience has been business and profit generation to date? Should they have corporate poverty departments? Can an emphasis on poverty alleviation help a corporation to make profits? This chapter explores these questions.

Here I focus upon large-scale corporations who have a presence in a developing country either through a wholly owned subsidiary, a joint venture or a major supplier. Thus I do not touch upon the vast majority of private sector activity of wholly owned domestic enterprises or, indeed, the private sector as such. A little thought and it can be noted that almost all poor people work in the private sector. Those who have jobs in the public sector are not among the very poorest and the unemployed, to a certain extent, have the 'luxury' of waiting for a job. The poorest of the poor have no such luxury.

An analytical framework for CSR and poverty

To examine the issue of CSR and poverty I turn to an analytical framework that covers both *supply* and *demand* responses. The *supply* response is equivalent to the development response, that is a growing and profitable company provides a supply of jobs and incomes – what I have called Type II development in earlier chapters. Consequently, to increase this supply requires specific conditions to allow the private sector to flourish.

Poverty and unequal conditions in many countries lead to instability, corruption and therefore much unreliability in negotiating contracts. This leads to higher costs in doing business and a general reluctance to work and invest in poor countries. Examples abound, but Singapore, near the top of Transparency International's corruption index, receives more than its fair share of private investment than, for instance, most sub-Saharan countries such as Nigeria, which finds itself at the bottom of the index.

Thus the supply of MNEs creates economic growth and employment. Large-scale MNEs may provide jobs directly but the overall number of workers in these organizations is probably not more than 100 million worldwide out of approximately 2.6 billion workers, that is something like 4 per cent of jobs.[5] There may be as many people again whose jobs and

---

[4] Shell Foundation (2005), p4.
[5] Assuming there are around 1000 MNEs with 100,000 employees gives a total of 100 million employees. With a world population of 6.5 billion and assuming about 40 per cent are in the labour force gives 2.6 billion workers (author's estimates).

livelihoods are created indirectly by the MNEs – such as suppliers or simply those benefiting from the wealth created.

However, it cannot be assumed that those who directly obtain jobs are those in poverty. Foreign investment is likely to attract and employ those with high skills rather those in destitution. It is mainly the indirect effects of MNEs that will provide some benefit to the poor – these will be working for the suppliers of suppliers (immediate suppliers of MNEs in developing countries are also likely to be highly skilled). Of the suppliers of suppliers it will be those in small firms or those in self-employment who will number among the poor. Consequently, foreign investment via MNEs will help the poor mainly through a 'trickle-down' effect. This way of doing business is unlikely to change simply because poor people are poor, because they don't have the skills necessary to help themselves out of their own poverty and, consequently, cannot provide the skills required by MNEs.

The *demand* response is a little more complicated. It is what is expected, or demanded, of companies so that they can operate freely. This is a bit of an oxymoron since 'expect' and 'free' are in opposition to each other. This demand is expressed through hundreds of rules and expectations. The corporate social responsibility movement is just one of many similar sets of expectations that run from initiatives such as the UK's Ethical Trading Initiative, the UN's Global Compact, the ILO conventions and standards to legally binding ones that are enshrined in company law and that come under the heading of corporate governance. Prominent in the demand response are the stakeholders of the organization. There is no accepted definition of who these are but they certainly include internal stakeholders such as owners, managers, shareholders and employees while the outside stakeholders – and this is more contentious – include suppliers, local communities, families, the environment (NGO community) and government. Each of these groups is expressing 'demands' on corporations with, perhaps, only the environmental group even mentioning the issue of poverty. The MNEs' response to these demands can affect long-term profitability, hence the increasing interest by MNEs in the various stakeholder groups.

There is also a third component related to poverty which is *both supply and demand* and this is when private companies develop initiatives directly aimed at the poor. In many cases this has come under the heading of 'business partnerships' where MNEs seek advantage through better public relations and understanding of local situations. But, normally, when one thinks of poverty alleviation, the private sector often escapes attention and the image of state-provided services is conjured up.

Yet the poor represent an enormous untapped resource for the private sector that is only just starting to be explored – I covered a number of case studies in Chapter 3 where companies have been active in nurturing microcredit programmes. The experience of credit programmes for the poor shows that these activities are both sustainable and profitable once the initial capacity building and investment has begun. Awareness by the private sector of this untapped potential is key for international organizations and donors as facilitators in helping the poor to help themselves. Much effort is expended here. Once the poor have their feet on the first rung of the ladder, this development process needs to be sustained through, for example, the continuing supply of credit from the banking system. Moreover when the poor have shown their creditworthiness through Grameen-type credit schemes, the culture of thrift is developed and credit records can be passed on to commercial, but not exploitative, lenders.

The dialogue between the private and public sectors was hardly in evidence even 10 years ago. For example, in a New York meeting held at the UN at the end of 1994, in preparation for the 1995 World Social Summit held in Copenhagen, the private and public sectors came together at a higher level than had been seen before. There, a number of high-ranking UN officials and some senior financial figures (Juan Somavia, then chairperson of the Social Summit and now ILO Director General; James Speth, then Administrator of UNDP; Marshall Carter, CEO of State Street Bank in Boston; former Citicorp banker Walter Wriston, and so on) sat down to see what common ground could be found between social development professionals and global bankers. The will was there, but the context was missing, according to Carter, who said, 'When we talked about our fiduciary responsibility – to ensure that stockholders are not exposed to undue risk – you could see the development people reaching for their dictionaries.'[6]

Since then, much has changed and the dialogue has blossomed into a series of global events known as Money Matters in the UNDP and a Money Matters Institute has been formed. Many other global fora have arisen in recent years to address these issues – the ILO Enterprise Forum held in 1996 and again in 1999 attracted over a thousand business and concerned individuals. The UN's Global Compact is yet another example of improving dialogue between public and private sectors as is the World Bank's Business Partners for Development programme. The UN's Global Compact covers the inter-related questions of human rights, labour standards and the environment. Businesses are expected to sign an agreement with the UN that they will 'embrace, support and enact' a set of nine principles related to these three themes. These latter themes are far from taking on board all CSR concerns – most stakeholders are missing, codes of conduct are absent and there is no requirement to produce a social report. Now the concern is whether these new initiatives are going to raise the costs of doing business around the world, which is something I look at next.

Labour market rigidities

A key economic concern is whether corporations that take on board 'ethical trading initiatives', 'core labour standards', 'stakeholder consultation'

---

[6] Lloyd Garrison (1997) 'Money matters to Marshall Carter – So does the developing world', *Choices* (UNDP), vol 6, no 3, pp4–9.

or even fully-fledged CSR in their dealings in developing countries will find themselves disadvantaged because they have become 'uncompetitive'. As Wolf noted:

> to the extent that companies feel obliged to operate with the same environmental standards and terms and conditions of employment worldwide, they are likely to harm the development of poorer countries, by ignoring the proper differences that operate in favour of less economically advanced countries. Similarly, to the extent that companies accept excessively costly operating practices, they are likely to be less competitive and less profitable, and so make a smaller contribution to the economy.[7]

If Wolf is correct, increasing levels of CSR in the operations of corporations in developing countries will lead to worsening levels of competitiveness, thereby less growth and increasing poverty.

This is the subject of an article by Ethan Kapstein of the INSEAD business school where he states:

> Consider the linkage of labor and environmental standards to multilateral trade agreements. Improving working conditions and air and water quality are laudable goals, and firms should do so whenever it is economically and technically feasible. NGOs can usefully contribute to that process by providing governments and firms with information, advice, and policy alternatives. But forcing the standards of industrialized nations on developing countries and the firms that operate in them could backfire by reducing investment and job creation. More workers would be chased into the informal economy, which has even lower standards, if any at all.[8]

Kapstein's argument is not altogether consistent with what is happening in practice. The Ethical Trading Initiative of the UK has attempted to include fair trading standards in trade.[9] It has been under attack since 'ethical' trade

---

[7] Martin Wolf (2001) 'Sleep-walking with the enemy', *Financial Times*, 16 May, www.ft.com.

[8] Ethan B. Kapstein (2001) 'The corporate ethics crusade', *Foreign Affairs*, September/October.

[9] Clare Short (1997) 'Development and the private sector: A partnership for change', at the Institute of Directors, 8 July, DfID, London, p13. See also Facilitator's Report (2002) 'The challenges of assessing the poverty impact of ethical trading: What can be learnt from fair trade initiatives and the sustainable livelihoods approach?', Department for International Development, 13 March, available on www.livelihoods.org/post/Docs/trade_pov.pdf, accessed 26 February 2006.

does not seem to apply to the UK's military-industrial complex. While the organization Fairtrade, based in Germany and owned by charities – among them Oxfam, Traidcraft and Banana Link – has, at least in part, evolved in response to the concerns expressed by Kapstein.

Fair trade is a subset of ethical trade in that it deals directly with producers of products, mainly agricultural products such as coffee, tea, fruit, wine, and so on. In the UK it has been expanding rapidly, despite the premium consumers must pay for Fairtrade products – according to *The Observer* in 2003, in the UK, there were just 150 Fairtrade products available and by 2005 the figure had risen to 1300.[10] Fair trade is a little difficult to define but it means that producers must sign up to Fairtrade's (or a similar) labelling system. One aspect of this system is a code of conduct for hired labour based upon ILO labour standards.[11]

Fairtrade is an example of CSR in action but, I believe, must balance the needs of the market with the need to protect both suppliers and consumers. How far along the route of codes of conduct, labour standards and rule-based product agreements one must go is still the subject of much debate and there is no easy answer. Wolf, for instance, says that a company that follows CSR policies will harm the development of poorer countries. Such a comment may not be well received by the Bhopal villagers who suffered the effects of Wolf-type conditions at a Union Carbide plant. There is no doubt that those countries who have labour costs that outrun labour productivity will suffer in terms of international competitiveness. It is true that CSR proponents have hardly dealt with that issue and that the international organizations who could debate the issue have largely ducked it – notably the WTO and the ILO. But enterprises in developing nations need to move toward acceptable CSR practices since 'beggar-thy-neighbour' actions where companies compete to pay the worst wages in appalling conditions will lead to reduced effective demand and lower levels of world trade.

On the issue of global standards, I agree with Henderson when he says:

> *The effects of enforced stringency and uniformity are especially damaging in labour markets. Regulations made in the name of 'social justice' or 'positive' human rights, whether by governments or businesses, can undermine freedom of contract and thus deprive people of opportunities. Those who suffer most from such actions are often the worst off.*[12]

---

[10] Andrew Purvis (2006) 'Ethical eating: How much do you swallow?', *The Observer*, London, 26 February.

[11] See   www.fairtrade.net/pdf/hl/english/Generic%20Fairtrade%20Standard%20 Hired%20Labour%20Dec%202005%20EN.pdf, accessed 27 February 2006

[12] David Henderson (2001) 'Misguided virtue: False notions of corporate social responsibility', March, London, UK, IEA (Institute for Economic Affairs).

I am very much in favour of labour flexibility in labour markets and, like, Henderson regard France's 35-hour week and forcing companies to pay doubled indemnities to fire workers (M&S was the starting point) as likely to reduce future levels of inward foreign investment in France. More recently, France has seen the higher unemployment that has resulted from these labour market rigidities and has started to allow more flexible labour contracts.

In fact the cost of labour often comes to be higher than its market price through market imperfections or through government intervention to put in place, for example, minimum wages. In the Philippines, for instance, minimum wages are above the market wage which has both positive and negative impacts. CSR proponents, again, have not discussed this issue, although the issue has been widely discussed outside that arena (see my discussion of the living wage in the next chapter). Clearly, CSR companies cannot give out wages above market wages for all the negative effects that that implies. However, over time a key way is to raise labour productivity in developing countries in order to pay higher wages and thereby increase effective demand. Keynes was also aware of the problems of inflation but, like myself, would not have had an economic policy totally dominated by interest rate and inflation considerations as we see in too many countries today. I have always been mystified why raised living standards, higher levels of employment in good jobs have not been the key targets rather than the dominance of inflation targets? Price inflation should, instead, be a process indicator rather than, seemingly, 'the' output or target to be achieved.

Although apparently self-evident, why is it important to look at labour productivity within and across countries? It is commonly accepted that under liberalization there will be a tendency for wages to match the marginal productivity of output. However, labour productivity and wages will be higher in one country than another. It is absurd to reduce all wages to the lowest common denominator so that domestic markets can clear to reach full employment while each country competes to be the lowest wage producer. What will happen is that labour productivity will tend to reflect relative factor endowments across countries. Moreover, those countries further up the technological frontier, due to investments either in technology or human resources or a combination of both, will have higher labour productivity and, consequently, higher wages. Thus a high relative wage is not a problem in itself. But if wages, and therefore labour costs, are higher than those expected by marginal productivity considerations for a given factor endowment then that country will become uncompetitive and exports as well as employment will suffer.

In developing countries, there is wide disagreement about the value of institutional interventions in labour markets of the type that may result from the application of CSR principles. Richard Freeman picturesquely points this out when he characterizes between, in the blue corner, the World Bank economists who see government regulation of wages, mandated contributions to social funds, job security and collective bargaining as 'distortions' in an otherwise ideal world and, in the red corner, ILO economists who stress the potential benefits of interventions, hold that regulated markets adjust better than unregulated markets, and endorse tripartite consultations and collective bargaining as the best way to produce full employment.[13] Freeman concludes there is little support for the former and little evidence for the latter view.

Freeman is struck by the extent to which the institutionalist perspective comes from Western Europe, where Germany, Austria and Scandinavia have provided reasonably successful (until more recently) institutional interventions in labour markets. Whereas the distortionist perspective comes from the Americas, where analysts contrast the largely unfettered American economy with state interventions in Latin America; these latter discussions might reasonably be described as activities at the 'meso' level of intervention because most countries have been operating under the 'macro' model of raising interest rates to cure inflation while conducting different meso level policies. The policy conclusion of this is not clear-cut since, as Freeman concurs, it depends on specific country experiences and the environment within which they are located. Thus the idiosyncrasies that exist in countries allow some interventions and institutions to work in some places but not in others.

The process of structural adjustment has been signalled to have both negative and positive effects on the labour market in developing countries.[14] There is not much doubt that, in the short term, the immediate effect of adjustment finds its way directly to the labour market – 'structural adjustment is common to developing and industrial countries, whether stemming from the changing international division of labour, the privatization of formerly public activities, debt repayment, anti-inflation policies, or shifts from planned to market economies. In all countries, the effects include displacement of labour ... that inevitably creates social hardship.'[15] This occurs as Government fiscal deficits are stabilized and public parastatals are restructured. This is a subject too long to be treated in depth here and the reader is referred to the texts cited in the previous two footnotes.

---

[13] Richard B. Freeman (1993) 'Labor market institutions and policies: Help or hindrance to economic development?' Proceedings of the 1992 World Bank annual conference on Development Economics, Washington, The World Bank.

[14] See for example ILO (1993) 'Patterns of employment growth under changing conditions of labor supply and demand', ILO Governing Body Report, GB258/CE/3/1, October; Tony Addison (1993) 'Employment and earnings', in Lionel Demery, Marco Ferroni, Christian Grootaert (eds) *Understanding the Social Effects of Policy Reform*, Washington, The World Bank, March; Guy Standing and Victor Tokman (1991) *Towards Social Adjustment – Labor Market Issues in Structural Adjustment*, Geneva, ILO).

[15] Stephen Mangum, Garth Mangum and Janine Bowen (1992) 'Strategies for creating transitional jobs during structural adjustment', Education and Employment Working papers, PHRD/World Bank, WPS 947, August.

Can a product-orientated approach reduce poverty? The fortune at the bottom of the pyramid

Prahalad and Hart, in their widely known work 'The Fortune at the Bottom of the Pyramid', also noticed that, of the world's 6.5 billion people, around 4 billion of them live on less than US$1500 per capita per year (real purchasing power parity values).[16] This pyramid has 75–100 million people in the top portion earning more than US$20,000 a year, then 1.5–1.75 billion earning between $1500 and $20,000 a year and the poor 4 billion earning less than US$1500 a year. With the majority of potential consumers being poor, Prahalad and Hart's argument is that an ignored source of market promise are the billions of poor who are joining the market economy for the first time.

Their argument is consistent with CSR in that by doing good to their consumers, in this case billions of consumers, MNEs can increase their profits – the prospective rewards they say include 'growth, profits, and incalculable contributions to humankind'. The key to unlocking this potential is for MNEs to use technology to produce affordable products for the poor. One example they give is the case of Hindustan Lever Ltd (HLL), a subsidiary of British Unilever PLC, which has been a pioneer in exploring markets at the bottom of the pyramid. It was slow to enter the market and it was only in 1995 when a local firm, Nirma Ltd, began offering detergent products for poor consumers, mostly in rural areas, that Unilever took notice. Nirma grew rapidly and HLL saw that its local competitor was winning in a market it had disregarded. HLL came up with a new detergent called Wheel, formulated to substantially reduce the ratio of oil to water in the product, responding to the fact that the poor often wash their clothes in rivers and other public water systems. HLL decentralized the production, marketing and distribution of the product to leverage the abundant labour poor in rural India, quickly creating sales channels through the thousands of small outlets where people at the bottom of the pyramid shop. HLL also changed the cost structure of its detergent business so it could introduce Wheel at a low price. HLL then registered a 20 per cent growth in revenues per year between 1995 and 2000 and its market capitalization grew to US$12 billion. Unilever has benefited from its subsidiary's experience in India and gone on to create a new detergent market in Brazil.

There are other opportunities too. These are not necessarily low-tech, since there are other ways to satisfy basic needs. Communication is a basic need, but half of the poor have never made a telephone call. Costs are high too. For someone in the US to call his/her banker in Switzerland can cost as little as 1 cent per minute, or even be 'free' if VOIP (Voice over internet protocol) is used. However, someone trying to sell gum in Somalia to a

---

[16] C. K. Prahalad and Stuart L. Hart (2005) 'The fortune at the bottom of the pyramid', www.digitaldividend.org/pdf/bottompyramid.pdf, accessed 24 February 2005.

developed country market would pay at least a dollar a minute – 100 times more! Part of this cost is institutionally driven, as many developing countries see telecommunications to be the preserve of the rich and therefore an alternative form of taxation. It also has to be admitted that individuals in many developing governments benefit hugely from either a direct, or an indirect, association with a telecommunication company.

Problems with Prahalad and Hart's concept

There are clearly many benefits for a MNE that develops their business at the bottom of the pyramid. Prahalad and Hart undoubtedly identify that there is wealth that can be both tapped and generated there. But there is also much wealth at the middle and the top of the pyramid that is even easier to access.

For purposes of calculation, I shall use the higher figures for the number of people and an average income level given in Prahalad and Hart's pyramid, as discussed above. Thus, I will consider 100 million people earning on average US$50,000 a year, 1.75 billion people earning US$10,750 a year and 4 billion people earning US$750 a year.

These figures immediately show that the third, poorest, tier contains 68 per cent of the world's population but *only* 11 per cent of its income. The richest tier or 2 per cent of the world's population have 19 per cent of the world's income and the middle tier or 30 per cent of the world's population have 70 per cent of its income. Even if I assume that the poorest tier earn as much as US$1500 a year (the top of the interval scale chosen by Prahalad) the figures do not change very much. The poorest tier then have 20 per cent, the richest tier 17 per cent and the middle tier 63 per cent of the world's income!

Thus it is not altogether surprising that the world's largest companies go where the income is to be earned, that is *in the richest and middle tiers where there is a higher concentration of richer people*. Obviously, the transaction costs for reaching middle-income consumers in the richer parts of the world are lower – why sell mobile phones across the vast Sahara desert when the sprawling metropoli of Tokyo, Milan or Beijing have a host of willing consumers? Prahalad and Hart's economics look faulty even using their own data.

Now I do not want to weaken Prahalad and Hart's argument and therefore convince the rich companies to ignore the bottom of the pyramid – particularly the necessary research, development and 'management' technology that Prahalad's ideas will bring – far from it, as will be seen below. But poor argumentation will not help the world's poor and there are at least four further problems with Prahalad's argument.

First, and this is an old chestnut in business circles, is that if business can make huge profits at the bottom of the pyramid, why do they not do that anyway? To a certain extent they have been doing what they can to make money for years. I remember travelling in Somalia in the mid 1970s (when the country had a functioning government under Siad Barre). The journey, a half a day north of the capital, required a 4×4 vehicle (needed, unlike the ridiculous trend for journeys in SUVs in developed countries where there are excellent roads) since the roads petered out halfway along the route. Then we walked for an hour, before taking a boat across a river where we were met by the heads of a village of about 1500 people. For their visitors, and we were numerous, Fanta was served! The Coca Cola Corporation had been there ahead of us. So, if there is a fortune at the bottom of the pyramid, why have the MNEs not been there already? Certainly, part of it can be explained by the fact that many have not thought of the possibilities.

But the costs of supplying goods and services to people without an awful lot of purchasing power are enormous. Prahalad and Hart do realize that building a complex commercial infrastructure for the bottom of the pyramid is a resource- and management-intensive task. 'Developing environmentally sustainable products and services requires significant research. Distribution channels and communication networks are expensive to develop and sustain.' Yet they also note that 'few local entrepreneurs have the managerial or technological resources to create this infrastructure'. MNEs can then help by transferring knowledge from one market to another, and can act as nodes for building the commercial infrastructure and providing access to knowledge, managerial imagination and financial resources. But why would MNEs do all this when it is easier to focus on where the money is at the top and in the middle of the pyramid?

Prahalad and Hart do not answer this but the CSR approach does give us, perhaps, a more complete answer. Today, the 4 billion poor have little to offer MNEs but, as their purchasing power takes off, they will become a bigger and bigger market for MNEs. It is part of the CSR argument that, through focusing more on their stakeholders, MNEs will see that it is in their own interest to promote development. This is argued in more detail below. But the weakness in Prahalad and Hart's argument is that their approach is essentially one of 'count, cost and supply' or what economists call a supply-side approach.

The second problem with the Prahalad and Hart approach is that it essentially ignores the demand side or how poor people will actually be able to earn income. The main argument for stimulating the demand side is to turn the poor into small-scale entrepreneurs and, to do this, Prahalad and Hart rely mainly on the idea of micro-credit. There is an enormous literature on this topic and, on balance, the literature demonstrates the success of such schemes.

This is because one of the key problems of under-development is the lack of access to credit at a reasonable real interest rate. This gap has begun to be closed through innovative schemes such as the micro-credit schemes pioneered by Mohamed Yunus and his Grameen Bank. Briefly, small groups of savers (largely women as they have been shown to be more careful than men) contribute as little as US$1 a week. Loans are then made to members of the group for as little as US$25 to purchase items, for example chicken wire to enclose chickens and prevent them gathering disease or being eaten by predators. Peer pressure is placed on the borrower to repay the loan according to a pre-determined schedule. Claims of up to 99 per cent repayment have been achieved and these monies then used to develop the wealth of the local communities. Nevertheless, real interest rates of the order of 33 per cent a year are thought to be the minimum to ensure the viability of such funds.

There are two problems with this approach: first it assumes that there is sufficient income within the local community to buy the products produced; second it assumes that the business plan submitted and accepted is viable, although the community frequently has no real experience of running a small business. But, a major difficulty has been the problem of success. Once a small micro-credit scheme starts to take off and larger and larger loans are required, links with more formal banks are required. But banks have been reluctant to loan at the bottom of the pyramid for the simple reason that they make enough money higher up where the costs of lending are lower, and the recipients more sophisticated. Of course, the actual cost of setting up a large loan is lower than that of a small loan. The small micro-credit groups succeed because many of their costs are covered through the voluntary contribution of time by the members of the fund. In a larger institution these costs have to be turned into real cash.

There is no magic formula for creating income (what economist call effective demand) for poor people. Most new employment in developing countries comes through small and medium sized businesses (SMEs). Of course, an SME needs a market and is greatly helped if it has links into a larger company. Consequently, efforts by large companies such as MNEs to improve the performance of their suppliers has all-round benefits. This is discussed later, but it is worth pointing out that supplier codes of conduct, although created with the best will in the world, can have the negative effect of making it very difficult for small companies to comply and, therefore, supply.

A third problem with Prahalad and Hart's approach is that they, like many others, have preached the virtue of technology as a tremendous help to those at the bottom of the pyramid. However, a walk around any poor area in the world will illustrate that technological fixes are few and far between. Nevertheless, technology can help in many areas – robust seeds (note the tremendous positive effect of new hybrids of rice that provoked the 'green revolution' in the 1960s and 1970s), cheaper telecommunications, more appropriate technology products (such as wind-up radios), rehydration salts to cure diarrhoea, a major killer of babies, improved technology in governance systems and security as well as management techniques themselves.

Fourth, Prahalad, in his book, rightly identifies the key problem as the one to create the capacity to consume but then identifies only a partial, and to my way of thinking, limited solution.[17] He notes that the traditional approach to creating the capacity to consume among the poor has

---

[17] C. K. Prahalad (2005) *The Fortune at the Bottom of the Pyramid: Eradicating Poverty through Profits*, New Jersey, Wharton School Publishing.

been to provide the product or service free of charge but rightly dismisses this since philanthropy, as I discussed in Chapter 5, might feel good but it 'rarely solves the problem in a scalable and sustainable fashion'.[18] Interestingly, Prahalad suggests meeting the consumer demand of the poor by packaging items in smaller quantities! But this solution is limited because the poor have unpredictable income streams. They are forced to make many trips to a store because they simply do not have sufficient cash in their hand-to-mouth existence and must therefore buy, for instance, one aspirin rather than a whole bottle at once. Yet, such a strategy will tend to keep the poor poor, simply because their transaction costs will be higher than those of richer folk for example, (i) in terms of time because they will have to travel more frequently and the shops are not always well placed for the poor, especially the women who have to shoulder the burden and (ii) because they cannot benefit from the economies of scale that buying larger quantities offers to the richer consumer. Finally, the implicit assumption is that the poor have lots of time. They do not, in general, since they spend enormous amounts of time trying to earn a living in very difficult and almost desperate circumstances.

So, is there a way out of this trap, what has been called in the past the *poverty trap*? The answer is 'yes', and much can be gained for the poor through the notion of corporate social responsibility which, as I argued in Chapter 1, provides a revolutionary basis for the way in which the main problems of world poverty and under-development can be tackled. And, this can be done through convincing large, medium and small players that there is a fortune to be gained by CSR.

What can happen when wages rise – the case of Gap

> *I do want to credit Gap. Even though Gap realizes there are some risks [of added scrutiny], they believe it's outweighed by the positive aspects of being transparent.* (Conrad MacKerron, group director of corporate social responsibility at the As You Sow Foundation)[19]

What happens when activists take it upon themselves to force the issue of higher wages in developing countries? One of the most famous cases is that

---

[18] Prahalad, *ibid.*, p16.

[19] Quoted in Jenny Strasburg (2004) 'Gap finds problems at thousands of its overseas factories, openness on work conditions praised', *San Francisco Chronicle*, 13 May 2004. The As You Sow Foundation is a San Francisco shareholder-consulting group that supports campaigns for improved corporate environmental and labour practices. It acted as a consultant for Gap's factory-monitoring report. See www.sfgate.com/cgi-bin/article.cgi?file=/chronicle/archive/2004/05/13/MNG6E6KL7E1.DTL, accessed 27 February 2006.

of the clothing retailer Gap, which was among the first enterprises in the US to draw up a code of ethics.[20] Gap bought in clothes from the Mandarin International Apparel Factory situated in the San Marcos free trade zone of El Salvador. It came to international prominence when a number of workers in Mandarin, an independent supplier to Gap, were dismissed for trying to set up a trade union in response to poor working conditions – more than 12 hours of work a day, overcrowded and overheated premises, coercive measures and very low wages of the order of $0.56 per hour. The National Labor Committee (NLC) of the US sounded an alarm and, although Gap was not the only enterprise working with Mandarin, the NLC focused pressure on the company. Because Gap was well known for living up to its public image, it became a target of the NLC campaign. Arguably, a company with a poorer image would have been less of a target, but then would not reap the same benefits of positive consumer reaction.

In the event, Gap at first cancelled its contract in El Salvador, but on reflection realized that this would not help to improve conditions there. It therefore signed an agreement with the NLC that it would renew its contract only if working conditions improved and the leaders of the trade union movement were reinstated. It also promised to give specific assistance to improve working conditions in Mandarin, and to have its code of ethics monitored independently – until then, monitoring had been carried out by employees of Gap. An independent group was formed to do this monitoring at the beginning, in conjunction with two established bodies, the Interfaith Center on Corporate Responsibility and Business for Social Responsibility. They established the main goals as being to:

- detect violation of Gap's code of ethics and applicable local law;
- promote practices leading to compliance with Gap's code of ethics and applicable local law;
- encourage training programmes for workers on the basis of their knowledge about their own rights;
- deter abuses against workers;
- provide a safe, fair, credible mechanism for dispute resolution;
- foster a productive, humane working environment;
- promote utilization of existing processes within the plant to resolve problems as rapidly as possible.

Gap's monitoring system at that factory continues to this day. However, while Gap received good publicity for this move, it failed to implement all the reforms; it put minimal resources into the monitoring system and reneged on its pledge to extend such monitoring to other factories in the region according to Global Exchange – an NGO pressure group set up to monitor the application of companies' codes of ethics in the US.[21]

---

[20] Based on Michael Hopkins, *The Planetary Bargain*.
[21] See www.globalexchange.org/economy/corporations/gap/overview.html.8.

With these resolutions and the establishment of the independent monitoring group, Gap has gone further than other US MNEs, which have developed codes of ethics but have not authorized an independent monitoring of their application. This agreement could provide a model for socially responsible enterprises, at least for their dealings with third parties. It also illustrates that the application of socially responsible principles is not a dream, and that one major company – and in fact there are many – is putting social responsibility for both itself and its contractors on a par with profit maximization.

That Gap will enhance both its public image and, consequently, its eventual profitability is something that may be expected. However, once a company becomes a target for activists the story continues. Yet, those who remain silent, such as Exxon in the US, tend to be ignored.

What impact on poverty does the Gap experience demonstrate? The direct impact will not be large since those who work for Gap will not, generally, be poor in absolute terms, such as those earning less than $2 a day. It may have a strong and negative effect on poor people, however. Companies such as Gap will find easier countries to work in than El Salvador. Higher wages for Gap employees may lead to increased demands from other workers in other industries, leading to wages rising above labour productivity and either inflation or unemployment or a combination of both may result.

Can CSR have a positive effect on poverty?

CSR is a good thing in itself, since it leads to better treatment of stakeholders from improved codes of ethics, better conditions for employees, the concerns of local communities being considered and less damage to the environment and so on. It also leads to increased allocations to Type III development actions. However, the direct impact of corporations on alleviating poverty – and remember I am talking about large MNEs and not the 'private sector' – is likely to be marginal on the *supply* side. This is because:

- poor people don't work directly for MNEs in general;
- MNEs do not create many jobs – even the largest corporations only employ about 100,000–200,000 compared to a world labour force of 2–3 billion;
- suppliers to MNEs tend to be hi-tech and do not employ poor people in general.

On the *demand* side there is more that MNEs can do, such as:

- making sure that products and production processes are safe;
- ensuring a pricing policy that poor people can afford (AIDS drugs are an obvious example);

- respecting the environment;
- having a development policy that focuses upon anti-poverty measures;
- working with the authorities and international organizations to ensure democratic environments, peace, lack of corruption, reduced bureaucracy and anti-discrimination.

In conclusion, there are a number of steps that corporations can take that will impact on reducing poverty. But these steps are unlikely to lead to major reductions in the numbers of people living in poverty, especially as the main focus of business is business which is where their experience lies – few within the walls of MNEs know anything about poverty alleviation programmes and, unfortunately, the rationale for MNEs to have such persons is not overwhelming. Neither do the above lists suggest that there is a lot of mileage in focusing upon anti-poverty measures with the exception of the last item above. Thus the case for a corporation to have a corporate poverty department is not strong since an emphasis on poverty alleviation is unlikely to help a corporation make profits. They may wish to do this for PR purposes but the direct business benefit is not high. I shall, nevertheless, argue in my last chapter that there is a good case for large corporations to have a 'development vision', which does not imply a development department, but simply a statement on what the corporation thinks it can do in the development arena, that is its Type III options.

On the other hand, the case for MNEs to embed CSR is much stronger. There are strong benefits across the board for each stakeholder who, in general, will not be in poverty. Consequently, even though it is certainly morally and ethically acceptable for corporations to be involved in poverty alleviation, the argument plays less well in the boardrooms in Dallas, Tokyo, Hong Kong and Jakarta simply because the impact on profits is marginal. As Björn Stigson, President of the WBCSD, remarked in a meeting in Geneva in 2006:

> *Where is the borderline for business engagement? Governments are having increasing difficulties making societies work. But what can we – as business – do and what can't we do? We need to have a discussion with the rest of society to determine where the borderlines between different actors lie.*[22]

---

[22] www.wbcsd.org/plugins/DocSearch/details.asp?type=DocDet&ObjectId=MTgy-MjM, accessed 25 February 2006.

8

Supply Chain Issues

When buying goods and services you are not just buying in those services you are in some respect buying in an element of your reputation. (Darren Ford)[1]

Introduction

Supply chains are important in CSR and development since the main contact between a corporation and a developing country will be through its suppliers. These will be as mundane as who is supplying the morning coffee to who, and how, the latest fashionable clothes are being supplied. The latter – with top brand names such as Armani, Emilio Zegna, Boss and so on stamped 'Italy' or 'Germany' – are, increasingly, largely made in developing countries. Only the high end (and high return) of design, colour, texture, advertising and marketing are done in the industrialized countries. And even these latter aspects are changing – already China is designing its own high fashion items and India is creating its own software products for example. In my lifetime, 'Made in Japan' has gone from implying cheap plastic toys to designating the latest computers, cars and electronic goods.

But corporations wield great power and the benefits bestowed on developing countries in terms of jobs and income (see below for more on this) can be hurt by the uncertainties and flexibility of corporate decision making. For instance, Anita Roddick of the Body Shop wrote about the alarming numbers of factories that are being closed down in countries such as Mexico because of companies shifting their supply contracts to factories in China where workers are paid 27c per hour instead of the US$1.27 an hour paid in Mexico.[2] Wal-Mart, the article reported, used 4400 factories in one Chinese province alone.

---

[1] Thanks to Darren Ford, Chartered Institute of Purchasing and Supply (CIPS) in comments on an earlier version, personal communication, 5 March 2006.
[2] Anita Roddick (2003) *The Guardian*, London, UK, 22 September.

What are the key issues?

There are at least four key issues:

- how far down the supply chain should CSR go?
- the relative importance of different suppliers;
- the extent of international standards;
- how important is CSR compared with seemingly lower priced options? Are buyers positive enablers of change?

How far down the supply chain?

How far down the supply chain should a company go to ensure that its social responsibility is inextricably linked with its reputation? And what is meant by a supply chain anyway? An excellent report by Insight from which I have drawn here, defined 'supply chain' as referring to all stages of the business process from sourcing raw materials to delivering the completed good or service to the customer.[3]

This broad, generally accepted, definition means that businesses at different stages in the process often use the term 'supply chain' slightly differently:

- In businesses where logistical accuracy is an important driver of profitability (for example in food retailing) the 'supply chain' may be used to describe the warehousing and distribution of product to the stores.
- Those companies manufacturing branded goods (for example cigarettes, branded soft drinks, branded household products and so on) sometimes use the term 'supply chain' to refer to the downstream part of the process: the mechanisms and partnerships by which the products are produced, stored, transported, marketed and sold to the consumer.

Corporate supply chains may be long and complex – a large general retailer in the UK may have in excess of 20,000 suppliers in a hundred countries. A multinational food producer may rely on hundreds of thousands of farmers. Other firms consolidate their buying, dealing directly with a handful of wholesalers or agents based in centres such as London or Hong Kong. Those companies, in turn, deal with thousands of factories and farms that rely on subcontractors and home-based workers to fulfil orders. Supply chains for surgical instruments, footballs and apparel have been traced back to workers' homes in villages in Pakistan, Bangladesh and Morocco.

---

[3] Insight Investment Management Limited (2004) 'Buying your way into trouble? The challenge of responsible supply chain management', *Insight Investment*, 33 Old Broad Street, London EC2N 1HZ.

Operating in these countries can therefore pose new and difficult cultural, operational, logistical and ethical challenges for companies.

Relative importance of suppliers

Important suppliers receive specific attention while suppliers of low value items that are not within the sphere of influence, or even noticed by a large corporation, will go elsewhere if the customer becomes too difficult and demanding. Yet, it is the small things that cause the great things to collapse – the piece of metal on the runway at Charles de Gaulle airport that caused Concorde's only fatal accident, the flap of a butterfly wing that can cause a hurricane some time later, the use of one under-age child in the production process that can lead to the collapse of a retailer's reputation, and so on. To date, those corporations who have applied the same CSR standards to their suppliers as to themselves, have not ventured far down the supply chain.[4] The most important suppliers are nurtured carefully but are also expected to follow the same, or similar, standards as the corporate purchaser.

International standards

Are external standards for supply chains such as AA1000, SA8000 or FLA (Fair Labour Association) vital for a company's reputation? Much has been said and written about these standards in both developed and developing countries. The key issue revolves around labour standards and for this most use ILO core labour standards (ICLS). However, these core labour standards are not particularly hard to achieve and they also apply to countries in general, not companies. But little or no research has been done to date on their use, effectiveness and impact on a company's bottom line. The ILO has been slack here since it is relatively easier for them – for political not technical considerations – to generate new labour standards rather than do the necessary analysis on the impact of its ICLS. ILO labour standards consist of 195 recommendations that are non-binding on member states, then 186 conventions that, when ratified by a country, are meant to pass into country law.[5] The ICLS consist of eight of these conventions.

---

[4] Darren Ford tells me that things are improving and he writes 'buyers are now conducting product analysis and realizing that small-value suppliers have signifcant risks and opportunities', personal communication, 5 March 2006.

[5] Some countries ratify conventions, pass them into law but do not report on their implementation – Uzbekistan for example. On the ILO website one finds 'The Committee notes with regret that, for the eighth year in succession, the reports due have not been received. It also notes with regret that the first reports due since 1996 on Conventions Nos 47, 52, 103 and 122 have not been received; nor have the first reports due since 1998 on Conventions Nos 29 and 100; nor the first reports due

The Insight report, cited above, noted that most companies have recognized that they face risks if labour standards abuses are discovered in their supply chains; some have acknowledged that they have a responsibility to stamp them out. As a starting point, many companies have begun to map out their supply chains and to identify the countries and/or suppliers where they believe the greatest risk to be of labour standards abuses occurring. Many have set up auditing systems to try to identify and (in some cases) rectify those problems. The most prominent of these are the standards based upon the ICLS: the SA8000 (Social Accountability) or the FLA standards.

The lack of a unifying framework for codes of conduct, the fact that one supplier may have to adhere to different codes for different buyers, make it uncertain where the future will lie. Clearly, the codes have some usefulness in that those who adhere to most of them will be careful about the ones they have not signed up to. Certainly, as one moves down the supply chain, interpretations become cloudier and cloudier. Darren Ford mentions a possible approach that he says is well known in theory, only practised by a few MNEs, and is known as Chaordic governance where there is no one strong party and a Memorandum of Understanding (MOU) is signed to that effect.[6]

The Insight report also added another dimension to the issue when it observed that up to now, Western companies that source from developing countries have been considered to be 'passive bystanders whose failure has been merely to turn a blind eye to abuses perpetrated by "ignorant" or "unprincipled" suppliers in developing countries.'[7] The report considered that some companies' own buying practices may have played a part in causing abuse even to the extent that corporate buyers' who increase price pressure, demanding ever greater flexibility and faster product delivery from suppliers, may be 'exacerbating labour standards problems and undermining their suppliers' ability to comply with buying companies' own ethical trading codes'.[8]

There are other issues as well as labour. Transparency in operations is one example. I looked at one instance of this, the EITI, in Chapter 3. In addition, there are all the issues associated with the other stakeholders of the supplier – local consumers (not all the output of a supplier necessarily goes to a single customer), the government, local communities, the environment (not covered in this book), local shareholders, local managers and so

---

since 1999 on Conventions Nos 98, 105, 111, 135 and 154. The Committee trusts that the Uzbekistan Government will not fail in future to discharge its obligation to supply reports on the application of ratified Conventions, in accordance with its constitutional obligations and, if necessary, requesting appropriate assistance from the Office.' The ILO is powerless in the face of recalcitrant governments.

[6] Darren Ford, personal communication, op cit.

[7] Insight Investment Management Limited (2004), p8.

[8] Insight Investment Management Limited (2004), p8.

on. Nevertheless, the main issue that has attracted attention has been the question of labour and this, obviously, is why most large corporations use suppliers in developing countries because of the availability of plentiful and low-cost labour. I look at this in more detail below.

How important should CSR be?

How much weight should CSR be given in the supply chain when a buyer is hard pressed to find a supplier at a competitive price? Buyers, to date, see CSR as 'not my job' and they are quick to shed anything that they believe gets in the way of top performance and indeed many are actively incentivized to do so. As the Insight report notes:

> *Buyers tend to be appraised on price, buying margin, cost saving, etc. They receive plaudits for introducing hot new ranges and exciting products at low cost. They are not encouraged to take a broader or longer view, to visit supplier factories or consider long-term intangibles, such as trust or company reputation. In some cases, where they have taken an interest in ethical or quality issues, buyers have found themselves forced into a type of 'doublethink'. They become aware of the problems in their supply companies, but they have little opportunity to do anything about it. In this case, knowledge becomes almost worse than ignorance, since it can lead to quite deep conflicts at a personal and motivational level.[9]*

It is likely that this latter perspective will change over time, as CSR bites and concerns in industrialized countries feed through the company and through consumers refusing to pay for products produced using exploitative practices. Buyers, too, can have a positive effect on change if they hold CSR as a model of good practice.[10] Change is coming slowly in this area, but already consumers have shown that they will pay a little more for goods they know have been produced 'cleanly'. But many companies, such as Wal-Mart, are still resisting this trend as our report on Wal-Mart in Chapter 3 demonstrates.

There are also pressures coming from government agencies. For example, a report by the Office of Government Commerce of the UK government, has addressed some of these issues.[11] The report emphasizes, with

---

[9] Insight Investment Management Limited (2004), p32.
[10] Thanks to Darren Ford, op cit., for suggesting this point.
[11] Office of Government Commerce (2005) 'Joint note on social issues in purchasing', Social procurement group, June, Trevelyan House, 26–30 Great Peter Street, London SW1P 2BY, www.ogc.gov.uk.

a somewhat bureaucratic tone, the fact that 'procurement staff need to be aware of social legislation, which might impose an obligation on them or on their relations with contractors in certain circumstances'.

Another well-known initiative coming from Government has been the UK's Ethical Trading Initiative (ETI).[12] ETI considers ethical trade – or ethical sourcing – to be the assumption of responsibility by a company for the labour and human rights practices within its supply chain. ETI uses a code of practice that sets out minimum labour standards, in turn based upon ILO labour standards, that they expect their suppliers to comply with. This initiative has not been without controversy, since the UK government has been widely criticized for its double standards in international trade: supporting, for instance, arms trading with a number of nasty regimes whose idea of a labour standard is how much bread and water is required to keep prisoners in forced labour just alive. One instance, in Uzbekistan, led to the UK ambassador, Craig Murray, being hounded out of office by identifying some dreadful labour and human rights practices of the Uzbek Government. Geo-political considerations – the large US airforce base in southern Uzbekistan – mean that issues such as forced labour, child trafficking and mistreatment of prisoners (that included boiling one poor unfortunate alive) were largely swept under the carpet by the UK government, presumably to keep their 'special relationship' with the US alive.

Certainly the personnel at ETI do not adhere to all, or even any, of the UK government's indiscretions. But they have lost considerable mileage because the probity of the UK government in its international relations has been questioned in several highly publicized cases in recent years.

What has been the development impact of supply chains?

MNEs are involved in job creation in two main ways – directly through job creation in the main company and indirectly through job creation among suppliers, distribution networks, public services and so on. Data on these two aspects are surprisingly scarce. A search of the literature showed that the topic was very alive in the early 1990s when there was a major report on the subject in 1994 by the Geneva-based UNCTAD (United Nations Conference on Trade and Development). However, little has been done since then.

The top 100 MNEs, according to the UNCTAD report, accounted for about one third of the combined outward stock of FDI stock of their host countries in the early 1990s.[13] They also accounted for about 12 million working people of which 40 per cent worked in their affiliates abroad. In

---

[12] www.ethicaltrade.org.
[13] UNCTAD (1994) *World Investment Report*, Geneva, UN, p208.

fact UNCTAD estimated that in 1992, of more than 70 million directly employed by all MNEs, only 12 million were employed in their foreign affiliates. Thus, in most developing countries the direct employment creation effects of MNEs are small – if we take a world labour force of around 2 billion,[14] the majority in developing countries, then only around 3 per cent of the world employed are employed by MNEs.

Indirect employment is, of course, a different matter. One aspect of this is the phenomenon of 'offshoring' where suppliers carry out services usually performed onshore by MNEs. These have been growing in number but it is probably no more than a few million. There are no global estimates although widely cited figures from McKinsey for the US predict that by 2015 roughly 3.3 million US business-processing jobs will have moved abroad.[15] As of July 2003, around 400,000 jobs had already moved from the US. But with around 140 million jobs in the US economy even by 2015 this will be only around 2 per cent of all US jobs.

Offshoring drew little attention when only blue-collar jobs were being lost since this was considered part of normal restructuring as developed countries moved away from unskilled to more skilled, brain intensive, production. Companies in the southeast US, for example, closed mills and factories as they shifted their textile manufacturing operations to China and Southeast Asia. More recently, the practice of offshoring has extended its reach to include so-called white-collar jobs. India has been a major beneficiary. By 2008, McKinsey forecasted, IT services and back-office work in India will increase fivefold, to a $57 billion annual export industry employing 4 million people and accounting for 7 per cent of India's gross domestic product.[16] Large companies have transferred their call centres to India, for example, where labour rates can be 50–80 per cent lower than US rates.

But most commentators believe that 'offshoring' is beneficial both to the sending and the host nation. The argument usually goes that increases in efficiency in the home market lead to lower costs that are then translated into higher growth. Such an argument is obviously not well received by workers, such as those in call centres, who have seen their jobs outsourced. These workers tend to be unskilled and therefore not open to retraining or finding other similar unskilled work. The CSR aspect of offshoring is not to stop the process but to assist those made redundant with socially responsible restructuring schemes.[17]

---

[14] A rough estimate by the author is that of the 6 billion world population in the mid 1990s around 40 per cent, or 2.4 billion, people are engaged in the labour force.

[15] http://news.com.com/Who+wins+when+jobs+move+offshore/2030-1014_3-5096283.html, accessed 28 January 2006.

[16] www.mapsofindia.com/outsourcing-to-india/future-for-outsourcing.html, accessed 28 January 2006.

[17] See George Starcher (2002) 'Socially responsible enterprise restructuring', October, Monthly Feature, www.mhcinternational.com.

One of the most discussed aspects of employment creation in developing countries is the establishment or expansion of export processing zones (EPZs). According to the above-mentioned UNCTAD report, in the early 1990s 200 EPZs in roughly 60 countries provided around 4 million jobs. It can be estimated that labour standards are severely lacking in these zones and that wages are among the lowest. That workers flock to them is a sign not of the EPZs' beneficence, but of the desperate conditions surrounding these areas and that for those seeking work a job is a job, however poorly paid. Despite the intense interest, the numbers are small – even if the numbers have doubled since the early 1990s, we are still talking about less than one fifth of 1 per cent of all jobs in the world.

Clearly, the key issue of the MNE role in employment is in the creation of indirect employment. The UNCTAD report estimated that this could be as high as two indirect jobs to each MNE direct job, making around 150 million jobs in all. Added to the 70 million jobs created by MNEs, this would give around 220 million jobs. If we assume that growth in the number of jobs was roughly the same as world population growth – around 2 per cent over the period 1992 to present, then a rough estimate of direct and indirect jobs provided by MNEs would add up to around 300 million jobs in 2005 or around 12 per cent of all 2.6 billion jobs worldwide (2.6 billion = 40 per cent of the world population in 2005 of 6.5 billion). Again, this is important numerically, but it is still only one in every seven to eight jobs worldwide. What is probably more important is that the 300 million jobs created worldwide by MNEs, directly or indirectly, are likely to be better paid than the average and, as world attention shifts to the quality of labour in developing countries, pressure is brought about to increase both the quality and pay of labour related to MNE operations.

What labour issues to consider?

An example of how purchasers can make a positive impact through tackling labour standards in the supply chain and focusing on supporting change over time comes from China. Research by an Impactt team led by Hilary Sutcliffe found that factory workers often put in up to 400 hours a month (12/13 hours a day or 80–90 hours per week), almost twice the legal limit.[18] They are often forced to work overtime and are given few, if any, days off per month. This leads, quite obviously, to reduced efficiency and increased accidents, worker dissatisfaction and high staff turnover.

The Impactt report noted that a range of external and internal supply chain practices drives excessive overtime. External factors include the buy-

---

[18] Hilary Sutcliffe (2005) citing Impactt, who published a public report on her Overtime Project in China, entitled 'Changing over time', available on www.impacttlimited.com.

ing practices of purchasing companies, which, as well as tight lead times and late sample approval, can include purchasers insisting that factories bear the air freight costs of late shipments.

The report went on to focus on the effect that internal drivers had on excessive overtime including: inefficient internal production systems; poor human resource management; and inadequate internal communications. Impactt worked with 11 purchasing companies and their supply partners over a period of three years to test the theory that by addressing drivers of overtime, working conditions can be improved and hours gradually reduced, while still maintaining wage levels. During the project, factories saw increased productivity, improved quality, steady or increasing pay and reduced worker turnover. Most also showed measurable reductions in working hours and an increase in the number of days off per worker per month, with significant progress being made towards compliance with the strict Chinese labour laws.

The greatest successes were achieved where changes were made in factory management commitment, openness to new working practices, commitment and involvement of purchasing companies, and transparency between all parties, rather than just focusing on productivity. The report challenged purchasing companies to work with suppliers over time, to provide support for changes and to develop more responsible buying practices. It promotes the message that the CSR approach to tackling labour practices can have a 'positive impact even in the most difficult areas and challenges companies to incorporate the changes throughout their supply chains' (p4).

The Insight report mentioned above identified a number of actions that a company could take in its supply chain to cover the key labour issues. These are:

1 *Devise a code of conduct*: Codes of conduct set out what the company believes are acceptable minimum standards. A company may devise its own codes or may implement a code that has been developed by an external organization, such as a trade association or the ETI, as mentioned above. Most codes are based on the set of internationally recognized labour standards enshrined in the ILO conventions (see Box 1).
2 *Carry out a risk assessment*: This is generally a desk-based assessment to determine which suppliers are most likely to contravene any of these standards.
3 *Train staff*: To ensure that buyers are familiar with the issues, that employees directly involved in the buying process have the skills they need and that the relevant managers in supplier companies understand the requirements, and that extensive and on-going training programmes are offered.
4 *Carry out ethical audits*: This involves visiting suppliers' production facilities, interviewing management and workers and assessing their compliance with the code of conduct. Audits can either be done by internal staff (typically product technologists or quality representatives, occasionally buyers) or by external specialists.

5   *Draw up improvement plans*: On the basis of the audit results, a list of suggested improvements is drawn up for the supplier to implement to meet the required ethical standard. Ideally the buying company works with the suppliers to help them achieve the required standards.

6   *Report/disclose*: Companies tend to place their supply chain policies and general information about the progress of their compliance programme into the public domain. Yet, the approach is very much one of the buyer finding a problem with the supplier, pointing it out to them and telling them to rectify it, or, in a best case scenario, working with them to do so. This approach does not look at the supply chain as an integrated system and most importantly does not look at how buying practices actually affect suppliers' ability to meet these standards.

Box 8.1 distils codes of conduct into nine key components,which include the ILO core labour standards, the four labour principles that are enshrined

---

Box 8.1 Issues typically included in corporate codes of conduct

1   Employment is freely chosen: Employers should not use prison labour or any other form of bonded labour. Workers should be free to leave when they please (after appropriate notice) and should not be 'tied in' by having to lodge their passports or ID cards. (GC, ILO, ETI)

2   Freedom of association: Workers should have the right to form and join trade unions and to bargain collectively. (GC, ILO, ETI)

3   Safe and healthy working conditions: Working environments and materials meet appropriate health and safety standards. (ETI)

4   No child labour: Children should not be employed below the legal minimum age and appropriate steps should be put in place to remove children from employment and guide them towards education. (GC, ILO, ETI)

5   Payment of a living wage: Workers should be paid at least the national minimum wage in their country, but preferably a wage that is enough for them to live on. Workers should also receive a pay slip and breakdown of their payment. (ETI)

6   Non-excessive working hours: Working hours should comply with national laws and in any case not be more than 48 hours per week plus a maximum of 12 hours overtime. Overtime should be voluntary and agreed in advance. (ETI)

7   No discrimination: Employers should not discriminate against workers on any grounds including race, ethnicity, gender, caste, union membership, with regard to recruitment, promotion, training or any other matter. (GC, ILO, ETI)

8   Regular employment: As far as possible, workers should be given proper employment contracts and full-time employment. Employers should not try to avoid payment of social security, sick leave and maternity and other benefits through subcontracting or labour-only contracting arrangements. (ETI)

9 No harsh or inhumane treatment of workers: There should be no physical, verbal or sexual abuse of workers. (ETI)

Notes: GC = UN Global Compact includes these labour issues. ILO = an ILO core labour standard. ETI = Ethical Trading Initiative base code.

Source: Insight and Acona (2004) 'Challenge of responsible supply chain management', p19.

in the UN's Global Compact, and the ETI codes (none is mutually exclusive). What is striking from this table is that neither the Global Compact nor ILO core labour standards cover all the key labour issues in the Box. Of course, many other items are included in the complete set of ILO labour standards that number several hundred. Thus, those companies that say they follow ILO core labour standards in fact do not address crucial issues such as the harsh treatment of workers, excessive working hours nor the payment of a living wage.

A living wage – what to pay?

There is much heat but little light on the issue of a living wage. It is easy to agree that workers should be paid a wage that allows them and their families to satisfy their basic needs. Some, such as Alvaro J. de Regili, argue that CSR without living wages is 'Irresponsible and Unsustainable'.[19] However he, as many others, does not define in any detail what he means. Clearly, the definition of 'exploitation' has had many variants. Most focus upon the vexed question of what a living wage is.

In most Western countries, a living wage is linked to the 'minimum wage' and is set mainly through negotiation or political pressure. The end result is usually a wage that provides a floor for companies and the public sector but is barely enough to cover basic needs, particularly housing rents. But the main problem is that there is no agreement on what are basic needs nor, in fact, can these be identified objectively. Analysts have struggled to identify at what level a poverty line should be set, but here again there is no objective way of setting such a line.[20]

Are all those who do not satisfy their *basic needs* in poverty? It depends on the definition of the poverty line and the level and composition of basic needs. Basic needs have been defined to consist of material needs such as

---

[19] For a discussion of living wage and CSR see for instance www.jussemper.org/Our%20CSR%20Concept/Resources/CSRwithoutLW.pdf, accessed 6 November 2005.

[20] For an attempt to define basic needs, indicators to measure them and the setting of basic needs levels or targets, see M. J. D. Hopkins and R. Van Der Hoeven (1983) *Basic Needs in Development Planning* (published for the ILO), London, Gower.

food, housing, clothing, safe water, adequate health and education; and non-material needs such as the right to participate, human freedom and social justice.[21] Some people may be in basic needs poverty – say below a housing poverty measure – yet exceed another measure such as food consumption. Are these people in poverty? As noted above, poverty and the setting of poverty lines are value judgements, so *there is no objective way of setting a poverty line*. If some countries wish to place all citizens who do not satisfy *any* basic need in the poverty category, then it is obvious that they will find many more poor than if they set the line on the basis of food consumption.

It is more pragmatic, as the World Bank normally does, to set a poverty line on the basis of food consumption because one does not then get into the debate on relative degrees of poverty. For instance, a household could be food poor but live in housing above a minimum level and, therefore, could be considered non-poor on housing criteria. An alternative is to consider a household or individual poor if for a chosen material basic need they are below the line on at least one criterion. But how can non-material needs be quantified? Even if we could obtain an agreed measure of 'freedom' or 'participation', whatever line were chosen could potentially include virtually the whole population of some African countries. It is probably better to be pragmatic and use a simple rather than a complex measure of poverty or of a living wage. Despite a lack of objectivity, many nations have striven to set a poverty line and its closely related component a minimum wage.

A report on Unilever activities in Indonesia found that, in the area of wages, there are cost pressures that force manufacturers to reduce wages below acceptable levels.[22] Additionally, overtime may not be remunerated at premium rates. Less obviously, cost pressures may lead directly to cutting corners in health and safety, and the use of vulnerable groups of workers. Moreover, Unilever found that despite the existence of a national definition of a legal minimum wage, it was difficult to judge the appropriateness of MNC wage levels within a given context. For example, how much above the legally required minimum wage was it appropriate for an MNC to pay?

Economists have long debated minimum wages and market economists (also known as neo-classicists) tend to have an unfavourable attitude to minimum wages. Ranis, for instance, argues that any continuing increase in real wages as a consequence of union and/or government pressure via minimum wage legislation is bound to be highly unfavourable to the maximum utilization of a relatively abundant unskilled labour supply.[23] In a review

---

[21] Also see Hopkins and Van Der Hoeven, *Basic Needs in Development Planning*.

[22] Jason Caly (2005) *Exploring the Links Between International Business and Poverty Reduction: A Case Study of Unilever in Indonesia*, An Oxfam GB, Novib, Unilever and Unilever Indonesia joint research project, first published by Oxfam GB, Novib, Oxfam Netherlands and Unilever in 2005.

[23] G. Ranis (1973) 'Unemployment and factor price distortions', in R. Jolly (ed.) *Third World Employment Problems and Strategies*, London, Penguin.

of the literature, Lopez remarked that a 'minimum wage not only generates aggregate income losses for society as a whole due to its distortionary effects but also is detrimental for workers themselves by reducing the level of training per worker, average lifetime wages and the number of workers receiving training'.[24]

There are at least nine arguments against the introduction of a minimum wage:

1   it would lead to more foreign and possibly illegal labour;
2   it is inflationary if set at a level above a market clearing wage;
3   it would give the wrong signals to labour during a time of high unemployment;
4   it could lead to less employment;
5   it may negatively affect young people getting a first foot on the ladder;
6   it will increase administrative costs through the need for increased labour inspection;
7   it tends to worsen income distribution;
8   those unemployed or in vulnerable groups are ignored;
9   it tends to encourage exploitation through forcing low-paid activities out of the public eye.

The main argument in favour of living or minimum wages is that they help to prevent the exploitation of labour at the lower end of the pay scale. But often in developing countries many if not most workers fall outside the formal sector covered by legislation and work in what is called the 'informal' sector where minimum wage legislation, if not all legislation, is ignored. Also, trade unions welcome measures that help them to negotiate pay scales. In fact many collective agreements explicitly have minimum wage clauses. But, again, trade unions normally cover only a small proportion of the labour force in developing countries and, obviously, don't spend a lot of time caring about non-unionized members who are quite likely to be in the informal sector.

So where does all this leave us? Pragmatism is the answer. In a country that has legislation for a minimum wage, companies cannot avoid paying such wages. This is not as easy as it seems either. Some countries have minimum wages that vary from region to region depending on local cost-of-living variations. Thus a MNE that pays a minimum wage across a country that satisfies one region may not satisfy the rules of another region. These complexities are lost on consumer groups in the MNE host country who may not understand these differences.

This still leaves the problem of a country that has no minimum wage or where the minimum wage, because of inflation for example, is very much

24 R. Lopez (1992) 'On-the-job training, minimum wages and the structure of production – a general equilibrium analysis', The World Bank, Working Paper, PHREE, September.

lower than perceived living levels. Should a minimum wage be adequate for a worker to satisfy his or her basic needs for, say, food, but what is the situation regarding his or her family? What happens when the worker is the only member of a family with a 'good job'? Again, pragmatism is the only answer. The 'living' wage should be adequate to allow a worker at least the following:

- daily basic food needs for the worker and their immediate family;
- basic rent in a modest home;
- presentable clothes for the worker and their immediate family;
- basic health and education for the worker and their family;
- transport to and from work.

The ETI would, in addition to the above list, add the legal provisions:[25]

- Wages and benefits paid for a standard working week meet, at a minimum, national legal standards or industry benchmark standards, whichever is higher. In any event wages should always be enough to meet basic needs and to provide some discretionary income.
- All workers shall be provided with written and understandable information about their employment conditions in respect of wages before they enter employment and about the particulars of their wages for the pay period concerned each time that they are paid.
- Deductions from wages as a disciplinary measure shall not be permitted nor shall any deductions from wages not provided for by national law be permitted without the expressed permission of the worker concerned. All disciplinary measures should be recorded.

The ETI additional provisions seem reasonable enough – with the proviso on what are basic needs – but they do not apply to the vast numbers in self-employment or to agricultural workers who are not covered by formal contracts. There is the crucial issue, too, of whether the living wage that results is more than the 'market wage'. If workers are willing to work for less than the market wage, companies will aim to pay only the lower wages – known as rent seeking. Certainly, as one moves away from more formal companies at the head of the supply chain to more informal companies further down, rent seeking will predominate. It may well be that rent seeking behaviour of this form will lead to bankruptcies of firms paying the 'living wage'. I discussed this issue in my book *The Planetary Bargain* where I argued that the movement over time should be toward a 'bargain' where companies agree not to undercut each other and that, eventually, 'rogue' companies would be outed.[26] However, sudden jumps in wages should not be intro-

[25] www.ethicaltrade.org/Z/lib/2000/06/livwage/index.shtml, accessed 29 January 2006.
[26] Michael Hopkins (2003) *The Planetary Bargain: CSR Matters*, London, Earthscan.

duced when the living wage is significantly above the market wage. This is inflationary as well as leading to uncompetitiveness of those firms who comply. Movements toward the 'living wage' need to be made over a period of time to prevent negative consequences. How long the period of time needs to be will depend on local conditions.

SMEs in LDCs

I demonstrated above, citing a decade-old UNCTAD report, that the quantity of employment in developing countries coming either directly or indirectly from MNEs is relatively small. The largest amount of employment in developing countries is in agriculture, the public sector and SMEs. With development, agriculture becomes more capital intensive over time and employment reduces. Public employment which, historically, has absorbed large amounts of labour also tends to reduce with development. As wages in the private sector improve and efficiency considerations lead to the reduction of public sector employment (no bad thing if this means a better paid and more efficient public sector) there is one main area of growth – SMEs. This, by the way, is not only true of developing countries: it also applies to developed countries.

Thus, the issue of SMEs and how they can be cultivated, grown and made more efficient is a major platform in any development effort. The two key areas that international agencies (and to a lesser extent LDC governments) have encouraged are access to credit and skill training that also includes entrepreneurial training. I showed, in the case studies in Chapter 3, that MNEs too have realized that this is a key area and have started to contribute to SME development particularly in the areas of credit and skill training. MNEs see this, quite appropriately, as a much better CSR contribution than pure philanthropy (Type III not Type I development).

But what about the CSR of SMEs themselves? One could easily argue that SMEs in developing countries (including small-scale farmers) have enough to worry about without being concerned with CSR. But much of CSR is commonsense, sometimes so blindingly obvious that it is ignored; for instance, identifying and treating your customers well.

Moreover, as Stephanie Draper observed, 'The fact that small businesses have a heightened requirement for good, multi-skilled employees, strong personal relationships and successful local engagement means that small firms can be a good environment for corporate social responsibility to flourish'.[27] Although she was writing about SMEs in the UK, there are clear parallels to SMEs in developing countries when she writes that the main motivational factors for small businesses to be socially responsible,

---

[27] Stephanie Draper (2000) *Corporate Nirvana: Is the Future Socially Responsible?* London, Industrial Society, p15.

based on interviews with managers and owners of small businesses, are as follows:

1 learning for staff – new skills and competencies can be developed;
2 improved culture – increased motivation and commitment of staff;
3 reputation – enhancing the firm's image locally;
4 recruitment – links with potential recruits;
5 productivity – gathering innovation for products and efficiencies;
6 corporate responsibility – personal satisfaction from discharging wider responsibilities;
7 customers – expanding the customer base.

For a local bicycle tyre repairer in Bangkok, the provider of fresh crushed juices by the roadside in Bogota or the market sellers of flowers in Nairobi, these may all seem to be very esoteric. However, each of these people could see their business improve through adopting at least some of the seven points listed above. For CSR to continue to flourish it has to be adopted, as it eventually will, by everyone all over the world.

Can impact be measured?

More precisely, can the CSR of suppliers be measured in any meaningful way? Can the impact of the development operations of large corporations also be measured?

To date, there has been little or no attempt to carry out any of these types of measurement. Darren Ford tells me that impact cannot be measured effectively until a 'level playing field has been created, regarding requirements from organizations in their reporting on the practices that they are adopting in their supply chain'.[28] There are, of course, surveys carried out to assess the development progress of nation states through national household surveys and censuses. There are also surveys of enterprises concerning their economic performance, which may include some questions on their social performance. Growing, too, are the reporting practices of major corporations who now report on their practices relating to the triple bottom line: environmental, social and economic. While this positive development should be applauded, it is important to remember that corporate reporting often covers what companies choose to disclose! Consequently a company's true performance may not be accurately reflected in the contents of their reports.

In an effort to minimize these differences the GRI has provided an avenue for corporations to report against a standardized set of indicators with their Sustainability Reporting Guidelines.[29] The Guidelines lay out principles on reporting, recommended content, and specific performance indi-

---

[28] Darren Ford, op cit.
[29] www.globalreporting.com.

cators for economic, environmental and social performance. While revision of the performance indicators remains ongoing, the economic section categorizes direct impact into indicators relating to customers, suppliers, employees, providers of capital and the public sector. Indirect economic impact, on the other hand, comprises only one indicator – EC13 – which calls for corporations to 'identify major externalities associated with the reporting organization's products and services'.

The confusion and lack of clarity surrounding indirect economic impact has been found to translate into comparatively poor or non-existent corporate reporting in the area. The significance of this relates back to the role of business in the objective of fulfilling the MDGs. The GRI succinctly states in their 2002 Guidelines: 'As governments and civil society begin to quantify progress against the MDGs, they will be looking to quantify the business contribution.'

What could a framework for reporting on the two questions noted above look like? A possibility is to use the framework I have proposed and used on numerous occasions to assess a company's CSR. Here I have adapted the framework to more closely refer to suppliers in developing countries.

I start with my basic theoretical framework, first developed in the US by Professor Donna Wood, and since applied by the author to dozens of companies. The work is described in detail elsewhere.[30]

Briefly, CSR is measured following a business organization's configuration on three levels:

1 principles of social responsibility;
2 processes of social responsiveness;
3 outcomes as they relate to the firm's societal relationships.

Level I: Principles of social responsibility

The level of application of these principles is institutional and is based on a firm's basic obligations as a business organization. Its value is that it defines the institutional relationship between business and society, and specifies what is expected of any business. This level of the CSR model itself is all about the relationship between business and society at large and it has three major elements:

1 *Legitimacy* concerns business as a social institution, and frames the analytical view of the inter-relationship of business and society.
2 *Public responsibility* concerns the individual firm and its processes and outcomes within the framework of its own principles in terms of what it actually does.

---

[30] Hopkins, *The Planetary Bargain.*

3   *Managerial discretion* whereby managers and other organizational members are moral actors. Within every domain of corporate social responsibility, they are obliged to exercise such discretion as is available to them towards socially responsible outcomes.

This level is typically found in the value, vision or mission statement of a company. In a developing country context, this book also calls for a statement of a corporation's development vision or plan (see Chapter 12).

Level II: Processes of social responsibility

Corporate social responsiveness is a business's capacity to respond to social pressures. This suggests the ability of a business organization to survive through adaptation to its business environment. To do so, it must know as much as possible about this business environment, be capable of analysing its data, and must react to the results of this analysis. But the environment of business is not static; it is a complex and ever-changing set of circumstances. This environment can be unchanged for decades, if not centuries, and then it falls apart and is reformed like a kaleidoscope with increasing rapidity. The ability to successfully scan, interpret and react to the business environment requires equally complex mechanisms.

Three elements are identified as basic elements of this level of the CSR model:

1   *Business environment scanning* indicates the informational gathering arm of the business and the transmission of the gathered information throughout the organization.
2   *Stakeholder management.* A stakeholder is defined as any group or individual who can affect or is affected by the achievement of the firm's objectives, for example: owners; suppliers; employees; customers; competitors; domestic and foreign governments; non-profit organizations; environmental and consumer protection groups; and others. Stakeholder management refers to mapping the relationships of stakeholders to the firm (and among each other) while finding, listening and meeting their needs, seeking to balance and meet legitimate concerns as a prerequisite of any measurement process.
3   *Issues management.* Having identified the motivating principles of a firm and having determined the identities, relationships and power of stakeholders, the key issues that the company deals with for each of its stakeholders can be identified. Often these issues are drawn from a number of stakeholder dialogues that the company organizes with its major stakeholders.

Level III: Outcomes

The main focus of measurement is the third level of the CSR model. To determine if 'CSR makes a difference', all the stakeholders relevant to an issue or complex of issues must be included in the assessment of performance using a number of impact measures. There are, again, three main categories:

1   *Internal stakeholder effects* are those that affect stakeholders within the firm. An examination of these might show how a corporate code of ethics affects the day-to-day decision making of the firm with reference to social responsibility. Similarly, it can concern human resources policies such as the positive or negative effects of corporate hiring and employee benefits practices.
2   *External stakeholder effects* concern the impact of corporate actions on persons or groups outside the firm. This might involve such things as the negative effects of a product recall, the positive effects of community-related corporate philanthropy, or assuming the natural environment as a stakeholder, the effects of toxic waste disposal.
3   *External institutional effects* refer to the effects upon the larger institution of business rather than on any particular stakeholder group. Several environmental disasters made the public aware of the effect of business decisions on the general public for example. This new awareness brought about pressure for environmental regulation which then affected the entire institution of business rather than one specific firm.

Applying the above CSR model: An example

An example of the way in which the model might be applied is given for Ben and Jerry's Homemade Ice Cream. Ben and Jerry's founder, Ben Cohen explained one aspect of the ethical principles of the firm.

> *Businesses tend to exploit communities and their workers, and that wasn't the way I thought the game should be played. I thought it should be the opposite – that business had a responsibility to give back to the community, that is because the business is allowed to be there in the first place, the business ought to support the community. What we're finding is that when you support the community, the community supports you back.*

This is a clear statement of principles which belongs in the first level of the CSR model. As stated, the principle fulfils both the institutional element (it acts to legitimize the institution of business) and the discretionary element (it directs the firm in a socially responsible path) and goes well beyond any legal requirements (the element of public responsibility).

At the level of processes of social responsiveness, corporate social responsiveness is a business's capacity to respond to social pressures. Ben and Jerry's social issues scanning is accomplished through a number of mechanisms ranging from direct community involvement through newsletters to special events sponsored by the company. The effectiveness of the scanning and issues management mechanisms can be seen in their funding of organizations as diverse as the Native American Community Board in South Dakota to the Central Massachusetts Safe Energy Project. We can see clear linkages from Ben Cohen's principles as stated to concrete corporate action.

Among the hundreds of issues which were raised at Ben and Jerry's, one specific *outcome* was carried out through its purchasing policies. The firm called on the Greystone Bakery in Yonkers, New York to bake its brownies, a firm that uses its profits to house the homeless and train them as bakers. This outcome is very specific and wholly measurable in a number of ways. One could simply measure the number of homeless people employed by the bakery and the number of trained bakers graduated by the programme. One might also look at how many are still employed at the bakery or in another company as bakers.

There is a clear causal linkage back through corporate mechanisms to ethical principles and the analytical framework can be seen to function. Further research could be done at Ben and Jerry's to cross-relate different elements and their indicators to determine how, for example, profitability is affected by the 7.5 per cent share of pre-tax earnings given by Ben and Jerry's to philanthropic causes. Conversely, one might take a proposed indicator such as 'outcomes of community involvement' and examine its statistical relationships to other indicators in other elements.

The first set of stakeholders in this process are external to the company – they are the homeless who take part in the training programme. A second group of stakeholders can be identified as the community from which the homeless are taken. Clearly, the bakery itself profits as a supplier to Ben and Jerry's and it, in turn, provides benefits to the stakeholders which are possible because of their business with Ben and Jerry's. As one aspect of a very successful social programme, this also benefits shareholders as the success of the firm grows. This is a classic case of new avenues of thinking leading to better profits, reputation and employment as well as a real improvement in the quality of life in the society in which Ben and Jerry's are operating.

What indicators to use?

The potential indicators are presented in Table 8.1. If you would like to apply a subset of these indicators to your company or institution they are available on the author's website,[31] where they can be used to rate any

---

[31] www.mhcinternational.com/rate_your_company.html; see 'rate your CSR'.

Hoplara, 2007

Table 8.1 MHCi CSR measurement – elements, indicators and measures

Elements of SRE model	Indicator	Measure
Indicators and measures		
Level I – Principles of social responsibility		
Legitimacy	■ Code of Ethics or Vision Statement	Published?
	■ Code of Ethics	Distributed to employees?
	■ Code of Ethics	Independent group does monitoring?
	■ Development vision published?	
Public responsibility	■ Litigation involving corporate lawbreaking	Amount, size?
	■ Fines resulting from illegal activities	Amount?
	■ Contribution to innovation	R&D expenditure
	■ Job creation	Number of net jobs created
Managerial discretion	■ Code of Ethics	Managers and employees trained?
	■ Managers convicted of illegal activities	Number, amount?
Level II – Processes of social responsibility		
Environmental scanning	■ Mechanism to review social issues relevant to firm	Exists?
Stakeholder management	■ Analytical body for social issues as integral part of policy making	Exists?
	■ Social audit	Exists?
	■ Ethical accounting statement	Exists?
Issues management	■ Policies made on basis of analysis of social issues	Firm's regulations and policies

Level III – Outcomes of social responsibility

Element of SRE model	Stakeholder g-roups (assumed)	Indicator	Measure
Internal stakeholder effects	Owners	Profitability/value	Share value, Return on Investment, etc.
		Corporate Irresponsibility or illegal activity	Fines, number of product recalls, pollution performance measured against some industry standard
		Community welfare	Amount of giving, programmes as percentage of earnings
		Corporate philanthropy	Amount of pre-tax giving to SD projects as percentage of earnings
		Code of Ethics	Published, distributed, trained
	Managers	Code of Ethics	Trained in code of ethics and apply in demonstrable and measurable ways
			Rank of manager responsible for applying code
	Employees	Union/staff relations	Evidence of controversy, good relations
		Safety issues	Litigation, fines
		Pay, pensions and benefits	Relative ranking to similar firms (measuring percentage spent on employee benefits, programmes, etc)
		Layoffs	Percentage, frequency, individuals chosen
		Employee ownership	Amount by per cent
		Women and minorities policies	Existence, rank with similar firms, litigation and fines
External stakeholder effects	Customers/ consumers	Code of Ethics	Evidence of application to products or services
		Product recalls	Absolute number, seriousness demonstrated by litigation or fines, percentage of total production
		Litigation	Amount of fraud, price fixing, antitrust suits
		Public product or service controversy	Seriousness, frequency
		False advertising	Litigation, fines

Natural environment	Pollution	Performance against index, litigation, fines
	Toxic waste	Performance against index, litigation, fines
	Recycling and use of recycled products	Percentages
	Use of eco-label on products?	Yes/No?
Community	Corporate giving to community programmes	Amount, percentage
	Direct involvement in community programmes	Number, outcomes, costs, benefits
	Community controversy or litigation	Number, seriousness, outcomes
Suppliers	Firm's Code of Ethics	Applied to all suppliers
	Supplier's Code of Ethics	Applied
	– Litigation/fines	Number, amount, outcomes
	– Public controversy	Amount, outcome
Business as a social institution	Code of Ethics	Published and applied
	Generic litigation	Amounts, number, outcomes
	Class action suits	Amounts, type, number, outcomes
	Public policy and legislation improved due to pressure from corporation	Yes or No
External institutional effects		

company. There are 20 questions based upon the framework described here and, since many require only a yes/no answer, the questionnaire only takes a few minutes to complete.

Concluding remarks

Primary suppliers have been covered in this chapter but little light has been thrown on how far down the supply chain a company must go to satisfy, at a minimum, reputation requirements. Pragmatism must be the guiding force in this discussion, since hard and fast rules are both difficult to draw up and even more difficult to apply. When standards are applied, there is much confidence to be gained through submitting to an independent audit. However, these are expensive and only the largest suppliers, or those with support from the parent corporation, can usually comply. There are also problems with the standards themselves. First, there are many of them and it is not easy to know which one to comply with. Second, even the most well-known standards do not cover all the main issues. For instance, the vexed question of the payment of a living wage is not covered by ILO core labour standards, nor is it covered by the other numerous labour standards developed by the ILO. Thus, even if a company says it follows ILO core labour standards (or for that matter other standards such as the UN Global Compact that say they apply ILO standards) it does not mean that all concerns are necessarily addressed.

Over time, as countries become richer – as they probably will without a catastrophe (although global warming seems to be one which man may be too late to control) – suppliers will be better able to observe acceptable standards of operation. However, one should not expect suppliers in developing countries to go too far too soon and the aspiration to observe at least core ILO labour standards may be as much as can be achieved in order to avoid the worst forms of exploitation.

9

CSR in developing countries

CSR is really about ensuring that the company can grow on a
sustainable basis, while ensuring fairness to all stakeholders.
(N. R. Murthy, Chairman, Indian IT firm Infosys)

Introduction

In this chapter the focus is on developing countries themselves and the
question being broadly examined is: What are home-grown companies in
developing countries actually doing on CSR and development? This is now
an heroic task. When I first started work on the *Planetary Bargain* nearly
10 years ago, I had one section on CSR in developing countries and it was
relatively easy to find specific developing country references. There, I covered what developing countries were doing on CSR and found that these
were mainly philanthropic interventions.

The quick reply to the question above is that quite a lot is being done
and, therefore, today the question has many more CSR activities to address.
My task is helped by the burgeoning number of regionally focused websites and newsletters devoted to CSR across the world from China, the
Philippines and India to Brazil. There is, in addition, a growing academic
literature on CSR in developing countries as interest in the whole field has
exploded. On the other hand, what CSR means across different countries,
what it means to companies in those countries and the general public varies
across the world.

To address the question posed, I have focused on what I consider the
key issues while providing a global spread. Further, given the rising power
and influence of just three countries, Brazil, China and India – countries
that also encompass nearly half of the world's population – I have explored
these three a little more than other countries and regional groupings.

There are three main aspects I shall cover in this chapter. First, what
are the overall trends in CSR in developing countries? Second, what are
home-grown companies in the countries themselves doing about CSR? The
chapter ends with some reflections on a number of my own ideas through
a dialogue with an informed observer of the field.

Trends in CSR in developing countries

Results from empirical analyses vary somewhat. There are those who find major differences of the treatment of CSR in developing countries, those who find some differences and those who find very little difference. For instance, according to an EIU survey in 2005, approximately 40 per cent of American and European respondents to the survey said that the main reasons for emphasizing CSR included the need to improve community relations and to deflect pressure from regulators, whereas, in Asia, where companies are less sensitive to community relations and where regulators are less powerful, only 33 per cent of respondents took this view.[1]

In an article addressing the hypotheses that CSR in Asia is 'not homogeneous but varies among countries' and that the 'variation is explained by stages of development', Chapple and Moon studied website reporting by 50 companies in seven Asian countries: India, Indonesia, Malaysia, the Philippines, South Korea, Singapore and Thailand.[2] The article concluded that CSR does vary considerably among Asian countries but that this variation is not explained by development but by factors in the respective national business systems. It also concludes, unsurprisingly, that multinational companies are more likely to adopt CSR than those operating solely in their home country and that the profile of their CSR tends to reflect the profile of the country of operation rather than the country of origin.

In another study, Jeremy Baskin found that CSR (he dropped the term 'social' and called it CR) in developing countries (especially South Africa, Brazil, India and parts of Eastern Europe) is more developed than is commonly thought, sometimes exceeding standards of some high-income countries.[3] Also examining corporate websites and annual reports of 127 leading companies in 21 emerging markets, Baskin found that there was 'not a vast difference in the approach to corporate responsibility between leading companies in high-income OECD countries and their emerging market peers'.[4] However, he found that three things stood out when looking in detail at the data on each company and country.

---

[1] The Economist Intelligence Unit (2005) 'The importance of corporate responsibility', London, January.

[2] Wendy Chapple and Jeremy Moon (2005) 'Corporate social responsibility (CSR) in Asia: A seven-country study of CSR web site reporting', *Business and Society*, vol 44, no 4, pp415.

[3] Based on an analysis of the corporate responsibility practices of 127 leading companies in 21 emerging markets across four regions: Asia, Latin America, Africa and Central and Eastern Europe by Jeremy Baskin (2005) 'Corporate responsibility in emerging markets', presented at Middlesex conference, London, 22 June.

[4] Companies from the following countries were analysed: Argentina, Brazil, Chile, China, Colombia, Czech Republic, Egypt, Hungary, India, Indonesia, Malaysia, Morocco, Mexico, Peru, Philippines, Poland, Russia, South Africa, Thailand and Turkey.

First, there was a striking difference between countries: a great deal is happening in countries such as India, Malaysia, Brazil, South Africa or Poland. By contrast the evidence from countries such as China, Russia or Egypt is of very little activity related to corporate responsibility.

Second, leading Brazilian, Indian and South African companies often seem to have more in common with each other than they do with companies in neighbouring countries. This is not always the case. For example, the evidence regarding the number of women on boards finds Latin American companies have more in common with companies in Spain and Portugal than with their peers in emerging markets in other regions.

Third, in most emerging markets there appears to be a substantial gap between companies doing a great deal (often at a similar level to their high-income peers) and those doing little or nothing. This gap appears greater than the gap within each of the high-income countries, with the possible exception of the US. In addition, it appears that as one starts to look beyond the very largest companies then corporate responsibility in emerging markets is far less common than, for example, among smaller and medium-sized companies in Western Europe.

Emerging market companies make up only 3.8 per cent of the FT500, the 500 largest globally traded companies.[5] Even using the much larger Dow Jones Global Index of 2500 companies, emerging market companies make up only 4.6 per cent.

Table 9.1 summarizes Baskin's analysis of the current state of CR (note his limited database that suggests his results must be treated with caution) in a number of emerging markets.

Baskin's research also showed that over two-thirds of the emerging market companies studied either 'produce a sustainability report or have a specific section on their website or in their annual report covering corporate responsibility'. While precisely comparable data for high-income OECD countries are not available, this is a high figure, and insofar as the conclusion is generalizable, suggests that emerging market companies do not see corporate responsibility as the preserve of the developed economies.

Some countries report to a greater extent than others – all but one of the 16 South African companies analysed had a specific corporate responsibility website. Even at the lower end, 56 per cent of Central and Eastern European companies analysed did so too; in short a clear majority of companies in all regions, as Figure 9.1 indicates.

Baskin asked the question: 'what is driving some emerging market companies (and countries) to engage with the corporate responsibility agenda?' His answer was that those emerging markets where corporate responsibility is more developed are those where:

---

[5] See http://news.ft.com/reports/ft500 for 2004 listing.

Table 9.1 *Summary of existing CR trends in emerging markets*

Region	Current state of CR	Key drivers
Central and Eastern Europe	Companies from Poland, Slovenia, Hungary and Czech Republic show most evidence of incorporating CR approaches Pockets of interest in many other states Disclosure is increasing overall Russia, Bulgaria and Estonia show least interest	Foreign ownership Accession (or the goal of accession) to EU membership Competitive advantage Influence of corporate governance codes
Africa and Middle East	South Africa has the most developed CR situation and SRI interest Minimal interest in CR elsewhere	Domestic pressure for CR Threat of regulation Significant SRI market Influence of corporate governance code
Latin America	Most activity in Brazil, Mexico, Chile, Uruguay, Argentina Focus is on CSI/philanthropy Some SRI funds emerging	Nascent public interest and domestic inequalities Regulatory pressures
Asia	Companies from India and Malaysia beginning to incorporate CR Pockets of interest elsewhere China has especially low take-up of CR	Global pressures Strategy for competitive advantage Strong external investor interest in corporate governance and SRI in Asia

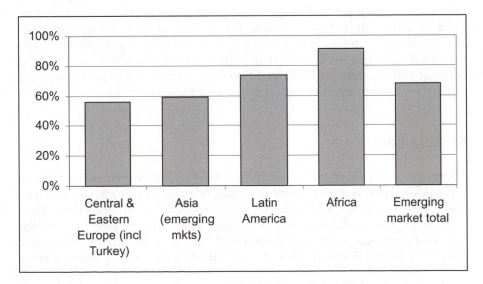

Figure 9.1 *Companies with public corporate responsibility reporting*

- the larger companies are strategically focused on being global or transnational players;
- regulators want to encourage corporate responsibility (often linking it to corporate governance);
- government sees corporate responsibility as part of a strategy to attract inward equity investment;
- civil society is relatively active on a range of social and/or environmental issues.

What are home-grown companies doing about CSR?

The emerging markets aside, CSR in developing countries, although growing in importance, is still not a high priority. There are at least two main reasons for this. First, development in developing countries has meant increased economic growth, more direct foreign investment, less debt, more employment, increased levels of basic needs, improved environment, less poverty and, more recently, better governance, transparency and reduced terrorism. Thus CSR is still not a development agenda item. Further, the general lack of democracy, a poor and controlled press (India is an obvious exception) and weak institutions have not put pressure on large local companies either to clean up their act or to be more involved in CSR and development. Second, when CSR has been an issue, the main contribution from such companies as Tata in India or wealthy banks in the Middle East has focused upon philanthropy.

Nevertheless, CSR in developing countries will change as globalization encourages greater dialogue through improved communication and large local companies will have to be involved to survive. Already, stirrings in developing countries have led to pressure to reduce corruption, and to increased vigilance on human rights. Regions vary however, so the next sections will examine some of the differences in how CSR is seen in selected regions and countries of the developing world.

Middle East

There are an increasing number of seminars and conferences on CSR in the Middle East as many countries struggle to escape from violence and under-development. Christophe Nicaise, regional director for Harry Winston, notes that a definite shift is taking place among companies in the Middle East, as corporate social responsibility takes on a more meaningful role.[6] The Harry Winston 'Paint a Smile' Rashid Pediatric Therapy Centre

---

[6] www.ameinfo.com/71357.html, accessed 29 November 2005.

project was the first CSR project run by Harry Winston in the Middle East and reflected its commitment to the Dubai community.

Nicaise writes that CSR is an integral part of Harry Winston's business practice, policy and operational strategy designed to address the ethical, social and environmental impacts of its business operations. Winston is acutely aware, Nicaise says, 'of the fact that CSR activities need to be constantly developing in pace with society, the environment and the corporation's business activities.'

Nicaise's example shows, and there are many more, that Type I or philanthropic contributions are still the norm for CSR in the Middle East, which is unsurprising given the strong influence of Islam and its equally strong focus on giving to the under-privileged. However, issues such as stakeholder dialogue, accountability and transparency that are inherent in the CSR approach are still some way away from being taken seriously across the Middle East.

Africa

Corporate social responsibility must be defined more widely than mere charitable cheque writing by corporates operating in Africa. CSR is more than philanthropy. There is an unfortunate tradition of corporates using philanthropy as a respectable means of buying off stakeholders to accept their operating practices.[7]

Many argue that it is trade and not aid that can unlock Africa's vast potential. The WBSCD, for instance (and this is a common enough viewpoint), insists that companies should urge governments to work toward removing distorting tariffs and establishing, as part of CSR, an open, transparent, rule-based global marketplace.[8] It believes that development benefits could be enormous, citing estimates that suggest that if Africa could just gain an additional one percentage point share of global trade, it would earn $70 billion more in exports each year, more than three times what the region currently receives in international assistance. Thus, the benefits of increased trade are much greater than the benefits of increased aid.

As the AICC notes, some of the key CSR trends in Africa are foreign, with the UK and the US setting the agenda.[9] A controversial point that AICC raises is whether this makes CSR a 'colonialist' concept. Clearly, if CSR is promoted by foreign advisers to cover developed country based corporations and their wholly owned subsidiaries, then CSR imperialism does not apply. But there are few, if any, corporations of that ilk. It is more

[7] African Institute of Corporate Citizenship (AICC) www.aiccafrica.com/PDF% 20files/AICC%20Press%20pack/CSR%20trends%20in%20Africa.pdf, accessed 30 November 2005
[8] WBCSD (2005) 'Business for development', Geneva, September, p77.
[9] See AICC web reference in note 7.

tricky when CSR is advocated by foreigners for key suppliers in developing countries to developed countries or wholly owned corporations that are based in Africa (or for that matter other developing countries).

Insofar as the products created by these latter companies are made for export then certainly the consumers of these products can ask whether they have been produced in a socially responsible manner and, if not, they can either buy elsewhere and/or bring pressure to bear on the local company. It would then be clear to the local company that not acting in a socially responsible manner would harm its reputation and its trading opportunities. Hence CSR and trade are closely interlinked and we are likely to see this discussed more in the future. But CSR is not just a stick; there is also a carrot effect whereby an enhanced reputation will lead to increased trading possibilities, increased profitability and the growth of companies in developing countries.

However this does not cover all the issues. First there are those large companies that only trade internally in Africa – local construction companies, SMEs that provide local services such as hairdressers, decorators, drivers and so on and, of course, the public sector that is not normally involved in commerce. Second, there are companies that produce products that may be consumed locally but are global goods. Oil is an obvious example where domestic production and domestic consumption from one company affect the global oil market (local production and consumption will produce downward price effects, albeit probably marginal) but it is only traded internally. Unfortunately, stopping such companies from using forced labour, starvation wages, sweatshops, child labour and other forms of exploitation could be seen as 'colonialist'. Happily, the international organizations do have a mandate, signed by most African governments, to halt such practices. Consequently, helping African governments and companies to become socially responsible does have a mandate and the 'colonialist' argument for most, if not all, CSR actions does not hold.

These issues, as one might expect, are hotly debated in the academic literature. In a 10-year review of research on Corporate Citizenship in Africa, Wayne Visser found that the few papers that do exist focus upon business ethics and, then, mainly on South Africa.[10] In his introduction to *Business Ethics: A European Review*, a special issue on Africa, Rossouw, cited by Visser, claimed that 'the first signs of academic life in business ethics on the African continent can be traced back to the 1980s' but he concedes that it remains fragmented and limited. Rossouw argues that CSR (he calls it corporate citizenship) in Africa has its own unique features, distinct from other regions in the world and observes that there are:

> *three areas that characterize business ethics in Africa: (1) On the macro-level, the influence of Africa's colonial and neo-*

---

[10] Wayne Visser (2005) 'Research on corporate citizenship in Africa: A ten year review (1995–2005)', International Centre for Corporate Social Responsibility, Nottingham University, UK.

colonial past; (2) On the meso-level, the moral responsibility of business towards the reconstruction of African societies; and (3) On the micro-level, the way in which individual businesses deal with affirmative action measures to overcome the consequences of historical racism, sexism and economic exclusion.[11]

Latin America and Asia

There are many activities in these two large regions and it would not be possible to cover all the various issues. So, here I will look at the three largest countries in these regions – Brazil, China and India – and map out what has been happening, briefly, in terms of CSR.

Brazil

In Brazil CSR programmes have tended to have the characteristics of 'social interventions'. These programmes are often designed and developed in the name of the firms, but in alliance with state agencies (at local or state level). President Lula, a strong trade unionist, has promoted the alliance of public social programmes and business social policy while at the same time coping with a move toward deregulation. Often these arrangements involve the mediation of business associations or institutes, which are already in place, to administer previous philanthropic donations to community programmes. But not all is as it seems to be in Brazil, as Emilio Klein remarks:[12]

> *... in that country everything is there on paper, perfectly neat and rational. But when you check the reality then things are very different. I would say that roughly in Latin America large corporations, and almost all enterprises, lack something that is essential in the background of your definition: fairness. They are unfair with their stakeholders, both inside and outside, and they can be so because they have all the power, including of course the government. If you add to that their short-term perspective, then you get what we get here. Employees, customers, purveyors or whatever, are being squeezed and pushed around by business, particularly those related to basic services (privatized), financial services and commerce.*

CSR is moving slightly away from pure philanthropy in Brazil, but the strong philanthropic concern of many people in Brazil is quite noticeable. It should

---

[11] Visser, 'Research on corporate citizenship in Africa', Introduction.
[12] Emilio Klein, personal communication, July 2006.

be pointed out that philanthropy is not the exclusive domain of business. Surveys cited by Cappellin and Giuliani for the year 2000 show, surprisingly for a developing country, that more than 70 per cent of the adult population donates goods and money to institutions or needy people.[13]

The same authors note that CSR became part of a broader strategy to gain legitimacy; a way of 'cleaning up the soiled image of entrepreneurs and companies that were regarded by many as responsible for the concentration of wealth and growing speculation in financial investment. Brazilian entrepreneurs could use CSR as a tool to restore the climate of trust among workers, enhance their competitive strategy and, above all, increase consumer loyalty and community acceptance.'

Right through Latin America there has been a strong influence of governments on the protection of workers within companies. This is promising, but care has to be taken that those workers *in* jobs do not benefit excessively over those *out* of jobs. One might also call this a 'Latin' phenomenon' since developed countries such as Spain and France also have strong worker protection mechanisms that are leading to poor labour market flexibility. Indeed the growth of the so-called 'informal sector' in Latin America can partially be attributed to the difficulty of obtaining 'protected' jobs in the formal company sector.

Concern with social issues in business in Brazil has a long history. One of the first groups to introduce social consciousness to the business field was the Associação de Dirigentes Cristãos de Empresas do Brasil (ADCE-Brasil), a branch of the International Christian Union of Business Executives (UNIAPAC). The ADCE was founded in São Paulo in 1961. In 1974, the association published an important document, Decálogo do Empresario, which contained, for the first time, an explicit proposal to link business management with social responsibility.

More recently, CSR activities have been promoted by the internationally well-known 'Instituto Ethos', which has encouraged firms not only to take a broader view of CSR but also to show how CSR can actually increase the owners' wealth. According to the mission of the institute, social responsibility should lead beyond the classic social investment model that is characterized by isolated initiatives related to the firm's economic objectives. Instituto Ethos offers its members services such as information on best practices and CSR, business networking, consultant expertise and publications. During 2000, it introduced a code of ethics for firms and published indicators of social responsibility.[14]

Voluntary codes of conduct have grown significantly around the world in the last two decades and, according to Cappellin and Giuliani, their codes are sometimes transferred from the parent company to the Brazilian factory.

---

[13] Paola Cappellin and Gian Mario Giuliani (2004) 'The political economy of corporate responsibility in Brazil, social and environmental dimensions', Technology, Business and Society Programme Paper Number 14, UNRISD, Geneva, October.
[14] See AICC web reference in note 7.

However, their research of 60 national and local business associations and of 12 national and international firms indicated that very few Brazilian companies have adopted a code of conduct.

When one thinks about social responsibility in Latin America, the first thought that comes to mind is 'corruption'. In Brazil, the problem has even involved its leaders – for instance, President Fernando Collor de Mello was forced out of office in 1992 on corruption charges. As the *Guardian* noted, 'There is little evidence that the private sector is taking a lead to prevent this state of affairs. While the majority (78 per cent) of Brazil's largest companies have anti-corruption codes, fewer than a quarter (22 per cent) report having investigated employees suspected of offering or receiving bribes. A smaller number still (14 per cent) have ever sacked anyone as a result.'[15]

Data published by Transparency International (TI), which since 1995 has published the Corruption Perceptions Index (CPI), show that bribery remains a major problem at all levels of public service throughout Latin America.[16] In a survey of 17 nations, only one came close to the upper limits: Chile, with 7.5 points out of a possible 10 but, even then, was still 17th out of 158 countries in 2005. Brazil showed some improvement during the three polls since 1995. In 1995, Brazil was considered one of the most corrupt of 41 countries (ranked 37). In the most recent poll (available in 2005) Brazil more or less maintained its middle-of-the-road position coming 62nd out of the 158 countries – note that our other two surveyed countries fared worse, with China in position 78 and India at 88.

According to Capellin and Giuliani, social responsibility is still considered to have limited usefulness. Three broad difficulties are identified. Union leaders recognize CSR as a positive approach, yet its application thus far has been limited. It has not reversed corporate agendas and practices vis-à-vis workers. Second, the approach of Brazilian firms to social responsibility does not yet include the trade unions as partners. Finally, in commitments to CSR, firms do not make room for a social monitoring mechanism. Hence corporate social responsibility does not overcome the classic unilateral business perspective. However, this view is not confined solely to Brazil. Many trade union organizations see CSR as a tool through which business can reduce the influence of trade unions. On the other hand those companies that have embraced wider discussions with trade unions have seen positive benefits, particularly in health and safety at work issues.[17]

China

There is increasing interest in CSR in China judging by the increase in news stories on the subject. As Chenyan Liu, for example, states: 'The [press]

---

[15] *The Guardian*, 25 July 2005.
[16] http://ww1.transparency.org/cpi/2005/cpi2005_infocus.html, accessed 3 March 2006.
[17] Personal communication from BAT's CSR manager, Adrian Payne.

messages are diverse, but the common theme in each of these pieces is that CSR isn't confined to one single aspect (as is often portrayed in the Chinese press). CSR is not a trade barrier, a certificate (i.e., SA8000), a burden or a slogan.'[18]

Nicola Macbean further notes, 'CSR has risen up the policy agenda as politicians and business leaders respond to criticism from consumer groups, NGOs and trade unions that big business is exploiting the vulnerable in its global search for profit.'[19]

But, does CSR mean the same thing in China as in the West? In the West CSR is seen as linking to all stakeholders and has led to the growing area of 'stakeholder dialogue'. The main stakeholders in the West are, inside the company, owners, company boards, managers, employees, shareholders, and outside the company, consumers, local communities, trade unions, suppliers and government. Clearly, since there are so many stakeholders, handling the information generated has become more and more difficult. In China, government is a key stakeholder – much more so than in the West – through the many SOEs (State Operated Enterprises) and, through its dominance of the Chinese State, in most decisions affecting the private sector.

In the West, too, there are many differing views on CSR. The most radical stance is that the only social responsibility of a company should be to make a profit. More tempered views argue that it is not profits that are the problem, since a company must make profits to survive. The issue is not profits at any cost but how profits are made. Exploiting the labour force to make profits is now generally frowned upon. And this is true right across the Western countries and is becoming more of an issue in China.

In China, the 1994 Labour Law established national labour standards including the payment of locally set minimum wages, a maximum number of hours overtime and health and safety requirements. But, according to Nicola Macbean, 'this and other employment legislation is poorly enforced and like many Chinese laws establishes programmatic goals rather than defendable rights'.[20] The department of labour administration at the local level is responsible for inspecting and supervising the application of minimum wages and other labour regulations with the local health department and environmental protection departments responsible for monitoring health and pollution aspects in the workplace.

Clearly, discussing CSR in 'China' is not an easy subject since the country is so large and diverse. The viewpoint on CSR in Beijing or Shanghai will change considerably as one moves away from the fast-developing east coast to the hinterland and, even more so, into the rural areas. Because of China's laws, it has been very difficult for rural workers to work in urban

---

[18] Chenyan Liu (2005) 'The spread of CSR in China', *CSR Asia Weekly*, vol 1, week 7, www.csr-asia.com, accessed 1 November 2005.
[19] Nicola Macbean (2003) 'China–Britain trade review', March.
[20] Nicola Macbean, op cit.

areas. This has led to a stark contrast growing between relatively developed urban cities and impoverished rural areas. Many workers in these latter areas have, more recently, been allowed into China's fast-growing industries that supply more developed markets and wages have gradually risen. However, China's 'pressure-cooker' polity is likely to lead to increasing problems from the rural areas if the distribution of income between rural and urban areas is not addressed rapidly.

So why would China be interested in CSR? There are perhaps six reasons:

1   *Reputation.* Increasingly consumers and investors require the companies they invest in to have a good reputation. If, at some point down the line, a company proves to be a rogue in some way, then consumers will flee, the value of the company will fall and investors will withdraw funds.
2   *Exploitation.* Overseas customers are more and more concerned that the goods they buy have been produced in harmonious environments where labour exploitation, child labour, environmental damage and so on do not exist.
3   *Supply chain probity.* The suppliers of both overseas business and domestic companies that supply overseas are increasingly being inspected as to their social responsibility. To date mainly the frontline suppliers have been under the microscope but as time goes on the suppliers of suppliers right down the supply chain will also be the subject of investigation.
4   *Corruption.* Transparency of operation and particularly anti-corruption measures are a major part of corporate responsibility. Corruption within companies leads to higher costs, more inefficiency and poor products and services.
5   *Foreign investment.* Investors will invest if they can be assured of good potential returns and stability. The stability of companies in which they invest is enhanced through transparency, lack of corruption and generally good CSR.
6   *Employee motivation* is enhanced with positive CSR policies. In the West the brightest skilled workers have shown their preference for working more with socially responsible companies than with others.

To convince China to move further down the CSR road, would introducing codes of conduct be the route to go? Clearly, the West has been very active in creating standards and codes of conduct. But, as Macbean has noted, this is not as easy to do in China since:

> *Supporting CSR principles by foreign companies in their operations in China can be highly problematic where activities span different working cultures and regulatory environments. Codes of conduct developed at head office do not translate easily into local practices and even languages. In Chinese the*

word 'stakeholder' (liyixiangguanzhe), a central concept in CSR, is a new term and few outside the social sciences recognize the word, let alone the meaning. At the heart of the criticism of social audits in China is the lack of independent worker consultation in verifying results.[21]

Disney, for example, found that it still could not satisfy its NGO critics even when it cancelled major production contracts with individual Guangdong suppliers. This led to an initiative by the International Council of Toy Industries to address the limited leverage of a single buyer to introduce an independent, ethical manufacturing auditing process that will be implemented by toy manufacturers representing more than 95 per cent of toys sold worldwide. The initiative has the public support of the Chinese and Hong Kong toy industries but, as Macbean argues, it is also likely to result in a consolidation of Chinese manufacturing into larger factories that can ensure good working conditions.

Perhaps the best way ahead is to try to rationalize codes of conduct with local laws in China. However, the mere inclusion in the law does not necessarily mean that the law is applied. Therefore many companies will find that best practices may well go further than basic legal requirements.

What more could be done to enhance CSR in China? A glance at the six reasons above illustrate that the business case for CSR is strong. So what are the key things that companies and the Chinese Government should look for when implementing CSR? A ten-point programme could look something like the following.

Action programme inside the company:

1   Develop a CSR strategy that includes an overall vision for the company's place in China. Decide what benefits and costs emanate from involvement in international initiatives such as the UN Global Compact, SA8000, ISO9000 and so on. Ensure there is a corporate commitment to CSR at board level and in management processes and local practices.
2   Investigate whether the company is paying a 'living wage' within the company and that it is paying its main suppliers properly and on time. If not, discover why not and then ask what steps should be taken to move towards this.
3   Work with trade unions and the government to ensure proper environmental and safety regimes within the company.
4   Ensure that CSR is not considered a luxury to add on later, that it is mainstreamed into the business model from the very beginning. Develop and apply indicators to monitor and evaluate the company's CSR strategy on a regular basis.

---

[21] Nicola Macbean, op cit.

Action programme outside the company:

5   Work with local UN and NGO organizations to increase the efficiency of development initiatives, including ensuring its tax contributions are used wisely.
6   Be pro-active in lending in-house training skills to a wider public.
7   Assist the creation and improvement of SMEs through the setting up of an advisory office and/or joining with other private sector or NGO partners.
8   Be involved in mentoring budding entrepreneurs.
9   Invest so as to support wider Chinese development objectives.
10 Ensure community or philanthropic company initiatives are sustainable in the development sense.

India

CSR is not a new term in India.[22] As far back as 1965, the then Prime Minister of India, Lal Shastri, presided over a national meeting that issued the following declaration on the Social Responsibilities of Business:

> *Business has responsibility to itself, to its customers, workers, shareholders and the community ... every enterprise, no matter how large or small, must, if it is to enjoy confidence and respect, seek actively to discharge its responsibilities in all directions ... and not to one or two groups, such as shareholders or workers, at the expense of community and consumer. Business must be just and humane, as well as efficient and dynamic.[23]*

The international CSR movement has certainly arrived in India. According to a report by the Centre for Social Markets for the International Finance Corporation (IFC), many leading foreign MNEs and domestic titans, pre-eminently members of the Tata Group, have been standard-setters on core CSR issues such as labour conditions, health and safety, environmental management, corporate governance and integrity.[24]

The Tata Group is, perhaps, the modern-day counterpart of the 19th-century Victorian industrialists and Quaker social reformers such as the

---

[22] CSM (2001) 'Corporate social responsibility: Perceptions of Indian business', Centre for Social Markets, July.

[23] *Ibid.*, p1.

[24] David St. Maur Sheil (2003) 'India: Report on SRI in Asian emerging markets', Centre for Social Markets, October, Report in Asian Emerging Markets, Sustainable Financial Markets Facility, SFMF, International Finance Corporation.

Lever Brothers and Cadbury family, who established company towns such as Port Sunlight and Bourneville in the UK. Indian families such as Tata and Godrej have a significant industry presence and reputation for social responsibility. One of the Tata Group of companies, Tata Steel, is the first in the country to produce a corporate sustainability report and it administers the only industry town in the world, Jamshedpur, which has received the ISO14001 environmental quality certification. Other companies have followed Tata's lead, such as Infosys, Ballarpur Industries Limited, Paharpur Business Park, Ford India, Samsung India Electronics and Cadbury's India. They have all produced environmental and social reports.

In recent years, too, some large and increasingly image- and market-conscious Indian companies have started signing up to voluntary international CSR initiatives. The UN Global Compact (www.unglobalcompact. org) is a good example. There are now some 87 Indian companies which have signed up to the Global Compact's nine principles on human rights, labour and the environment. Nevertheless, in India, as elsewhere, the IFC report above notes that the verification of corporate commitment to voluntary efforts is still a long way off.

There is some progress. The above-mentioned IFC report stated that the Confederation of Indian Industry (CII) (www.ciionline.org) – India's largest industry body – has taken a lead in promoting CSR among its membership. It has adopted a set of Social Principles with UNDP India and has appointed CSR officers in its regional offices. This has set a positive example to other industry bodies in India such as FICCI (Federation of Indian Chambers of Commerce and Industry), which have also held CSR-related events.

In 2001 a survey sent by e-mail by the Centre for Social Markets (CSM) to a cross-section of Indian businesses began by asking whether the terms 'Corporate Social and Environmental Responsibility' or 'Corporate Citizenship' meant anything to the respondent. If so, what? And, what relevance did they have for the respondent's company? Of those that replied, one in eight stated that CSR meant little to them. CSR was most commonly understood as a commitment or obligation to society. A total of 56 per cent of those who responded to this question made a link between community responsibilities and corporate citizenship.

The second survey question focused on the social responsibility of Indian companies. Respondents were asked to explain what they saw as the social responsibility of their company. They were also questioned on whether their company was living up to its responsibilities, and whether they felt more societal and business awareness of social responsibility was needed.

A total of 39 per cent of respondents referred to their social responsibilities as the creation of employment, developing proper promotional and training opportunities, and ensuring good working conditions. Approximately half of the survey respondents stated that they have a responsibility to help with social problems in India. On stakeholders, customers were clearly considered to be the most important followed by employees, share-holders and investors (banks) in that order. The community got a medium ranking, and unions and regulators were ranked as the stakeholders of least importance. The state was referred to by over a quarter of respondents as an obstacle to successful business. Problems included unclear, unpractical and poorly monitored regulations, poor infrastructure, a complicated tax system, and too much bureaucracy. There were also references made to cleaning up the corporate governance structure and clamping down on corruption.

Finally, survey respondents were asked which companies they considered to be models in their sector both in India and internationally. Of note, Infosys, Tata and Wipro were mentioned several times as models.

A dialogue on CSR and development

So CSR has made only halting progress within developing countries. The torch is still being held by the MNEs. But not everyone believes that MNEs hold the key to development. A dialogue reproduced here, between Nigel Carter, formerly of BP and the author, identifies some of the outstanding issues:[25]

NC: My background lies with BP and, especially, ten years living and working in Africa. I was, therefore, very interested in your paper but, on hearing it, slightly anxious as to the message you were giving.

MH: BP is now engaged in many countries in socio-economic 'development' – I think BP were involved only sporadically in development but these days have a slightly better appreciation.

NC: I have inferred that you generally seek to promote (multinational) corporations as the preferred vehicle for promoting wealth in newly developing countries.

MH: I would 'prefer' countries to sort out their own problems but my point is that the UN and governments have failed and therefore the residual is the private sector. I think the corporate sector can do much more but I don't rule out other mechanisms, hence I don't see corporations as the only route.

---

[25] Personal communication from Nigel Carter, 5 October 2005, following a presentation of my ideas in a speech at the University of Geneva, Geneva, 19 September 2005, and reproduced with Nigel's permission. His views are personal and do not reflect those of BP or his current employer.

NC: What was not clear to me was whether you thought that all corporations should be so involved, or whether, as I believe, it must be entrusted to those that are 'on the ground'?

MH: I think all corporations should consider where they are on the development issue and then fathom out what they can do.

NC: My belief is that the corporates will only be in a country if (1) they perceive a market for their goods, or (2) there are opportunities – mostly natural resources and labour – to exploit. Even if they are there, there is a prerequisite for them to conduct themselves in a responsible way – avoidance of corruption, resistance to the over-exploitation of access to foreign exchange, unfair transfer pricing, fair employment terms, among others. Many cooperates operate as parastatal companies with a substantial, if not preponderant membership of local appointees, fronted by a foreign national as chief executive. This does not preclude the abuse, albeit possibly only modest, whereby the local appointees enjoy access to foreign exchange, foreign trips and 'brown envelopes' which might not otherwise be reasonably accessible to the executives of quite large national organizations in those countries.

MH: I think this is the conventional view of the corporate world. The longer term view that I am advocating sees large corporations more actively involved in development.

NC: Before we give corporate 'carte blanche' to promote wealth, we need to ensure that they are operating in a sustainable and socially responsible way.

MH: I don't see why there needs to be different stages, the two aspects you mention can proceed hand-in-hand.

NC: I would just add a word on the debate about the exploitation of cheap labour. If companies are paying their employees a fair market rate in the countries in which they operate, this is not exploitation. If they are, as BP were, keen to demonstrate consistently that their pay levels were in the 'upper quartile', this is even better. If, for example, as Nike found to their cost, they are paying marginal rates, then they should rightly be condemned.

MH: Knowing what is the 'market rate' is not easy. Should the market rate be above the minimum wage? What happens when it is below? If the market wage is below subsistence living, is that acceptable? I firmly believe that wages should at least evolve to the point where they allow basic needs to be met in developing countries but, then, what is meant by basic needs? [I covered this issue in the previous chapter.]

NC: I hope that this adequately explains my angst.

MH: I think your view is very common, which doesn't mean I don't respect it. I have been surprised by how much companies have taken development on board in their operations – look at Microsoft and WHO for instance, or BP in Azerbaijan and Colombia.

Concluding remarks

The problems of under-development are huge. Related are other socio-political issues creating havoc – for instance, drug cultivation in Colombia, Bolivia, Ecuador, Afghanistan; conflict in Iraq, Afghanistan, Lebanon, Somalia, Congo, Sudan, Kashmir; expanding, rather than reducing, numbers of nations with nuclear weapons and the ability to deliver them; concerns about global warming and so on. It might therefore seem academic to worry about CSR, even more to believe that CSR can provide a route out of all these issues. There is no magic silver bullet to solve all these complex problems and issues. Yet CSR, when applied in developing countries, as it inevitably will, provides a peaceful approach to resolving problems. As companies and institutions reflect more on their social responsibilities the room for conflict must be reduced. If I could ask corporations in developing countries to ask their stakeholders to think for one minute about their social responsibilities at least once a year, I am convinced the world would become a better place.

10

Limitations of International Agencies

It's an open question whether Bolton's [US ambassador to the UN in 2006] throwing all the cards up in the air is meant to improve the council or to prove that the U.N. can't reform itself and therefore should be abandoned. (Kenneth Roth, executive director of Human Rights Watch)[1]

Introduction

It is curious for me to write under the above title, given that I have been involved in the development activities of the United Nations, its agencies, its development banks as a researcher and then consultant for several decades. In fact, given the strong negative pressure on the UN that is prevalent, particularly from the powerful Republicans in the US (as the above quote highlights in a nutshell), my overall impression is that it does a good job on development, even at times outstanding, with the very small resources at its disposal. But, as I shall argue here, its impact on development is, unfortunately, a mere drop in the ocean. I shall use 'UN' in the following to abbreviate for all its agencies.

Size of UN

One of the problems is that the UN is actually a small organization. The total operating expenses for the entire UN system – including the World Bank, IMF and all the UN funds, programmes and specialized agencies – came to some $18.2 billion a year at the turn of the 21st century. This is less than the size of many MNEs – General Electric, for instance, had a market capitalization of US$350 billion in 2004, and Exxon Mobil had

---

[1] Warren Hoge (2006) 'U.S. Isolated in Opposing Plan for a New U.N. Rights Council', *New York Times*, 4 March 2006.

profits of around US$32 billion in 2005 – and is dwarfed by military expenditure – US$80 billion a year just on Iraq by the US in 2005. The budget for the UN's core functions – the Secretariat operations in New York, Geneva, Nairobi, Vienna and five Regional Commissions – is $1.25 billion a year. This is about 4 per cent of New York City's annual budget – and nearly a billion dollars less than the yearly cost of Tokyo's Fire Department. It is $3.7 billion less than the annual budget of New York's State University system.[2]

Despite allegations of an increasingly bloated UN, there are fewer posts today than in previous years. The UN's budget for 2004–2005, for example, provides for 9288 positions, compared with 10,021 posts in 1996–1997.[3] Yet for over a decade, the UN has faced a debilitating financial crisis and it has been forced to cut back on important programmes in all areas. Many member states have not paid their full dues and have cut their donations to the UN's voluntary funds. As of 31 December 2004, members arrears to the regular budget topped $357 million, of which the US alone owed $241 million (68 per cent of the regular budget).

Self-fulfilling prophecy

However, therein lies at least one of the UN's major problems. As anyone reading this book will know, a declining or stagnant organization is a very difficult place within which to work. The constant barrage of criticism, led by the US, going as far back as the dawn of the UN,[4] has not helped the organization and it is not surprising that the most hostile administration ever to internationalism, the 2000–2008 Bush administration, can report that the UN organization 'suffers from poor management, 'dismal' staff morale and lack of accountability and professional ethics'.[5] The US, of course, also pays the lion's share of the UN budget – 22 per cent of the UN budget, down from 25 per cent a few years ago and is therefore, easily, its most influential member. Consequently, one could argue that the current dismal state of affairs among the UN and its agencies stems as much from the poor service of the US than from almost any other country.

In a declining organization, job security is the main threat and what happens is that those lucky few who have so-called 'permanent' contracts survive while all the transient staff – young people with precarious contracts, consultants and so on are quickly chopped. But life and ideas come

---

[2] See www.ldb.org/vl/top/unfacts.htm.

[3] See www.un.int/usa/fact3.htm.

[4] The UN HQ was placed in New York in 1948 mainly to placate the US amid fears that the US would withdraw from any body that would become supra-national to it.

[5] Report of Congress mandated panel cited by Warren Hodge, *New York Times*, 13 June 2005.

into an organization through these latter people. The ones who stay are often not the most competent, frequently being placed in senior posts simply because they are related in some way to one incompetent dictator or politician and because the SG of the UN has his own debts to pay (patronage, for instance, to those who elected and support him).

The Peter Principle flourishes in the UN's system where everyone rises to their level of incompetence – remember that the Peter Principle promotes competent staff until they become incompetent and then they don't get promoted anymore. In the UN system, many senior positions are filled, by sideway movement, with incompetent people so there the Peter Principle works at double speed.

One area that has escaped much of the incompetence of the UN is in the so-called 'field'. In countries remote from the centres of the UN, surprisingly competent people can be found aided and abetted by young interns, JPOs (Junior Professional Officers, mainly from the developed countries) and the like. Occasionally, of course, the centre decides to reduce its own incompetence by sending an incompetent to head a field post. Often their negative effects can be nullified due to competent local staff who run the local office in spite of, rather than with, the new incompetent. Happily, the incompetent, not being a workaholic, will spend time enjoying the privileges of the position – being driven to 'important' meetings by the UN dedicated driver, travelling to 'important' conferences, especially those in attractive places and so on.

But does it matter?

If it is assumed that the UN is ineffective, the fact it is becoming smaller in staff and more incompetent should not really matter. However, no one seriously disputes the lofty ideals of the UN nor that it allows all the nations in the world to have a forum to attempt to resolve problems and issues which they would not otherwise have. But one cannot assume that the growing difficulty of the UN to deliver its programmes is both harmless or that someone else such as an NGO or private sector organization can take up the slack.

Take, for instance, the UNHCR (United Nations High Commission for Refugees) that has the job of coping with cross-border movements of, in the main, persecuted people. Among other agencies such as the Red Cross, International Organization for Migration, OCHA and the like, the UNHCR has a poor reputation for delivery, its staff are rarely respected and incompetence is rife. For instance, one staff officer involved in managing a major initiative financed by the EU to assess the status of a certain group of refugees attempting to enter Europe was so out of depth that she had to hire a full-time assistant to do her job for her. She spent more time worrying about the daily allowances of consultants, travelling on 'mission' and gossiping in the corridors than doing her job. She was not allowed to hire competent people because she was forced to choose from several hundred 'floaters' with permanent contracts in the UNHCR, but without jobs since they had returned from the 'field' but did not have the necessary competence for available jobs and were simply supernumeraries to the capacity of absorption of the organization. Her boss was seriously ill and could only come into the office occasionally but, perhaps a blessing in disguise, he could not travel. The upshot is that the project became seriously behind schedule, costs increased, and the main people who suffered were the poor refugees who cannot be helped due to project delays. This is just one more story to add fuel to the critics of the UN.

Reform is required. But as will be seen next, reform revolves around transparency and accountability and not around how the work is carried out and the disastrous personnel policies of the organization. Furthermore, there is no easy way to replace the UNHCR. Private companies will see no profit in dealing with refugees except of course to deliver services that are paid for by the UNHCR and donor countries.

Is more transparency and accountability the answer?

The new mantra is the title of this section. No organization escapes from this mantra these days and it has even found its way into the CSR of organizations. I wonder how much effort has been expended by the new CSR organizations such as AccountAbility[6] to balance the costs of increased accountability against benefits, and to whom? There are none that I know of.

When the Minister of State for Work and Pensions was pressed in the summer of 2005 during the ILO summer conference (by the author) to explain why the UK, along with the US, had vetoed the ILO budget, he explained that it was because there was a need for more 'transparency and accountability (T&A)' because there was too much waste. In principle this sounds fine but in practice these simple ideas drive the organizations into the ground through giving more power to the bureaucrats to control and less to the innovative thinkers. An insider in the ILO told me that the 2005 budget process had tripled the use of senior staff who had to be taken away from more productive duties. Thus the mantra of T&A is driving the UN organizations into more bureaucracy and less delivery, which is not quite what is intended. Clearly, a serious rethink is required by those sanctimonious bodies who are calling for more T&A, without considering what is involved.

One organization approaching sclerosis because of the double mantra is the EU. It sits on a pile of cash that it finds difficult to get out of the door.

---

[6] See www.accountability.org.

To preserve T&A stemming from a series of so-called scandals (one 'non-scandal' which led to the folding up of a totally innocent scheme for the training of statisticians was that of Eurostat), its tendering system is perhaps the most complicated and, one might say petty, of all international organizations. No company can bid and be accepted for even a small contract, say one of €100,000 without having proved it has handled such contracts before. It might be argued that this is good, because it would not be appropriate for companies with zero experience to bid and win contracts. Yet, most new employment comes from small companies (with less than ten employees) who therefore have little chance of getting on the EU ratchet.

So, what happens in practice is that large companies, which have the resources to devote full-time individuals to bid for contracts, become successful. These companies tend to become 'body shops' where they put together collections of individual professionals whom they know about but who do not work for them. The larger companies cream off the benefits (mark-ups on individual fee rates) and force down the salaries of their hires. The latter, who cannot get a step on the ladder, are forced to accept lower and lower fees over time. Indeed, should a small firm manage to win an EU contract, they may wait a long time to be paid, even as they fill out all the lengthy forms that ensure 'transparency and accountability'. The EU then finds itself with a mountain of cash that it cannot get out of the door because of its cumbersome tender and bid process.

The UN's main development arms

The UN has two main development arms – the World Bank and the UNDP.[7] They work largely in competition with each other. The World Bank does not consider itself part of the UN system even though, for instance, its staff travel on the highly prized UN passports (aka laissez-passer). The World Bank is largely insular to outside influences, as can be noted when looking through its published output – rarely do these documents refer to outside (i.e. outside the World Bank) sources. Its head is nominated by the US and, consequently, the World Bank's policies are closely aligned with those of the US. The 2005 appointment to be head of the World Bank, Wolfowitz, caused a stir in development circles since some parties believe him to be the man behind the Iraq war and therefore he was not seen as someone likely to bring harmony into the World Bank's relations with developing countries. The main industrialized countries realized the potential harm that the new

---

[7] There are, of course, many aspects to 'development' and it is addressed in many of the UN regional arms (such as its Economic Commission for Latin America), its specialized agencies (such as the World Health Organization or International Labour Organization) or its offshoots such as UNESCO.

man could bring and, for the first time ever, invited him to Europe to be 'interviewed' by the main EU countries. But the 'interview' process was a sham, since there was little doubt that the EU countries (even France and Germany who have different axes to grind) would go along with the US and Wolfowitz was duly appointed.

The UNDP is the main development arm of the UN in the sense that it promotes human development in all the 170 countries or so where it operates. It has a pitifully small budget, averaging something like $3 million per country. These funds are more often than not supplemented by the local national governments – in richer developing countries such as the UAE these support the whole budget. Alternatively, in countries such as Honduras with a regular budget of around $3 million, up to US$300 million has been raised through partnerships with the private sector. These figures can be misleading, since UNDP will often only take a percentage of these funds for development activities. The main difference between the UNDP and the World Bank is that the former has representatives from all countries and operates a one-country-one-vote rule, while the World Bank is influenced by one-dollar-one-vote; that is, the richer countries have a larger say in its affairs. More recently the development models portrayed by the World Bank and the UNDP have converged, particularly since the UNDP was headed by a former World Bank official, Mark Malloch Brown, who then went on to be Deputy to the UN Secretary-General, and was immediately followed by yet another former World Bank official – Kemal Dervis.[8]

The development policy of the two arms

Both development arms – the World Bank and the UNDP – have been promoting the private sector in their development efforts and, in the last few years, a greater emphasis has been placed on the notion of CSR. The World Bank has at least five units that deal with CSR issues, while the UNDP has been content to work under the umbrella of the UN Global Compact, of which more below.

The development models that each follows are different. The World Bank (and the IMF and WTO – the so-called Bretton Woods organizations named after the location where they were first mooted) have, for the past 20 years or so followed the 'Washington Consensus', which is essentially a free market model based upon the Chicago school of monetary economics. All countries wishing to receive either World Bank or IMF support must make vigorous efforts to allow the market its full potential while reducing

---

[8] Which does not mean to imply that they have not done a good job, both former World Bank officials continued, and even expanded a little, the positive development work of the UNDP.

the power and reach of the public sector. In theory this sounds promising, however, in practice few countries had the necessary institutions in place to develop the private sector and 'sleights of hand' by many countries led to loans being received and quickly transferred to the overseas bank accounts of the controlling despots. Realizing that their strategy had not succeeded in every case, the new 'mantra' is one of democracy, transparency, anti-corruption and, wait for it, 'accountability'. Again, in theory, this all sounds well and good but, in practice, the need for increased T&A is likely to lead to increased bureaucracy and less efficiency. This is precisely what the Bretton Woods institutions do not want. The conventional wisdom of these institutions continues, as remarked by Jan Vandemoortelle of UNDP, 'to perceive poverty reduction as a universal "good" that will result as an automatic by-product of economic growth and macro-economic stability. Governments and their partners find it difficult to translate the concept of "pro-poor growth" into practice'.[9]

The UNDP meanwhile is on the sidelines and playing a more complex game. It cannot ignore the Washington consensus yet it tends to be much more pragmatic in its dealing with developing countries. Arguably, this is because the organization is closer to the field with offices in nearly every developing country (only over the past decade has the World Bank been implementing this model) and therefore deals with more practical problems of development than just loans and credit. Also, the influence of the US is less, so the UNDP's Executive Board[10] is composed of a wider variety of developing countries and is more subject to the one-country-one-vote philosophy of the UN than the one-dollar-one-vote dominance of the Bretton Woods organizations.[11]

Critics of the UNDP development model might say it is too focused on improving the efficiency of governance, reducing poverty through public programmes and working with radical NGOs. Certainly, the UNDP must have its programmes approved by the host government but then, so does the World Bank. The devil is in the detail. The World Bank deals with the

---

[9] Jan Vandemoortelle: 'A Look at MDG progress', *Sustainable Development International*, 13th edition, 1 March 2005, available on: www.sustdev.org/index. php?option=com_content&task=view&id=365&Itemid=34.

[10] The UNDP Executive Board is made up of representatives from 36 countries around the world, who serve on a rotating basis. Through its Bureau, consisting of representatives from five regional groups, the Board oversees and supports the activities of UNDP, ensuring that the organization remains responsive to the evolving needs of programme countries. (Source: www.undp.org)

[11] Who Runs the World Bank Group? The World Bank is run like a cooperative, with its member countries as shareholders. The number of shares a country has is based roughly on the size of its economy. The United States is the largest single shareholder, with 16.41 per cent of votes, followed by Japan (7.87 per cent), Germany (4.49 per cent), the UK (4.31 per cent) and France (4.31 per cent). The rest of the shares are divided among the other member countries. (Source: www.world-bank.org)

most 'important' institutions of a country, such as its central bank, ministries of economy and finance, and thereby has more influence. Furthermore,
the revolving door of these latter ministries often means that their key staff
have just worked for the Bretton Woods institutions or are just about to.
The UNDP tends to deal more with the 'weaker' ministries of education,
health, labour, environment and its main government counterpart is the
ministry of foreign affairs or relations which, in turn, has less influence in
the country. In turn this means that the UNDP, dealing with weaker ministries, has more potential to propagate its ideas and therefore may even be
more successful in influencing development.

The UN's impact on meeting the MDGs

The Millennium Development Goals (MDGs) arose in 2000 as key targets
for the development community. They consist of eight main goals:[12]

1 Eradicate extreme poverty and hunger
2 Achieve universal primary education
3 Promote gender equality and empower women
4 Reduce child mortality
5 Improve maternal health
6 Combat HIV/AIDS, malaria and other diseases
7 Ensure environmental sustainability
8 Develop a global partnership for development.

Associated with these goals are 18 targets, of which the two that explicitly
mention the private sector are:

■ Target 17: In cooperation with pharmaceutical companies, provide
  access to affordable, essential drugs in developing countries.
■ Target 18: In cooperation with the private sector, make available the
  benefits of new technologies, especially information and communications.

In turn, each target has one or more associated indicators to assess progress
leading to a total of 48 indicators.
    The idea is useful as it provides a target that allows the mobilization
of funds and guidance for the development community. The main problem
is that one country that satisfies one criteria is likely to have also satisfied
others. On the other hand many countries pay lip service to signing up
for the goals, even to the extent of changing their laws but, in practice, do
nothing.

---

[12] The full details are available on http://ddp-ext.worldbank.org/ext/MDG/home-
Pages.do.

In terms of whether countries have themselves progressed in meeting the MDGs, we can turn to a paper by the technical head of MDG analysis at the UNDP, Jan Vandemoortelle. He noted that:

> *only a quarter of the required progress was achieved in the 1990s. Progress towards gender equality in primary schooling was on-track but for the wrong reason. Enrolment increased modestly for girls but stagnated for boys. Hence, the apparent improvement in the ratio between girls and boys depicts a misleading picture.'* ... *the world is not on-track to meeting the global MDG targets by 2015 ... The 2015-targets will remain elusive without substantial increases of foreign aid from wealthier nations. Sadly, aid efforts declined by one-third in the 1990s. But the adoption of the MDGs seems to have reversed the trend. Official Development Assistance (ODA) has increased in recent years. Five countries already meet the international aid target of 0.7 per cent of gross national income; three of them are now aiming for an aid level of 1 per cent. Six others have set specific deadlines for reaching the 0.7-target.*[13]

Little mentioned is that the private sector was also once involved in the 0.7 target. Harris Gleckman, one of the founders of this idea, noted that the mantra of 0.7 per cent for development has focused attention on governmental contributions to development.[14] But the original proposal was 1 per cent of GNP, which was to be composed of both governmental *and* private sector contributions. Over time, the 1 per cent became, in the public mind, 0.7 per cent; and the private sector match was forgotten, although it was never formally reduced and the private sector contribution was never formally rescinded from intergovernmental negotiations.

Returning to the MDGs, Vandemoortelle notes that, more depressingly, 'Anti-poverty strategies look strikingly similar, even for countries that face very different challenges. By and large, the targets have not enlarged pro-

---

[13] See footnote 9.

[14] Harris Gleckman in 'One Percent for Development: The lost history of a 0.3 per cent of GNP standard for MNEs, and an argument for its resurrection', Financing for Development Co-ordinating Secretariat, Department of Economic and Social Affairs, New York, United Nations, 2005 (Gleckman@un.org). This paper was prompted by a question asked of the Conference Secretariat during the Financing for Development (FFD) preparatory process. The delegates asked, what was the origin and rationale for the well-known 0.7 per cent for development – where did this crucial number come from? A quick poll of colleagues in the FFD Co-ordinating Secretariat and the Department of Economic and Social Affairs produced a series of tantalizing leads but no clear unequivocal history of this classic development target.

poor policy choices at the country level; neither have they influenced the conduct of the international aid business.'

So can business provide the way forward for the MDGs? Undoubtedly the main effort will be with the public sectors but, as a recent report 'Business and the Millennium Goals: A framework for action' developed by the UNDP and the IBLF noted: 'most companies can have some impact on development and can make a contribution in the following spheres of influence:

■ core business activities – in the workplace, the marketplace and along the supply chain;
■ social investment and philanthropy activities;
■ engagement in public policy dialogue and advocacy activities.'[15]

On 14 June 2005, business executives from over 30 countries joined UN Secretary-General Kofi Annan, President Jacques Chirac and Prime Minister Tony Blair in a meeting to emphasize and clarify the role that business must play in achieving the MDGs. The report of that meeting, organized under the auspices of the UN Global Compact, noted that in 'today's global society, business interests increasingly overlap with development objectives; however Government efforts have not effectively taken this transition into account and, therefore, the full potential of the private sector remains untapped.' Its report further noted that:

> *Government, business and civil society must work together to reach the MDGs. Based on historic roles, Government and civil society are assumed to be the natural actors for carrying out development-related activities. It is only more recently, as the pace of globalization has quickened, that the existence and success of responsible businesses has been acknowledged as a positive force in spurring development and improving human conditions. Now, it is time for Government and civil society to welcome business to the development table. Without a bounty of cross-sector partnerships – taking advantage of each group's strengths and resources – and a more distinct role for business in the development agenda, the task of raising living standards for billions of humans will not be realized. Identifying clear methods and mechanisms for cooperation and dialogue among sectors is the only way to meet the MDGs.[16]*

Alert readers will notice that both reports were issued under the auspices of the UN's Global Compact, which will be discussed further below. But what

---

[15] www.unglobalcompact.org/content/NewsEvents/mdg_bus/mdg_jamshed.pdf.
[16] www.unglobalcompact.org/content/NewsEvents/mdg_bus/mdg_paris.pdf.

is clear is that governments and the UN, despite valiant efforts, are failing to meet the MDGs and that is why a call to business has been made.[17]

ILO and CSR

The ILO World Commission on the Social Dimension of Globalization distinguished between corporate governance and CSR as two essentially different concepts. The former, the Commission states, is 'essentially concerned with issues of ownership and control of enterprises' but it then cites OECD principles of Corporate Governance, that good corporate governance 'helps to ensure that corporations take into account the interests of a wide range of constituencies, as well as the communities within which they operate'. The Commission defined CSR to be 'the voluntary initiatives enterprises undertake over and above their legal obligations'. The Commission report reflects the IOE's view that CSR is a set of 'initiatives by companies voluntarily integrating social and environmental concerns in their business operations and in their interaction with their stakeholders'.[18] Moreover, in the IOE's own submission to the World Commission the IOE sees CSR to be 'a core aspect of business activities throughout a company and recognizes CSR as a means of engagement with stakeholders in the various markets in which a company operates'.

It is interesting that the World Commission document and IOE both see the legislative part of business in society as corporate governance, while the voluntary part is CSR. This latter view is controversial. A major concern for multinationals is the issue of legislation. Many of the bigger companies, in fact, welcome some legislation since it helps to create a level playing field. But the question is not whether CSR should be voluntary or not but where on the scale between no legislation and total legislation the pointer should be set. For instance, many companies are happy with rules about child labour and approach the ILO for guidance. But as Philip Jennings, the General Secretary of Union Network International, noted:

> *Companies and governments overwhelmingly want the public both to believe in the ethical corporation and at the same time do not want to provide new legal backing for tighter ethical behaviour... But the ethics genie is out of the bottle and its operational principles are proving difficult to control. Another*

---

[17] A report on the relative contributions of a company and an NGO to the MDGs has been supported by Novib Oxfam Netherlands and ABN Amro Bank, and carried out by Dutch Sustainability Research. (DSR) (2005) 'Measuring the contribution of civil society and the private sector to achieving the Millennium Development Goals', November, The Netherlands, NCDO.

[18] International Organization of Employers: 'Corporate Social Responsibility: An IOE Approach', 21 March 2003, Geneva.

big change is that workers and citizens as stakeholders can now be involved directly with powerful corporations. Traditional global standards (ILO/OECD) are mainly administered through governments: their exercise is remote and complex.[19]

Both the ILO and the IOE insist on voluntary initiatives for CSR. Yet, there will always be both voluntary and prescriptive rules for corporate behaviour, including for social aspects since there is always some social legislation which limits what corporations can do or obliges them to do something such as respect for minimum wages. Thus defining CSR as a set of voluntary initiatives misses the point that there is a dividing line between voluntary and obligatory. Both the ILO and the IOE would make a useful contribution by being clear on which issues require legislation and which do not. To a certain extent, the CSR and legislation issue is a red herring since the most important point is that countries often have excellent social legislation but, in practice, the legislation is ignored.

What is clear is that ILO has been left behind, to date, as a major contributor to the debate on CSR. The ILO tends to be reactive rather than pro-active. On the other hand, ILO work covers a substantial amount of the CSR ground, particularly related (but not confined) to the labour area, without calling it such. The ILO could make a major contribution both to the debate and improving people's lives through focusing its efforts.

So what does business think?

An online discussion in July 2005 on business and the MDGs was organized by the World Bank expressly to discuss the MDGs with business. A number of useful conclusions resulted and I have chosen a few that corroborate many of the ideas in this book and also illustrate what business is thinking.[20]

John Banda, General Manager from JJ Enterprise, highlighted problems of working with the government of Malawi including time delays, the problem of working with well-funded NGOs that are hesitant to work with small firms in Malawi, and the problem of working with local banks that often take too long to approve working capital loans to provide quick service to the NGOs. John Banda's Keys to Success of Any Partnership are:

- transparency and accountability to both parties;
- achieving the intended goal of the partnership;
- accepting each other's ideas if they are constructive;

---

[19] Philip J. Jennings, UNI General Secretary, Union Network International; www.union-network.org/uniindep.nsf/0/0240DE313E8F1A64C1256E5A0043FA88?OpenDocument.
[20] See www.businessandmdgs.org/.

- being flexible to change if there are unforeseen circumstances;
- communicating immediately all urgent matters.

Raul Martinez is the Director of Institutional Development for CEMEX in Mexico. CEMEX is a leading global producer and marketer of cement and ready-mix concrete products. He encouraged companies to clearly define their vision for CSR. In 2005, CEMEX called for the creation of innovative products that generate social and environmental benefits such as concrete pavements that utilize used and crushed tyres, helping to eliminate a waste problem for most cities, and reducing product costs at the same time.

CEMEX also learned how low-income populations build their homes in Mexico and found that finance was the critical challenge for these communities to be able to buy construction materials to build their homes. In response, CEMEX developed a savings and credit programme that allows poor people to save money, but also to obtain credit based on their own savings. Thus far, more than 112,000 low-income families have borrowed more than 45 million dollars which have allowed the construction of the equivalent of 75,000 new rooms of 10 square metres.

Raul Martinez also addressed the issue of the potential impact of businesses around the world to reduce poverty by noting that generalized and extreme poverty was the normal condition of human existence for thousands of years. Some 200 years ago, private enterprises – fuelled by the industrial revolution – began to change things.

> *The most important social responsibility task for the private sector is to manage our companies efficiently in order to grow, to create more jobs, to pay taxes religiously, and to create value for all stakeholders.*
>
> *This is not intended to be a Friedman-style statement that the responsibility for a company is nothing but to generate profits, but if companies are to prosper, the most important condition is to have a government and a social system that applies fiscal, legal, educational, security, and credit frameworks that strongly support business activities. If this had been done worldwide, I assume that over a billion people would not be living in extreme poverty.*
>
> *Philanthropy (a little help for some in need) is good, but nothing but an aspirin.*

To reduce poverty worldwide to minimum terms, in a couple of decades, businesses should be called to action the same way that proletarians were called to unite and fight more than a century ago – 'Companies of the world, unite yourselves and fight for better conditions to grow and invest in the developing countries.'

Once countries in need understand that they must change (that must be our fight), things will improve. At the same time, companies must look to their operations and aim to give their working families a good life in which to learn, enjoy what they do, get back home early and educate their children, and seek to protect the environment. They must make sure that stockholders and investors have good returns and transparent information. They must make sure that all taxes are paid on time, and put pressure on government to use those resources properly, fighting corruption. These and many other things are important to create a better world and to make sure that nature will be conserved the way it should be.

Jim Forster of Cisco Systems emphasized that declining costs of communication contribute positively to economic development and emphasized his point by noting that African universities' Internet access is 40 times more expensive than that for US universities.

Dr Andreas Bluethner of the division of European Governmental Affairs for BASF, a chemical company, suggested that a global public–private partnership organization that responds to solutions proposed to global challenges would be useful to corporations, and suggested that partnerships work best when there is:

- transparency;
- trust;
- management of expectations;
- partnership building and management skills;
- available resources;
- internal and external communication;
- an ability to 'translate' between different organizational cultures.

Edward E. Miller, President and General Manager of GTB in Santa Cruz, Bolivia, wrote that 'The level of confidence GTB has reached in its relationship with the indigenous communities has contributed towards the company's maintaining the gas pipeline without the common social conflicts present today in Bolivia. This *building trust* relationship has contributed towards the indigenous communities' families benefiting from the permanent and temporary job opportunities that were generated by the company.' The key to the success of this partnership with the indigenous communities was 'building trust' and the identification of mutual benefits: the gas pipeline's normal operation = a stable business for GTB = employment and development programmes for the communities = greater welfare for the indigenous families.

As for the key to successful partnerships, Mr Miller said that for these programmes to work, a top-down commitment from the highest levels of management has to be established with weekly reporting inside the organization required from the manager responsible for the project as well transparency and clarity on what can and cannot be done.

Michael Spenley is Group Head of Accountable Sourcing for Littlewoods & Shop Direct Group, the UK's largest home shopping online retailer of clothes and items for the home. Mr Spenley was candid that his business is 'not doing enough' for development:

> *We have a somewhat reluctant positioning on CSR, although*
> *we do focus on ethical and accountable sourcing... We have*
> *not issued a social report since 2000, having partially lost our*
> *way on development issues during prolonged culture change*
> *in the organization...Many employees within our organization*
> *would like to do a great deal more to provide a definable mea-*
> *surable contribution towards the MDGs. However, we are a*
> *business primarily. We must keep one eye on the horizon and*
> *maintain a balance with commerciality/profitability.*

Mr Spenley was pleased with the United Nations Global Compact, stating that UNGC has acted as a catalyst for actions contributing to development within the company:

> *Communications from the UNGC come to me and to our*
> *CEO, and often from the office of the UN Secretary Gen-*
> *eral. I'm not sure about your companies, but here that means*
> *action (!) and letters filter down to my level covered in red pen*
> *instructions or questions from my CEO.*

Importantly, he noted that the major hurdles regarding becoming involved in development work are the cost, limited resources, perception of limited benefit, and low priority in relation to commercial projects.

Dr Ethel M. Cormier of the Procter & Gamble Nutrition Science Institute indicated that their experience in working with government, non-profit organizations, NGOs and multilateral institutions has been mixed. She stated that diversity of strength is important in the partnership as well as not changing the players involved. Importantly, she writes, 'I have seen this work best when all players felt on the line and responsible for the end goal or outcome. This is either a self- or top-down generated pressure.' Also, she states that the first set of barriers that normally have to be removed are the behavioural preconceptions that each group has about the other:

> *Governments assume that private sector companies are not*
> *appropriately concerned about consumers and the environ-*
> *ment. The public sector believes that the private sector is*
> *focused only on profit, but has a useful deep pocket to fund*
> *their projects. The private sector thinks that governments and*
> *multilateral institutions have such complex and inefficient*
> *bureaucracies that getting anything accomplished and espe-*
> *cially in a timely way is near to impossible. Or, they believe that*
> *changes in government administrations will lead to changes in*
> *leadership, focus and previous decisions. Of course, these are*
> *generalities that have been based on real events.*
> *A second barrier is our preconceived and sometimes unreal-*
> *istic expectations of each other. For example, NGOs, gov-*

*ernments and multilaterals often want partnering private sec-
tor companies to focus only on the lowest economic groups.
This normally translates to an unrealistic business proposition
resulting in a consumer price for a product that not only does
not cover the cost, but loses money for the company. Companies, on the other hand, with social initiatives want local
governments to help them with reaching the public (manufacturing, marketing, awareness, distribution, etc) in unfamiliar
markets. Again, this is not always the skill set of those entities.*

Dr Cormier listed her keys to successful partnership:

- taking time to define the objectives, goals and measures;
- taking time to define the structure (e.g. decision making, communication), roles and responsibilities;
- taking time to develop more than surface relationships with partners so
  that trust and openness is possible;
- understanding the culture of the partnering organizations and supporting the partner based on this understanding;
- over-communicating.

In answer to what the private sector can do to reduce poverty in the world,
Michael Spenley wrote that the most obvious steps to poverty reduction
would be:

- providing a living wage to all workers who produce goods for sale;
- making consumers aware of their responsibilities to the planet;
- bringing an end to throw-away consumerism where most consumers
  want the cheapest goods possible;
- reversing the trend from the importance of cheap to the importance of
  value.

Importantly, Mr Spenley wrote, 'A developing world where young women
sew clothes for Western consumers but can't afford to clothe themselves,
where teachers teach in schools but can't afford to educate their own children and where construction site workers help build skyscrapers in capital
cities yet live in shanty towns must not be accepted as reasonable by business leaders.'

Edward E. Miller wrote that the world's best minds have been struggling
with the private sector's role in reducing poverty for decades. He submitted that the private sector must help communities write their own business
plans for improvement projects and provide corporate governance through
the completion of the project: 'Reducing poverty in the world does not
require large amounts of cash when the private sector becomes an active
partner that is fully committed to helping people help themselves.'

James P. Clark is Chairman of the World Technology Network (WTN), a global association of the peer-nominated, peer-elected and most innovative people in science and technology (www.wtn.net). An annual panel session focuses on issues involved in the MDGs, and their annual World Technology Awards programme includes award categories such as social entrepreneurship, policy, education, law and environment in addition to information technology, biotechnology, communications technology, materials, energy, space, health and medicine.

WTN has partnered with UNOPS, UNESCO, UNDP and UN DESA. Clark comments:

> *Our interest and commitment has been there from the start but in our experience, our UN-related partners have been logistically and culturally incapable of actually doing much effective work. Our experience working with various development-work partners, particularly multilateral institutions in the UN system, has been consistently disappointing. I have met some people who seem wonderful and experienced and enthusiastic at the start of a partnership, but when actual hard, detailed work has to be done, they or their colleagues seem to disappear.[21] This causes all sorts of problems including:*
>
> - *the deliverable we had hoped to achieve is less good than it might have been because we end up doing all the work without our partner(s)*
> - *the reputation of the UN and development work in general sinks even lower in the minds of the people we are trying to encourage to become involved.*

Mr Clark indicated that the number one reason some partnerships are more effective than others is that 'the key players/leaders have decided to devote whatever-it-takes resources of time and effort to get the project off the ground and to monitor it as it proceeds. It is that attitude that filters down through everything else that happens.'

He said that accountability of the key players/leaders is also key. 'If a project fails to achieve its goals, a thorough investigation needs to occur and someone needs to be judged. Too often in the UN system, either a bad project is forgotten by everyone (by mutual agreement) or the project managers are simply found new jobs elsewhere in the UN system where they can be ineffective on someone else's turf.'

So, is the UN Global Compact the, or an, answer? This is considered in the next section.

---

[21] I put this down to the three Ms: Meetings, Missions and Meandering that includes sick leave and multi coffee breaks!

The UN Global Compact

The UN Global Compact has grown rapidly since its inception at the World Economic Forum in Davos by Kofi Annan in 1999. It consists, as can be seen in Box 10.1, of four main actions expected of a company.[22]

There is nothing particularly controversial about these for participating companies, of which around 1700 have signed up to date. One frequent criticism heard is that companies obtain benefits by being seen to be associated with the UN but that there are no binding obligations on them to do anything. On the other hand, other than being 'seen' in supposedly good company there is nothing much that companies get out of the Global Compact.

Nevertheless, today, the UN Global Compact is the world's largest corporate citizenship initiative with more than 2000 participants from over

---

Box 10.1 UN Global Compact activities for companies

To participate in the Global Compact a company:

1   sends a letter from the Chief Executive Officer (and where possible, endorsed by the board) to Secretary-General Kofi Annan expressing support for the Global Compact and its principles;

2   sets in motion changes to business operations so that the Global Compact and its principles become part of strategy, culture and day-to-day operations;

3   is expected to publicly advocate the Global Compact and its principles via communications vehicles such as press releases, speeches etc.;

4   is expected to publish in its annual report (or similar corporate report) a description of the ways in which it is supporting the Global Compact and its ten principles. This 'Communication on Progress' is an important tool to demonstrate implementation through public accountability.

The Global Compact offers engagement opportunities to all participants through the following:

■   *Dialogues*: Action-oriented meetings that focus on specific issues related to corporate citizenship, globalization and sustainable development.

■   *Information sharing and learning events*: Local information sharing and learning events whereby participants share experiences and lessons related to Global Compact issues. Companies are also invited to develop and share examples of good corporate practices and lessons learned on the Global Compact website.

■   *Partnership projects*: The Global Compact encourages participants to engage in partnership projects with UN agencies and civil society organizations in support of global development goals.

---

[22] See www.unglobalcompact.org.

Box 10.2 Global Compact Principles

Human Rights
Principle 1: The support and respect of the protection of international human rights.
Principle 2: The refusal to participate in or condone human rights abuses.

Labour
Principle 3: The support of freedom of association and the recognition of the right to collective bargaining.
Principle 4: The abolition of compulsory labour.
Principle 5: The abolition of child labour.
Principle 6: The elimination of discrimination in employment and occupation.

Environment
Principle 7: The implementation of a precautionary and effective approach to environmental issues.
Principle 8: Initiatives that demonstrate environmental responsibility.
Principle 9: The promotion of the diffusion of environmentally friendly technologies.

Anti-Corruption
Principle 10: The promotion and adoption of initiatives to counter all forms of corruption, including extortion and bribery.

---

80 countries, including business, labour and civil society (the UN's euphemism for NGOs).

As far as the 10 principles are concerned, there is nothing particularly controversial with, perhaps, the main exception being the labour principles 3 and 6. However, to date, there are no data generally available to judge how far companies have gone in adhering to the 10 principles and, in particular, the labour principles (Box 10.2).

The way forward for the UN Global Compact has been subject to many criticisms and comments.[23] For example, Jeremy Hobbs of Oxfam (a UN Global Compact member) has observed that there are businesses within the Global Compact that agree with many counter-arguments but they need support against outside pressure on four critical issues: (1) performance standards; (2) an ombudsman or mechanism for registering complaints; (3) transparency of practices (including how a corporation becomes a member, and how or why they would be removed from the Compact); and (4) the full adoption of the UN Norms on the Responsibilities of Transnational Corporations.[24]

---

[23] See, for instance, www.globalpolicy.org/reform/business/2004/0623countersummit.htm.
[24] In the discussion recorded in the previous footnote: www.globalpolicy.org/reform/business/2004/0623countersummit.htm.

Hobbs further noted that there are some companies in the Compact that support the norms, but US businesses have been especially 'aggressively opposed'. Currently, there is no Compact evaluation of which company is violating basic rights, or how the rights are being violated. Interestingly, the Compact has quietly begun to delist companies that are egregious violators (described as 'freeriders'), but this process has been 'very mysterious and quiet'.

As a supporter of the UN Global Compact, this author actually mooted the need for a 'compact' between business and the UN as long ago as 1994 when working for the UN Human Development team. These ideas eventually found their way into the first edition of my book, *The Planetary Bargain: CSR Comes of Age.*[25] Consequently I am a strong supporter of the UN Global Compact but would like it to include *all* stakeholders following my definition of CSR in Chapter 2.

As I wrote in 2002, the UN's Global Compact sets standards for company behaviour to only three stakeholder groups: labour, environment and the community (human rights).[26] I also noted that, and this is true today, there is no doubt that the GRI is currently the most widely encompassing of them all. It has been brave enough to attempt to devise a set of indicators so that companies can report on progress to meeting 'triple bottom line' objectives. The GRI, however, is also not without its critics[27] and my own view is that there are simply too many indicators in the GRI package to be particularly useful – so 'most' companies can say that they cover 'most' GRI indicators making for a patchy effort and not easily allowing inter-company comparisons. Furthermore, many of the indicators are highly inter-correlated and therefore redundant.

---

[25] In fact in a project for the UN in 1994 [Michael Hopkins (1994) 'Role of the private sector in the UN', Report to Head of Human Development Team, New York, UNDP], I had suggested the need for a compact between business and the UN and wrote at that time 'What, then, could a social agreement or compact contain and to whom should it be directed? There are perhaps, three main actions. First, at the international level there is a case for vigorously pursuing a minimum priority set of labour standards to include in international agreements in the WTO. Second, private companies should be encouraged to work toward a set of minimum working conditions that all will respect. Rather than doing this through legislation and given that it is in the self-interest of the private sector to do this, the leading figures in the major companies in the world should be brought together to thrash out a gentlemen's agreement. The United Nations can help to draw up the agenda for such a meeting. Third, individual nations should work actively to agree and to respect a minimum number of labour standards.' However, I make no claims to be the originator of the GC. It is probable that Kofi Annan's 1999 Davos speech was stimulated by similar thinking some five years after my own contribution.

[26] www.mhcinternational.com, Monthly Feature, September, 2002.

[27] See for instance Mallen Baker (2002) 'The Global Reporting Initiative – Raising the Bar too high?', August, www.mallenbaker.net.

Notwithstanding my own critique of the UN, I did note that I felt it was doing many excellent things but, simply, did not have the power and reach of the MNEs to be particularly effective. Could, therefore, the UN Global Compact address my main concerns? It has certainly gone further in recruiting companies than I originally imagined. However, the limitations of the UN and the strong negative influence of the US will continue to hinder its being able to adopt a global reach even with the large companies that work with it. Many companies, of course, will simply seek the reflected 'glory' of working with the UN, while others will seriously pursue the 10 principles. But these are clearly not enough, since they only partially cover all the stakeholders involved and, even if fully implemented, would more than likely not lead to great progress in achieving the MDGs.

Insiders in the Global Compact (Georg Kell the current head and two consultants) have also noted the limitations of the Global Compact. They write that:

> there is an ambivalence about the Global Compact. On the one hand, it generates a network of concerned companies and relevant others. On the other hand, it is set in the nationally based and bureaucratic context of the numerous agencies of the United Nations, each with its own mandate. On the one hand, it is an experiment in learning, networking and the development of a global conversation about human rights, labour standards and environmental protection. On the other hand, its success will only be accepted by some external critics if it can be shown to have clearly achieved improvements against the Millennium Development Goals or diminish what many perceive to be the problems of globalization. The longevity of the Global Compact experiment and the idea that the Global Compact may evolve a life of its own, and leave its mother ship – the United Nation – means that ownership could disperse away from the United Nations.[28]

So would specific initiatives be an answer? Next I look, briefly, at one such initiative called Business Action for Africa (BAA).

Business Action for Africa

In a meeting in July 2005 led by Mark Moody-Stuart, former Director of Shell and Chairman of Anglo-American plc, a group called Business Action for Africa (BAA) was launched. It is a business campaign to support

---

[28] Malcolm McIntosh, Sandra Waddock and Georg Kell (2004) *Learning to Talk*, Sheffield, Greenleaf Publishers, p18.

Africa's development, and brought together over 330 African and international companies from 36 countries. Their premise is that 'business should be an active partner with governments, donor institutions and other parts of civil society in supporting sustainable development in Africa'. The meeting was opened with a welcome address from Prime Minister Tony Blair, President of the G8, and closed by President Obasanjo of Nigeria, Chairman of the African Union (AU) and NEPAD Heads of State and Government Implementation Committee and Secretary of State for International Development, Hilary Benn. President Mwanawasa and Deputy Prime Minister Lehohla addressed the meeting together with Ministers from Algeria, Cameroon, Egypt, Rwanda, Senegal, South Africa and 80 private sector speakers.

The meeting illustrates my point that business is more and more concerned with development issues. However, the dominance of the meeting by government statesmen with no significant CEO present except Mark Moody-Stuart shows that the movement has a long way to go. More aid and philanthropy might be welcome but have not been successful so far. However, some progress was made when the meeting noted that the:

> *Government should try to step back from those areas in which business can better deliver. Too often well intentioned efforts by government stifle business, over regulate, and tax out enterprise. African governments need to give greater priority to removing impediments to doing business and improve the investment climate for domestic and foreign investors – by creating societies based on the rule of law, transparency, pluralism, rules on fair competition, and efficient public sector management.*

There is no doubt that corruption in African societies has been one of the main sources of under-development and that there is much to do. But corruption cannot be removed overnight and more 'T&A' might not necessarily do the trick. But the move is in the right direction and is one step on the road to alleviating poverty.

One area where there has been progress in involving the private sector in development has been in the area of Private–Public Partnerships (PPP). How much of an answer to development can PPP be?

Private–public partnerships

Partnerships involving corporations, governments, international organizations, and non-profit or non-governmental organizations have attracted much attention from researchers and policy makers in recent years, most noticeably after the Johannesburg World Summit on Sustainable Development in 2002. However, the majority of private sector businesses do not collaborate in partnership with these groups. Why is this? What are the key

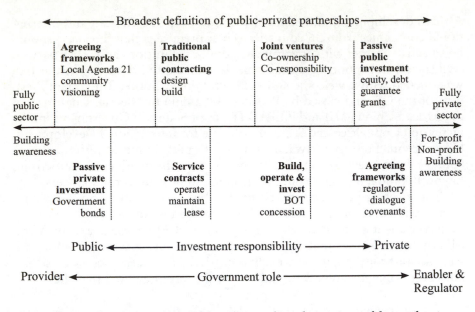

Figure 10.1 *Spectrum of possible relationships between public and private environmental service providers*

issues that need to be discussed so that more businesses emerge to play a more active role in the challenge to reduce poverty across the globe?

The term 'public–private partnership' (PPP) describes a 'spectrum of possible relationships between public and private actors for the cooperative provision of infrastructure services'[29] (see Figure 10.1). The only essential ingredient is some degree of private participation in the delivery of traditionally public-domain services. Private actors may include private businesses, as well as NGOs and community-based organizations (CBOs). In this context, CBOs typically represent directly one or several communities, while NGOs are intermediaries between government and communities, and often provide communities with technical and financial assistance for the development of their projects. Through PPPs, the advantages of the private sector – innovation, access to finance, knowledge of technologies, managerial efficiency, and entrepreneurial sprit – are combined with the social responsibility, environmental awareness and local knowledge of the public sector in an effort to solve urban problems.

Although governments and private firms have long worked together under simple arrangements that typically involve purchasing private sector products for public services, both parties are reluctant to enter into

---

[29] Drawn from Elizabeth Bennett, Peter Grohmann and Brad Gentry (1999) 'Public–private partnerships for the urban environment options and issues', PPPUE Working Paper Series Volume I, Yale University for the UNDP, New York, and available on www.undp.org/ppp/library/publications/working1.pdf1.

more complex relationships, such as those presented by the provision of infrastructure services. Governments are often concerned that private businesses will take advantage of them, while businesses tend to consider government approaches to be burdensome and a waste of time. So, what does it take to coax these groups off their traditional paths and persuade them to work together to address urban environmental problems? Generally, it takes a widely acknowledged crisis – one that multiple groups acknowledge as affecting their core interests. In the case of urban infrastructure, the substantial problems facing so many cities constitute such crises and have been key drivers in the formation of new PPPs.

Efforts to implement these partnerships at the local level, however, face many challenges. For governments, the challenge is to find ways to fulfil their responsibility for ensuring that all citizens have access to basic services, while meeting the needs of private investors. This implies a new and often difficult transition for many governments, from provider and manager of basic services, to enabler and regulator. For private firms, the challenge is to be convinced that investing in any particular project offers more attractive returns than other available investment opportunities. Drawing that conclusion depends on the firm's comparison of the potential returns against the potential risks, including both country risk (reflecting the general frameworks established by governments for any private investment in the country) and project risk (reflecting the specific characteristics of the investment opportunity offered by governments).

Overcoming these challenges is further complicated, however, by a range of gaps in the capacity of both public and private actors. Major gaps include:

- the reciprocal mistrust and lack of understanding of each other's interests and needs across the public and private sectors;
- the absence of locally available information on, and experience with, arranging sustainable partnerships;
- the underlying legal, political and institutional obstacles to forming effective public–private relationships.

These gaps often lead to lengthy negotiations, increased transaction costs and make smaller projects much less attractive to potential international and larger national investors.

A well-known PPP is the Private Finance Initiative (PFI) which was a creation of the Conservative government in the early 1990s and has since been enthusiastically embraced by the Labour Government of Tony Blair.[30]

Governments and local authorities have always paid private contractors to build roads, schools, prisons and hospitals out of tax money. But in

---

[30] BBC News Online 'What are public–private partnerships?' Wednesday, 12 February 2003, 18:58 GMT.

1992, the Conservatives hit on a way of getting the contractors to foot the bill. Under PFI, contractors pay for the construction costs and then rent the finished project back to the public sector. This allows the government to get new hospitals, schools and prisons without raising taxes. The contractor, for its part, is allowed to keep any cash left over from the design and construction process, in addition to the 'rent' money.

However, critics say that the government is just mortgaging the future – and the long-term cost of paying the private sector to run these schemes is more than it would cost the public sector to build them itself.

In summary the lessons learned from PPP have been:

■ Partnerships are formed among organizations, but succeed because of individuals.
■ A strong leader must champion the partnership goals with vision, energy and enthusiasm.
■ The vision must be shared.
■ Decisions must be made jointly.
■ Money contributed from all partners helps facilitate any project.
■ Visible senior-level organizational support conveys the organization's commitment to other partners and to the general public.
■ Organizations should consider new ideas and approaches, share responsibility, and play an active role.[31]

Concluding remarks

This chapter has illustrated my thesis that the United Nations' family has been a leader in development efforts since it was set up after the Second World War. It has shown leadership in ideas – more recently the UNDP Human Development Reports and the World Bank Development Reports – and has also shown an ability to innovate – the MDGs and the UN Global Compact are two examples. It has also shown itself more and more open to embracing collaborations with the private sector. However, its lack of resources and the politicization of its actions by powerful member states have left it in poor shape to tackle the pressing issues of under-development today. As T&A bites through misdirected assistance, it will see its power to influence development continue to reduce. At the micro level, large corporations are doing more and more to assist in development. It is at the macro, policy level where corporations are reluctant to act but where their critics urge them to perform – oil company receipts that are retained in developing countries continue to be managed poorly in encouraging development. Some hesitant progress has been made through such initiatives as the Extractive Industries Transparency Initiative (EITI).[32] The macro level,

---

[31] See www.businessandmdgs.org/.
[32] See www.eitransparency.org.

therefore, is an area where the UN family can be a partner to corporations and it is likely to grow in importance. But the UN family must continue to innovate, otherwise corporations will simply go their own way in promoting development.

11

Socially Responsible Investment in Developing Countries

A primary role that SRI funds can play within the corporate sector is to encourage more transparency and the wider adoption of environmental and social reporting. SRI funds can therefore play a role in drawing together the ongoing corporate governance initiatives with the environmental and social trends that are also taking place. (International Finance Corporation)

Introduction

Socially responsible investment (SRI) is one of the fastest growing forms of investment. In the US alone, according to the Social Investment Forum,[1] from 1995 to 2003, assets involved in social investing, through screening of retail and institutional funds, shareholder advocacy and community investing, have grown 40 per cent faster than all professionally managed US investment assets. Investment portfolios involved in SRI grew by more than 240 per cent from 1995 to 2003, compared with the 174 per cent growth of the overall universe of assets under professional management.

In 2005, a study gathered the views of 42 SRI thought leaders via half-hour interviews.[2] The study concluded that: 'What we will witness over the decade is a gradual shift from SRI as an instrument of moral philosophy for moral investors to SRI as an instrument for mainstream investors who are not interested in morality itself but recognize that immoral behaviour of companies will hurt their investments.'

---

[1] 2003 Report on Socially Responsible Investing Trends in the United States, Social Investment Forum, www.socialinvest.org, accessed 25 November 2005.
[2] 'The Future of Socially Responsible Investment: Thought Leader Study', see www.socialfunds.com/news/article.cgi/article1832.html, accessed 30 November 2005.

SRI in developing countries

The UK Social Investment Forum defines SRI to be investment where 'social, environmental, ethical and corporate governance (SEE/CG) considerations are taken into account in the selection, retention and realization of investment and the responsible use of rights (such as voting rights) attaching to investments. SRI combines investors' financial objectives with their concerns about SEE/CG issues'. SRI covers investment by financial institutions in developing countries such as investment funds, stocks, loans and the like as well as investment by MNE in their own operations.

Does this mean that developing countries will now receive more in investment funds than ever before? A related question is whether SRI is bringing in more investment to developing countries than would be the case with aggregate investment anyway? An even more difficult question to fathom out is whether the poorest people in developing countries are benefiting more than would otherwise be the case from socially responsible investment funds? Although we know that foreign direct investment (FDI) in developing countries is increasing, we cannot answer either of the two questions posed. We do know that FDI is increasing rapidly to China, India and Brazil and that the flows to Africa are very small in comparison.

Further, which parts of FDI are 'socially responsible' and which are not is a question that available data cannot answer. Nor can it tell whether the new vogue of CSR concerns is actually leading investors to invest more in developing countries than would otherwise be the case. McKinsey, for example, have produced a massive 500-page report on Investment by MNEs in developing countries.[3] They adopted a case study approach but did not cover socially responsible investment. Moreover, despite writing over 500 pages, their main conclusion did not produce anything particularly innovative, with statements such as 'MNEs improve living standards in developing economies'.

The UKSIF notes that Western banks are increasingly expanding their services into developing countries and that many of these banks have joined the Equator Principles (EP) that provide a 'framework for financial institutions to manage environmental and social issues in project finance'.[4]

The EP principles, as we noted previously, started with 10 of the largest banks and most have since joined. Opinion is divided on the efficacy of their progress and some NGOs have already been critical of progress. In 2004, BankTrack, a consortium of global NGOs that tracks the social and environmental impacts of the private financial sector, released a report that assessed progress.[5] The report, 'Principles, Profits, or Just PR? Triple

---

[3] McKinsey (2003) *New Horizons – Multinational Company Investment in Developing Countries*, San Francisco, October.
[4] UK Social Investment Forum, Just Pensions Report, No. 11, Financial Services, October 2005, p4.
[5] According to a report in www.socialfunds.com/news/article.cgi/article1436.html, accessed 15 December 2005.

P investments under the Equator Principles', criticized the EP banks for financing projects that violate EP standards, and for a lack of transparency about implementation of the EPs.[6] ('Triple P' stands for the balancing of people, planet and profits.) The report cited specific projects financed since the launch of the EPs that contravene multiple EP standards, such as the $3.6 billion Baku-Tbilisi-Ceyhan (BTC) oil pipeline from the Caspian Sea in Azerbaijan to the Mediterranean in Turkey.

SRI impact on development

The impact of socially responsible investment on living standards is hard to quantify. However, some intend to try. For instance, in an analysis of the impact of the London Principles,[7] one of the principles covering CSR, Principle six, states:

> *Exercise equity ownership to promote high standards of corporate social responsibility by the activities being financed. Business risks from supply chain employment conditions, local community impacts and other 'social development' issues have increased in recent years. One of the roles of equity investors, as owners, is to protect investment returns by ensuring these risks are managed through high standards of corporate social responsibility.*

The intent was to put in place mechanisms to ensure continuing progress in the financing of sustainable development by UK-based financial institutions. The authors of the report found that it was difficult to 'accurately assess their impact' and stated that 'this has been the least satisfactory outcome of the project thus far and perhaps reflects an overly ambitious aim, made in the visionary atmosphere around Johannesburg in 2002. On reflection, the LP project in isolation may not be able to establish mechanisms that ensure continual progress. Effective progress is dependent on many factors, some of which lie outside the scope of any one initiative. However, we aim to explore the feasibility of establishing supplementary mechanisms and processes to encourage progress.' The report ended with the cryptic note: 'LP mechanisms impact unclear. Good progress by signatories, but less impact on wider financial system.'

One can sympathize with the authors of the report and it is all too rare, unfortunately, for principles to be properly evaluated once set up. Part of

---

[6] www.banktrack.org/fileadmin/user_upload/documents/0_BT_own_publications/PPP_report_0406_final.pdf, accessed 15 December 2005.
[7] 'London Principles Pamphlet: 3 years on from Johannesburg Summit', Forum for the Future, London, 2005.

the problem could be that the 'social' has less prominence than the 'environmental'. Three of the LP principles were devoted to environment while only one to social. This illustrates the dominance of environmental thinkers over social thinkers in the preparation of advisory reports – one of the two authors of the report was the well-known environmentalist Jonathan Porritt.

SRI companies

A number of companies have grown up in recent years to harness investment into socially responsible products. No complete list exists although membership in organizations such as the UK Social Investment Forum runs to 165 members among which there are banks and building societies (8), investment management institutions (53), social finance organizations (6), independent financial advisers (17), professional advisory firms and research providers (40) and 41 others.[8] Perhaps the best one could say is that the field is growing in number and diversity of interest.

Outside the UK, social investment can be found in many industrialized countries especially Canada and the US, with activities increasing in South Africa, the Netherlands, France, Spain, Portugal, Australia and Germany. However, developing countries such as Brazil, China and India have few if any SRI funds located in them – an aspect that will be discussed further below.

Despite the rapid growth of SRI, conventional investors are still only dimly aware of the area. For instance, a lecture was given at the Institute of Business Ethics in London in December 2005 by Lord Griffiths, a former Vice Chairman of Goldman Sachs and Chairman of a Commission on debt set up by the shadow Chancellor of the Exchequer in the UK. In response to a question by the author on whether his Commission had covered socially responsible investment, he replied blankly that he was not sure what was meant by SRI!

Further, as noted by the US NGO, Social Funds, investing distinguishes between SRI research, which factors social and environmental considerations into investment decisions, and 'mainstream' research, which focuses purely on financial factors.[9] An example is the company Innovest, based in the US, and founded a decade ago by CEO Matthew Kiernan. It has defied convention by straddling the divide, integrating social and environmental sustainability considerations directly into financial analysis. As Kiernan remarked:

---

[8] See www.uksif.org/Z/Z/Z/dir/type/index.shtml#a4, accessed 15 December 2005.
[9] See www.greenbiz.com/news/news_third.cfm?NewsID=29209, accessed 28 November 2005.

Rather than conceiving of ourselves as having both feet in the neoclassical SRI tradition, which I see as a vertical slice of the investment universe, we see ourselves as a horizontal slice across the board really representing what we firmly believe to be the leading edge of where the mainstream is going. The social logic behind this decision was that I felt if we could deflect the trajectory of the $40 trillion mainstream investments toward sustainability by even one degree, we would have mobilized an awful lot of capital – maybe even more capital than the traditional SRI space.[10]

Kiernan was hard-pressed to identify Innovest's direct competitors – 'not traditional SRI research firms such as KLD Research & Analytics or the Ethical Investment Research Service (EIRIS). Generation Investment Management and Sustainable Asset Management (SAM) both integrate sustainability factors into financial analysis, but neither truly compares to Innovest'.

Although few, if any, SRI firms target developing countries, an indirect fund (launched by Innovest) is the 'Global Compact Plus' analytical tool, which allows investors to assess the sustainability performance of companies participating in the United Nations Global Compact – the voluntary framework of social and environmental commitments. Three factors distinguish the new tool. First, it focuses on sustainability risks. Second, it focuses not on what companies say they are doing, but on what they actually are doing ('there's always going to be a gap between what they say and what they do, so if all you know is what they say, you're really investing with one hand tied behind your back,' Kiernan points out). And third, it rates and ranks companies directly against their same-sector competitors.

Some well-known companies are entering the SRI field. HSBC Investments have observed that demand for socially responsible investments (SRI) has increased substantially in recent years, especially in Europe, the US and, more recently, Asia.[11] HSBC has a small SRI team of five based in Paris, comprising analysts, and marketing and fund managers. Their SRI analysts conduct research based on input from general global equity analysts and their own external rating agencies. In addition, all HSBC's European equity analysts provide input on socially responsible investment factors as part of their research process.

The HSBC team uses the traditional screening machinery to decide which SR stocks to invest in, or not, as the case may be. They employ a negative screening approach to agree with their client a list of stocks to be avoided. Then they use a positive screening process with two steps:

---

[10] See www.greenbiz.com/news/news_third.cfm?NewsID=29209, accessed 28 November 2005.
[11] See   www.hsbc.com/hsbc/csr/ethical-finance/products-and-services/sustainable-investing, accessed 27 November 2005.

defining an SRI universe from the overall universe (performed by their SRI analysts) and then stock picking from this SRI universe based on financial data. I would prefer not to include any stock of investment instruments that did not have decent prospects. I don't see why SRI should mean investors should not get a decent return on their investment!

HSBC does say that its SRI team has a programme of ongoing meetings with a large number of companies on social and environmental issues, and at those meetings their fund managers and analysts 'may also raise concerns about companies' corporate governance.' By the end of 2004, HSBC had some US$1 billion in ethical and SRI assets – albeit only representing less than 1 per cent of their US$204 billion of total assets under management.

Corporate Social Investment

Corporate social investment (CSI) is the term often used to describe a company's investment in a range of community activities. It is, therefore, more limited than CSR. Research on CSI by Jeremy Baskin, reproduced in Figure 11.1, shows that 'emerging market companies are almost as likely as high-income OECD countries to report on their corporate social investment … and they are more likely to have extensive CSI programmes in place'.[12]

Baskin believes that companies in Latin America and Africa are more active because high levels of income inequality, and often weak state provision of social services, 'impel[s] companies in poorer regions to be more active'. It may, he believes, also explain the lower levels of reported CSI in Asian emerging markets and Central and Eastern Europe, where social inequality is generally less extreme.

Although CSI is more limited than CSR, according to my definition of CSR, it goes beyond charitable activity and includes issues with a direct and sustainable impact on a society's stakeholders. South African firms, for example, donate significant amounts to education, black education having been severely neglected under apartheid, and the country still has many skill shortages to overcome. Another common CSI activity of South African firms involves work related to HIV/AIDS – South Africa has one of the highest incidences in the world, not helped by President Mbeki, who, until recently, downplayed HIV/AIDS with disastrous results. An example that shows even sympathetic companies have difficulties implementing relief programmes if a government refuses to acknowledge the problem.

According to Baskin, the mining company Goldfields is a fairly typical example of good practice. Each year it sets aside 0.5 per cent of pre-tax

[12] Based on an analysis of corporate responsibility practices of 127 leading companies in 21 emerging markets across four regions – Asia, Latin America, Africa and Central and Eastern Europe by Jeremy Baskin (2005) 'Corporate responsibility in emerging markets', presented at Middlesex conference, London, 22 June.

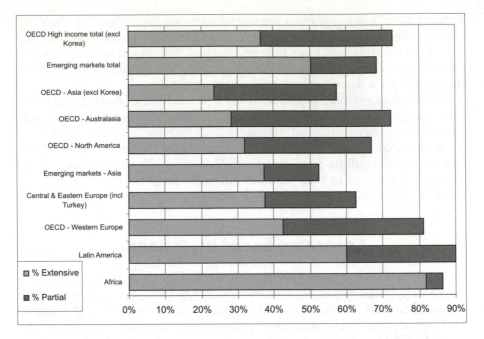

Figure 11.1 *Extent of reported Corporate Social Investment (CSI)*

profits – in 2004 this amounted to ZAR10.2 million (about $1.3 million). The company's focus is on the provision of primary health care facilities and infrastructure as well as health care education, including HIV/AIDS; primary, secondary and tertiary education; social development projects; and environmental education – all Type III activities. Funding is distributed evenly between the communities in which its mines are located and more remote communities where, as a consequence of the migrant labour system, many of its employees have their families and homes.

SRI within developing countries

SRI within developing countries, as compared with SRI from rich to poor countries, is under-developed.[13] As the IFC (International Finance Corpora-

---

[13] Emerging market data in this section are based on original research designed and undertaken by Jeremy Baskin with assistance from M. R. Castro (February/March 2005). He used OECD data based upon that from the London-based SRI consultancy EIRiS. Note that in all cases:

■   OECD Western Europe excludes Iceland and Luxembourg.
■   OECD Asia does not include Korea and therefore only comprises Japan.
■   OECD Australasia covers Australia and New Zealand.
■   OECD North America covers US and Canada. Mexico is included under emerging markets.

tion of the World Bank) notes, for the most part, investors actually in Asia have hardly acknowledged SRI and nor have they accepted, or understood, the longer term advantages of SRIs compared with more traditional forms of investment.[14] In fact, research commissioned by IFC on the SRI industry in 2003 indicated that SRI assets amounted to only $2.2 billion in all emerging markets, including Asia. That is less than one-tenth of 1 per cent of the worldwide total. Only $1 billion in SRI assets is held by developing country investors.

In India, for example, the IFC report observed that SRI 'is still relatively unknown and not well understood in India. While SRI volumes and values have increased globally, the Indian financial markets have not been proactive in attempting to introduce it to India or make it available to domestic investors.'

In China, the same report remarked that 'the concept of Socially Responsible Investment (SRI) is still in the very early stage of being introduced into China'. Two decades of fast-paced economic reform and rapid economic growth have left numerous environmental and social problems in their wake. However, the government and increasing numbers of ordinary people realize the importance of following a more balanced development track despite the overall emphasis on economic growth. A number of companies have also started adopting more socially benevolent and environmentally responsible practices. There are no SRI funds and there has been little incentive given the relatively low income of people working in the caring professions, such as nursing and teaching. However, this may change as many innovations are happening in the fund market, including the entry of foreign fund management companies and the need to encourage people to make their own retirement savings.

In Brazil, social objectives have been high on the agenda particularly under President Lula. Brazil is faced with huge social and economic problems most notably its poor distribution of income and high levels of poverty. Nevertheless, even in Brazil, SRI is progressing slowly. SRI activity in Brazil was said to have got underway in 2001 with the launch of an SRI service by Unibanco – one of the largest financial institutions in Brazil.[15] Unibanco

---

- Africa covers companies from Egypt, Morocco and South Africa.
- Latin America covers companies from Argentina, Brazil, Chile, Colombia, Mexico and Peru.
- Emerging markets Asia includes companies from China, India, Indonesia, Malaysia, Pakistan, Philippines and Thailand.
- CEE includes companies from Czech Republic, Hungary, Poland and Russia, and also Turkey.

[14] David St. Maur Sheil (2003) 'India: Report on SRI in Asian Emerging Markets', Centre for Social Markets, October, Report in Asian Emerging Markets, Sustainable Financial Markets Facility, SFMF, International Finance Corporation.

[15] See www.socialfunds.com/news/article.cgi/article479.html, accessed 20 December 2005.

has offered research reports on the social and environmental performance of Brazilian companies with the aim of eventually putting pressure on some major companies to consider the multiple benefits of improving their social and environmental business practices.

More recently, in 2005, the Brazilian stock exchange, Bovespa, launched a socially responsible index similar to the FTSE4Good index. Not without controversy, since Ciro Torres, from IBASE (the Brazilian Institute of Social and Economic Analyses) argued that the index lacked stakeholder input from NGOs, trade unions, environmental and consumer organisations.[16] He also pointed out that the index included companies involved in the tobacco, arms and alcohol industries.

Microcredit

Closely related to the issue of SRI is microcredit. Most new employment is generated in private small and medium sized companies (SMEs) either in the formal or the so-called informal sector. Microcredit is the fuel used to make these SMEs grow – a properly designed credit programme can help the poor to start small-scale activities that gradually lead them into sustainable business activities. The UN reported that, by the end of 2004, more than 92 million families – most of them living on less than a dollar a day – benefited from microcredit.[17] The Microcredit Summit Campaign, launched in 1997 by representatives from 137 countries, noted that the number represented a seven-fold increase from the 13.5 million borrowers counted in the campaign's first year.

Even large corporations have been promoting microcredit. BP, as part of its CSR programme to stimulate community involvement during work on the Baku-Tbilisi-Ceyhan (BTC) pipeline project, worked with FINCA – a micro-finance institution in Azerbaijan – to provide microcredit as an effective way of ensuring that small businesses could develop along the route of their pipeline. The repayment rate for the BTC-funded part of FINCA's portfolio has to date been 100 per cent among 4380 clients.

According to the 2005 UNDP Human Development Report, the reach of microfinance has made 'impressive gains, yet setbacks and challenges still impede advancement. For instance, less than 1 per cent of World Bank funding goes to microcredit.'[18] (Richard Weingarten, executive secretary of the UN Capital Development Fund, said, 'The demand for microfinance services remains largely unmet, especially in Africa.')[19]

---

[16] See www.ethicalcorp.com/content.asp?ContentID=3932, accessed 20 December 2005.
[17] See www.microcreditsummit.org/enews/2005-12_index.html, accessed 4 March 2006.
[18] UNDP (2005) *Human Development Report*, Oxford, Oxford University Press.
[19] www.ipsnews.net/news.asp?idnews=31341, accessed 10 March 2006

The UNDP report showed that 90 per cent of current microfinance clients are in Asia, with 10 per cent spread across the rest of the world. In Africa, just 8.5 per cent of the potential market is currently being served, leaving 91.5 per cent of the poor without access to financial services. In Latin America and the Caribbean, only 11.6 per cent are covered.

Microcredit was given its greatest impetus in the 1970s in Bangladesh when the Grameen Bank, started by Muhammad Yunus, began giving small loans to those people too poor to be eligible for credit from other banks. As a young economics professor at Chittagong University in Bangladesh in 1976, Muhammad Yunus lent $27 out of his own pocket to a group of poor craftsmen in the nearby town of Jobra.[20] To boost the impact of that small sum, Yunus volunteered to serve as guarantor on a larger loan from a traditional bank, kindling the idea for a village-based enterprise called the Grameen Project. Today, Yunus' Grameen Bank has lent more than $5.1 billion to 5.3 million people. The poor, contrary to conventional belief, are efficient and thrifty, capable of high marginal rates of saving, productive investment and asset creation with low capital intensity. The Grameen experience has been repeated across Asia and Africa by such NGOs as CASHPOR.

Nevertheless, microcredit schemes vary greatly. The Grameen Bank only lends to those poor people who are prepared to form small groups of borrowers. A default by any member falls on the entire group. In this way the lack of collateral for potential borrowers is substituted by community and peer pressure to pay back loans. Because of the time required to set the credit mechanisms in process, a grant from the UNDP, or similar body, is useful in the first instance to begin the capacity formation process. A BP scheme, using a different model, essentially finances small companies that are already in existence and also helps them prepare business plans and provides training in business practices.

Women are particularly careful borrowers and the experience of the Grameen Bank has shown that poor women will invest funds profitably to pull their families out of poverty and to improve the prospects of their children. Moreover, in the process of poverty reduction through this system, not only is the family's material condition improved but also the women's social position in the community. Indeed, there seems to be an almost inelastic demand for credit among the rural poor in Asia up to effective interest rates of 40 per cent.

The two main objections to credit for the poor are, first, that the poor cannot be trusted to pay back loans and, second, if the scheme is so attractive then private money would be involved rather than sitting on the sidelines. The Grameen experience is putting to rest the first objection. The second is more difficult to lay aside. Grass-roots lending practices require banks to go to the people and then to carefully nurture regular payments

---

[20] See www.businessweek.com/magazine/content/05_52/b3965024.htm, accessed 20 December 2005.

and peer group pressure in paying back loans. Intensive training is also required for the staff of the banks. These up-front costs have not been welcomed by commercial banks who are used to lending to large borrowers with substantial collateral. However, as the Grameen experience takes root outside Asia and given the enormous number of potential borrowers, the commercial banks are beginning to take notice. As this snowball effect gathers pace, the Grameen way of extending credit to the poor could be one, or even *the*, way to alleviate poverty.

Lipton has given a list of rules for successful pro-poor credit.[21] These are:

1   Respect fungibility. Borrowers usually know the best use of funds.
2   Focus extra lending (or incentives to provide it) upon the poor – but not by targeting it directly on persons, let alone households labelled poor by lenders.
3   Avoid lending rules that discriminate against the poor.
4   Poor people lack collateral so protect the lender's capital by other means.
5   Keep down the transaction cost of lending, especially as a share of loan size, and for poor borrowers.
6   If local supervision (e.g. peer group monitoring) is not to lead to risks, adopt an organization to keep the lender's portfolio diverse by location and sector of activity.
7   Avoid monopoly of lending – formal lending, moneylenders and NGOs are complementary.
8   Before the State acts to increase credit supply, ensure that unmet need (or demand) exists for credit to finance either producer goods or consumption smoothing and that meeting such demand has a satisfactory financial, private economic and social return.
9   Subsidize administration and transaction costs of lending agencies readily but temporarily, capital loans very sparingly, and interest rates hardly ever.
10 Don't politicize or otherwise soften repayment – although comprehensive credit insurance (with the expense met by borrowers overall) may be sensible in some cases.
11 Good economic returns to credit (and good repayment) are likelier if there is adequate infrastructure and education.
12 Lending institutions gain by insisting that members save before they borrow.
13 Create incentives for lenders to expand where, and only where, they succeed; some do better by providing credit alone, others by combining it with other inputs.

---

[21] M. Lipton (1996) *Successes in Anti-Poverty*, Issues in Development, Discussion Paper No. 8, Development and Technical Cooperation Department, International Labour Office, Geneva.

Concluding remarks

Clearly, investment analysts wish to see the 'business case' for social investment and are not carried by the 'moral case'. However, mainstream analysts are only slowly seeing the business case because:

■ investors are still mainly interested in making profits or driving value;
■ SRI is imperfectly understood and its impact not well measured to date;
■ there is a political tinge of social democracy and even socialism/green party sympathy;
■ there remains a belief that it is government's responsibility;
■ there is opacity of company reporting;
■ there is a perception that major SR issues are beyond company control.[22]

In an article several years ago I argued that business and investment analysts could take a number of steps such as:

■ understand and popularize available standards;
■ contribute to debate on business performance and CSR;
■ communicate perceptions to businesses they analyse;
■ state their ideological beliefs on CSR openly.[23]

The evidence for progress by hard-nosed business investment analysts is still not there, despite the evident progress on the sums of money heading in the SRI direction. It is only a matter of time before mainstream analysts will ignore SRI at their business peril.[24]

---

[22] Robin Marriott (2006) 'Ethical investing means long-term', *CityAM*, 3 March, p16.
[23] Michael Hopkins (2001) 'CSR Investment – the next "dot.com" boom but without the crash', www.mhcinternational.com/social_investment.htm, MHCi Monthly Feature, November, accessed 4 March 2006.
[24] I wrote this conclusion on 4 March 2006 sitting only a few blocks away from Canary Wharf, the new financial centre of London, if not the world. Each time I jog around the new, gleaming skyscrapers there, I wonder if any flashing buttons are working in the way I suggest here. To date my invitation to the hallowed floors that blaze with light until the early hours has not been forthcoming.

12

Main Actions for Companies Involved in Development

The true enemies of capitalism are not those who regulate or moderate. Instead the enemies of capitalism are the poverty, ignorance, corruption, short-sightedness, and exploitation that prevent the world's peoples from being free moral agents and living lives of dignity and respect ... together we must build a new understanding of business-society relationships in the global context.[1]

CSR and international development: Are corporations the solution?

In many ways, the large corporations have taken over from governments and the UN. But this is not always a positive situation. In this book I have shown that MNEs are starting to outspend governments on development, are much richer than the UN, have a global reach and are being involved in development in ways hardly thought of even a decade ago.

Yet corporations are responsive to their shareholders, in general, not to democracy. Most, of course, respect democratic institutions and contribute, financially, to the democratic process. But then, many would argue that these latter contributions serve to support only those parts of democratic institutions that are favourable to corporations. Evidence for this is not hard to find. The powerful Republican lobbyists in the US have just about squeezed out Democratic party lobbyists, and this is a story that has still escaped all the headlines. Certainly, one could not argue that the responsibility of corporations to their shareholders makes them democratic only to the extent that their shareholders represent the community at large. This is evidently not the case with most shareholder groups dominated by insti-

---

[1] Donna J. Wood, Jeanne M. Logsdon, Patsy G. Llewellyn, Kim Davenport (2006) *Global Business Citizenship: A Transformative Framework for Ethics and Sustainable Capitalism*, Armonk, New York, M. E. Sharpe, p224.

tutional investors – many of whom fail to turn up at shareholder meetings and prefer to deal with the chairman of the board directly.

There is, of course, another major area where corporations cannot entirely take over from governments and the UN, and that is in the area of global politics. The war on terror, at first sight, seems to be conducted outside the remit of large corporations. And the UN is hardly involved either. Iraq is the major issue of our times and the UN manifestly failed to have much influence. The US and UK decision to go to war in Iraq started by using the UN and its machinery, but when this failed the invasion and its consequences went ahead anyway. Whatever the merits of the case – and my own view is that the superpowers should have persisted with the UN before the invasion and should also have prepared much better for the aftermath when they actually did go to war – corporations did turn out to be more powerful than both governments and the UN. Bob Herbert of the New York Times tells us why:

> *Dwight Eisenhower, the Republican president who had been the supreme Allied commander in Europe in World War II, and who famously warned us at the end of his second term about the profound danger inherent in the rise of the military-industrial complex. Eisenhower delivered his farewell address to a national television and radio audience in January 1961. 'This conjunction of an immense military establishment and a large arms industry is new in the American experience,' he said. He recognized that this development was essential to the defense of the nation. But he warned that 'we must not fail to comprehend its grave implications'.*
>
> *'The potential for the disastrous rise of misplaced power exists and will persist,' he said. 'We must never let the weight of this combination endanger our liberties or democratic processes.' It was as if this president, who understood war as well or better than any American who ever lived, were somehow able to peer into the future and see the tail of the military-industrial complex wagging the dog of American life, with inevitably disastrous consequences.*
>
> *The endless billions to be reaped from the horrors of war are a perennial incentive to invest in the war machine and to keep those wars a-coming. 'His words have unfortunately come true,' says Senator John McCain. 'He was worried that priorities are set by what benefits corporations as opposed to what benefits the country.'*
>
> *The way you keep the wars coming is to keep the populace in a state of perpetual fear. That allows you to continue the insane feeding of the military-industrial complex at the expense of the rest of the nation's needs. 'Before long,' said Mr. Jarecki in an interview, 'the military ends up so overempowered that the rest of your national life has been allowed to atrophy.'*

In one of the great deceptive maneuvers in U.S. history, the military-industrial complex (with George W. Bush and Dick Cheney as chairman and C.E.O., respectively) took its eye off the real enemy in Afghanistan and launched the pointless but far more remunerative war in Iraq.

The military-industrial complex has become so pervasive that it is now all but invisible. Its missions and priorities are poorly understood by most Americans, and frequently counter to their interests.[2]

The chilling words of Herbert provide the background to how some large corporations have become more powerful than democratic institutions, including the UN. In the case of Iraq, this power has obviously not helped development. But it does imply that the more we can hold corporations responsible for their actions the less likely that large corporations like Halliburton, Bechtel or the Carlyle Group can benefit, and influence hugely, our political processes. Halliburton, which had US vice-President Dick Cheney as one time CEO, built the Guantanamo prison compound for terrorism suspects and donated $709,000 to political campaigns between 1999 and 2002. Bechtel, considered the largest contractor in the world, donated $1.3 million to political campaigns between 1999 and 2002 and is the earlier employer of former Defense Secretary Caspar Weinberger, former Secretary of State George Schultz and former CIA Director William Casey.[3] The Carlyle Group had former UK Prime Minister John Major as Chairman of its European Group until 2004, and he continues to serve as a consultant on energy matters.

The UN, of course, suffered badly. Its special representative for Iraq, Sergio Vieira de Mello, was killed when the poorly protected UN HQ in Baghdad was severely bombed in July 2003. The UN continues to be involved, to this day, but its presence is largely based in safer Jordan as its diplomats and civil servants have, for whatever warped reason, become 'legitimate' targets of war.

Could CSR have prevented the Iraq war? Yes. The relations between Halliburton, Bechtel, Carlyle and many other corporations in a CSR world would have been intensively examined. Stakeholders would have been held publicly accountable and socially irresponsible actions such as supporting war efforts for personal gain would have been stamped out. Is this naive? Perhaps. But right now, large corporations are more powerful than the UN, and more powerful than many nation states. Therefore, CSR is even more of an urgent issue than it has ever been before.

---

[2] Bob Herbert (2006) 'Ike Saw It Coming', *New York Times*, 27 February.
[3] Diana B. Henriques (2003) 'Which Companies Will Put Iraq back together?' *New York Times*, 23 March.

What are the main actions that corporations could take to enhance development under a CSR framework?

There are actions both within the MNE itself, touching its internal stakeholders, and actions outside the MNE, reaching toward its external stakeholders. Most, if not all, of an MNE's actions affect development in some way; some more than others, of course. For instance, good governance of a company, written and applied in a code of conduct for boards of directors, will impact on development more marginally than direct community-level interventions. Although, clearly, a company policy at board level to assist development would be no bad thing.

An MNE looking at its involvement in development could approach the issue in one or more of three main ways. It could:

1 simply say that it is focusing on profit maximization for its shareholders and claim that development is none of its business;
2 work on a partial approach, such as with the UN Global Compact and support that process;
3 engage fully with its stakeholders and explore options for furthering development efforts while ensuring that the actions it takes are fully in line with preserving shareholder value.

The argument in this book is that the third approach is in the long-term interest of MNEs and, of course, is crucial for development to move faster than it has to date.

So, what could the key areas of MNE involvement in development be? There are actions both inside and outside a corporation and these are discussed in the next section.

Development actions inside the company

A fully-fledged approach

The adoption of a fully-fledged approach to CSR within a company has a number of benefits. The demonstration effect of good internal CSR policies should not be forgotten even though these are indirect and hard to measure. CSR policies inside a company can be a lightning rod for other companies both in the location where the MNE is based as well as its overseas locations. CSR also makes good business sense in multifarious ways. For instance, consumers develop a higher degree of identification with companies that have good policies and practices.

Environmental and health standards

Companies which maintain environmental and health standards; propagate transparent business practices; protect human rights at the workplace; and work against corruption are widely respected and appear as more attractive to shareholders, reduce the possibility of industrial action and maintain a working environment that leads to higher worker productivity.

Anti-corruption

A strong anti-corruption culture needs to be built within the organization through active support from the senior management. Today, anti-corruption is widely discussed both inside companies and in their dealings with the outside world. Companies, too, see the overwhelming advantages of good governance in the countries where they work overseas and, in particular, the advantages of working with a government that is implementing anti-corruption policies. Much corruption occurs between external sources of finance and the host government. Thus it takes two parties to maintain an anti-corruption stance. The line between corruption and accepting small gifts or hospitality is sometimes blurred. On the larger stage, many companies are almost forced to pay bribes or kick-backs to win contracts. And this is not only the case in developing countries, industrialized countries have also not been blameless as we know with the Enron scandal, the Crédit Lyonnais scandal affecting top government officials in France, Volkswagen in Germany and so on. Even a single dubious payment can come back and haunt a company or individual down the line, as in the case of David Mills, an international corporate lawyer who hit the headlines in the UK through only the whiff of impropriety in one of his business dealings with the Italian government. It not only dented his formidable reputation, impacted badly on his marriage but threatened the career of his wife, Tessa Jowell, a Secretary of State in the Blair government. Just as with payments to blackmailers, once started the web of deceit and intrigue can be hard to break. Thus, each company should have a set of guidelines and business principles which must be followed by all staff. This code of conduct needs to be followed at all national and international offices which the company may have. Local business practices and culture must not influence or change the organization's guidelines. The system of internal communication and training has to be strengthened to keep all staff aware of the policies and principles.

A vision statement

Companies should create a vision statement on how the MNE can (and does) assist in development. This does not mean simply listing a number of philanthropic activities that the company intends to carry out. Development requires careful thought on how, once an injection of funds has been made, development initiatives can be sustainable, that is continue without the requirement for additional funds. Too often, company development initiatives have been dominated by generic global initiatives that are not tailored to suit specific circumstances.

Development actions outside the company[4]

Private sector participation for poverty alleviation

There is not an awful lot a company can do to reduce national poverty itself. However, working with national governments to work out how best the private sector can stimulate economic growth for poor people is in the interest of both the government and the company. In addition, public–private partnerships for tackling man-made or natural disasters can also speed up reconstruction activities.

Raising skill levels

Improving people's skills in a myriad of ways is undoubtedly the best way to create development. Education, training, skill development and capacity development are all aspects of the same issue – improving human skills. MNEs with their wealth of experience in in-house training have an enormous amount to contribute. At a minimum MNEs could be involved in a national training policy to ensure that private sector needs are incorporated in government training plans. It may be surprising to some, but many government training schemes in developing countries have little contact with private sector needs. MNEs can also set up, perhaps in partnership with others, courses and organizations to create training for sorely needed skills.

SMEs

Small and medium sized enterprises (SMEs) are where most new employment occurs in developing countries. MNEs have a role to play either directly through assisting SMEs to improve their management, marketing, technological and financial skills, or indirectly through ensuring that SMEs

---

[4] Asia conference on MDGs under the framework of the UN Global Compact: 'Global Compact regional conclave', 8 March 2005, Jamshedpur, India, www.unglobalcompact.org/content/NewsEvents/mdg_bus/mdg_jamshed.pdf.

as suppliers are not subject to complex contractual paperwork and, once hired, are paid rapidly.

Self-help

Helping people to help themselves is a key mantra to encourage development (or to use current jargon, sustainable development). Assisting budding entrepreneurs, or even existing ones, through mentoring can help launch new businesses, improve existing ones or even assist government departments to improve their efficiency.

Investment in developing countries

It is essential, of course, to invest in developing countries and work toward allowing their exports to be freely imported into the rich countries – a huge and controversial issue that will play out for many decades to come. Will not these new imports hurt local markets in industrialized countries where the MNEs are located and many of their staff? Once again, this is an issue that is currently being discussed vigorously in the development literature. This author's view is that the rich countries will innovate more quickly than developing countries simply because of their higher level of skills and continue to move into brain-intensive knowledge industries. As the developing countries start to move into these markets, too, the economic growth that is being created will allow room for many and there is no particular reason for unemployment to rise drastically. This, though, is another story.

Links with the local community

To many, CSR is simply working with the local community. Clearly, improving local conditions is in the interest of MNEs to enhance reputation and preserve harmony. Assistance to local communities can also help to improve purchasing power that leads to an expansion in the market size. But these actions are not as easy as they seem on the surface. Three questions that are not easily answered are: Where does the role of the MNE start and stop vis-à-vis the local community? What are the key issues to be involved in? Should MNEs be involved in human rights and, if so as many think, what are the limits?

Philanthropy

Philanthropy has always been a big part of MNEs' actions in LDCs. But few philanthropic actions are sustainable in the sense that once the project has finished, will the project and its related activities continue? As discussed in Chapter 5, this author is very sceptical of philanthropic activities. The test of a 'philanthropic' project is that the intervention must lead, as far as can be judged, to a sustainable, that is developmental, result.

Development assistance

Development assistance is key in many countries. This would best be done with existing development agencies such as the UNDP who have vast experience in development. Clearly, MNEs should not replace the UN nor government's own efforts. Simply, the power and wealth of MNEs need to be harnessed in positive development efforts. Should these efforts be in addition to the taxes that MNEs pay anyway? There is no easy answer. But many taxes that MNEs pay in developing countries are misused. A democratic government will tend to use tax revenue in ways that benefit its electorate so as to ensure re-election next time around. Yet most governments in developing countries are not democratic. So should MNEs be involved in those countries and, if so, what should they do exactly? First, MNEs should evaluate their position based on existing relations with the government. Clearly, if a host government simply says that how it spends the taxes paid is not the business of the MNE, then the MNE can decide whether to stay or leave. Second, where possible the MNE can, at least, assist the government in ensuring that tax revenue is used effectively to promote development. MNEs have vast experience in tax issues and could well lend some of this experience to develop capacity (better governance) within government. Third, when MNEs carry out their own development projects these should draw upon the development experience available in NGOs and local UN offices, such as the UNDP. Fourth, MNEs are not the government and obviously cannot, nor should not, carry out the major programmes of the government such as education, health, security or employment systems. But MNEs can be involved as an agent of positive change through lending their expertise to improving efficiency in government programme delivery. Fifth, if more than one MNE is involved in a developing country they should work together to ensure increased efficiency of development programmes in the host country.

But how much will all this cost? How much of its time and money should an MNE invest in any of the above-mentioned activities? There is no easy answer to this question. It is worth bearing in mind, however, that an MNE is involved in many of the above-mentioned processes as much by default as through a clearly thought out strategy. An MNE has to be continually involved with the host government negotiating all sorts of deals from land acquisition to taxation to import and export. Often these discussions will influence government policy and changes will be made. So what I am suggesting here, at least as a first step, is to place the myriad of discussions with government in an overall development framework. The more transparency the better, since the MNE will then be seen to be working in the country's best interest rather than colluding in smoke-filled darkened rooms. Thus, the MNE strategy in any particular country could be framed with a clear idea as to the benefits and costs of its intervention in terms of its own bottom line and also in terms of its benefit to development. Some of these are highlighted in the table below.

Table 12.1 *Corporate social development in LDCs*

Actions	Benefits to MNE	Disadvantages to MNE	Benefits to development
1. Anti-corruption culture embedded throughout organization	a. Reputation enhanced b. Costs of delivery of services and products reduced	More difficult to win contracts	Increased efficiency as poorly managed projects are eliminated and good projects properly monitored
2. New investment in LDC	a. Take advantage of cheap labour b. Closer to raw materials	1 Increased costs of ex-patriate managers and local training 2 Increased costs in management 3 Need to deal with host government and local institutions	1 Increased employment and incomes 2 Enhanced external trade position
3. Improving community relations	Reputation enhanced	1 Increased costs 2 Increased criticism if badly designed	Well-designed projects can create sustainable development
4. Philanthropic actions	Reputation enhanced	1 Increased costs 2 Will need to continue pay-offs if project design is non-sustainable	One-off actions are rarely sustainable
5. Development assistance	International reputation enhanced	1 Accused of becoming a new UN 2 Entering unfamiliar territory	1 Obtain expertise from practical managers 2 More resources available than from international public sources 3 Less strings tied to development assistance
6. Capacity development	Reputation enhanced	Few if existing skills are used but there is a management cost	Sustainable training can never be lost, essential for development

To conclude, in a nutshell what could a 10-point programme be for MNEs involved in developing countries (and just about all MNEs are involved either directly or indirectly)?

Summary of possible development actions

Inside the company

1   Develop a CSR strategy that includes an overall vision for the company's place in development. Decide what benefits and costs emanate from involvement in international initiatives such as the UN Global Compact, SA8000, ISO9000 and so on.
2   Investigate whether the company is paying a 'living wage' within the company and is paying its main suppliers properly and on time. If not, why not, and then ask what steps should be taken to move towards this.
3   Work with trade unions to ensure proper environmental and safety structures within the company.
4   Monitor and evaluate the company's anti-corruption policy on a regular basis.

Outside the company

5   Collaborate with the government in the host country to see how the government's anti-poverty policy can be enhanced. Work with local UN and NGO organizations to increase the efficiency of development initiatives, including ensuring that its tax contributions are used wisely.
6   Be pro-active in lending in-house training skills to a wider public.
7   Assist the creation and improvement of SMEs through the setting up of an advisory office and/or joining with other private sector or NGO partners.
8   Be involved in mentoring budding entrepreneurs.
9   Invest so as to support the development objectives of the host country.
10 Ensure community or philanthropic company initiatives are sustainable in the development sense.

Conclusion

Are corporations taking over from governments and the UN in terms of development? The many examples and issues discussed in this book show clearly that MNEs are very much involved in development. Over time, they will be more involved in development than ever before and in ways that are hard to imagine today. Moreover, there is a real chance that MNEs with their wealth and global reach can do much more on development than the UN has achieved to date. The book is pessimistic about the chances for the UN, simply because it has become a political football. MNEs might, eventually, convince host governments that the UN is too important to fail. CSR will ensure that corporations will be involved in development and they will see that supporting the UN's development efforts will, also, be in their own best interest.

Index

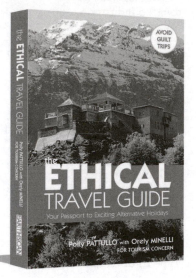

The Natural Advantage of Nations
Business Opportunities, Innovation and Governance in the 21st Century

Edited by Karlson 'Charlie' Hargroves and Michael Harrison Smith

Forewords by Amory B. Lovins, L Hunter Lovins, William McDonough, Michael Fairbanks and Alan AtKisson

'I am particularly pleased with the new book, *The Natural Advantage of Nations,* which will, in effect, follow on from *Natural Capitalism,* and bring in newer evidence from around the world'
AMORY B. LOVINS, Rocky Mountain Institute

'This is world-leading work, the team deserves the loudest acclamation possible'
BARRY GREAR AO, World Federation of Engineering Organisations

'A seminal book, a truly world changing book... As part of the process of pulling together the people whose ideas they wanted in the book, [the editors] have pulled together a whole movement'
L. HUNTER LOVINS, Natural Capitalism, Inc

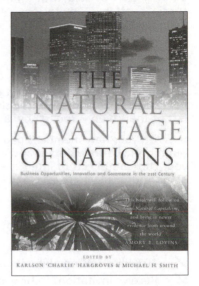

This collection of inspiring work, based on solid academic and practical rigour, is an overview of the 21st century business case for sustainable development. It incorporates innovative technical, structural and social advances, and explores the role governance can play in both leading and underpinning business and communities in the shift towards a sustainable future.

The team from The Natural Edge Project have studied and incorporated key works from over 30 of the world's leaders in sustainability. The book is also supported by an extensive companion website. This work takes the lessons of competitive advantage theory and practice and combines them with the sustainability paradigm, in light of important developments in economics, innovation, business and governance over the last 30–50 years.

Far from being in conflict with economics and business practices, this book demonstrates how we can improve the well-being of society and the environment while driving innovation in an increasingly competitive world.

Hardback 1-84407-121-9 Published January 2005

HOW TO ORDER:

ONLINE www.earthscan.co.uk
CUSTOMER HOTLINE +44 (0)1256 302699
EMAIL book.orders@earthscan.co.uk

Join our
online community
and help us save paper and postage!

www.earthscan.co.uk

By joining the Earthscan website, our readers can benefit from a range of exciting new services and exclusive offers. You can also receive e-alerts and e-newsletters packed with information about our new books, forthcoming events, special offers, invitations to book launches, discussion forums and membership news. Help us to reduce our environmental impact by joining the Earthscan online community!

How? – Become a member in seconds!

>> Simply visit **www.earthscan.co.uk** and add your name and email address to the sign-up box in the top left of the screen – You're now a member!

>> With your new member's page, you can subscribe to our monthly **e-newsletter** and/or choose **e-alerts** in your chosen subjects of interest – you control the amount of mail you receive and can unsubscribe yourself

Why? – Membership benefits

✔ Membership is free!

✔ 10% discount on all books online

✔ Receive invitations to high-profile book launch events at the BT Tower, London Review of Books Bookshop, the Africa Centre and other exciting venues

✔ Receive e-newsletters and e-alerts delivered directly to your inbox, keeping you informed but not costing the Earth – you can also forward to friends and colleagues

✔ Create your own discussion topics and get engaged in online debates taking place in our new online Forum

✔ Receive special offers on our books as well as on products and services from our partners such as _The Ecologist_, _The Civic Trust_ and more

✔ Academics – request inspection copies

✔ Journalists – subscribe to advance information e-alerts on upcoming titles and reply to receive a press copy upon publication – write to info@earthscan.co.uk for more information about this service

✔ Authors – keep up to date with the latest publications in your field

✔ NGOs – open an NGO Account with us and qualify for special discounts

Join now?
Join Earthscan now!

| name |
| surname |
| email address |

Earthscan Member
[Your name]

My profile
My forum
My bookmarks
All my pages

www.earthscan.co.uk